Beyond Bilingualism

MULTILINGUAL MATTERS SERIES

Series Editor
Professor John Edwards, *St. Francis Xavier University, Antigonish, Nova Scotia, Canada*

Other Books in the Series
Language Attitudes in Sub-Saharan Africa
   E. ADEGBIJA
Language Planning: From Practice to Theory
   ROBERT B. KAPLAN and RICHARD, B. BALDAUF Jr.
Language Reclamation
   HUBISI NWENMELY
Linguistic Minorities in Central and Eastern Europe
   C. BRATT PAULSTON and D. PECKHAM (eds)
Quebec's Aboriginal Languages
   JACQUES MAURAIS (ed.)
The Step-Tongue: Children's English in Singapore
   ANTHEA FRASER GUPTA
Three Generations – Two Languages – One Family
   LI WEI

Other Books of Interest
Bilingual Education and Social Change
   REBECCA FREEMAN
Encyclopedia of Bilingualism and Bilingual Education
   COLIN BAKER and SYLVIA PRYS JONES
Foundations of Bilingual Education and Bilingualism
   COLIN BAKER
Languages in America: A Pluralist View
   SUSAN J. DICKER
Language, Culture and Communication in Contemporary Europe
   CHARLOTTE HOFFMANN (ed.)
Policy and Practice in Bilingual Education
   O. GARCIA and C. BAKER (eds)
Teaching and Learning in Multicultural Schools
   ELIZABETH COELHO
Teaching and Assessing Intercultural Communicative Competence
   MICHAEL BYRAM

Please contact us for the latest book information:
Multilingual Matters, Frankfurt Lodge, Clevedon Hall,
Victoria Road, Clevedon, BS21 7HH, England
http:/www.multilingual-matters.co.uk

MULTILINGUAL MATTERS 110
Series Editor: John Edwards

Beyond Bilingualism

Multilingualism and Multilingual Education

Edited by

Jasone Cenoz and Fred Genesee

MULTILINGUAL MATTERS LTD
Clevedon • Philadelphia • Toronto • Sydney • Johannesburg

Library of Congress Cataloging in Publication Data

Beyond Bilingualism: Multilingualism and Multilingual Education/Edited by Jasone Cenoz and Fred Genesee
Multilingual Matters:110
1. Education, Bilingual–Case studies. 2. Multilingualism–Case studies. 3. Language and education–Case studies. I. Cenoz, Jasone. II. Genesee, Fred. III. Series:
Multilingual Matters (Series): 110
LC3715.B49   1998
370.117–dc21   98-22406

British Library Cataloguing in Publication Data

A CIP catalogue record for this book is available from the British Library.

ISBN 1-85359-421-0 (hbk)
ISBN 1-85359-420-2 (pbk)

Multilingual Matters Ltd

UK: Frankfurt Lodge, Clevedon Hall, Victoria Road, Clevedon BS21 7HH.
USA: 325 Chestnut Street, Philadelphia, PA 19106, USA.
Canada: OISE, 712 Gordon Baker Road, Toronto, Ontario, Canada M2H 3R7.
Australia: P.O. Box 586, Artamon, NSW, Australia.
South Africa: PO Box 1080, Northcliffe 2115, Johannesburg, South Africa.

Typeset by Solidus, Bristol.
Printed and bound in Great Britain by the Cromwell Press.

Contents

Introduction

A great number of people are multilingual and use more than two languages in their everyday life. The languages they use have different statuses as majority/minority languages both in their community and internationally and some of the languages are used primarily in the private domain while others are used primarily in public domains, such as work or school. Multilingualism is not exceptional but more frequent than might be commonly thought. In fact, 'To be bilingual or multilingual is not the aberration supposed by many (. . .); it is, rather, a normal and unremarkable necessity for the majority in the world today' (Edwards, 1994: 1). Community multilingualism can be the result of historical, political or economic movements such as imperialism, colonialism or immigration. There is a growing need for individual multilingualism as a result of increasing communications among different parts of the world and the need to be competent in languages of wider communication. The use of minority languages and interest in their maintenance and revival is also creating situations in which more than two languages co-exist and are necessary in everyday communication, the languages of the community and a language of wider communication. Individual multilingualism is also promoted by multilingual education. Whereas learning second and additional languages in school has traditionally been associated with the social elite and the hallmark of a well-educated person's background, the increasing recognition and use of world languages as well as minority languages is making multilingualism a desired educational aim for many individuals in many communities around the world.

It has been customary to use the term 'second language acquisition' to refer to the acquisition of languages other than the first language without distinguishing between the acquisition of a second language and 'multilingual acquisition', that is the acquisition of additional languages. In a similar vein, the extensive research on the effects of bilingualism on cognitive development devotes very little attention to the effects of bilingualism on multilingual acquisition. Nevertheless, multilingual acquisition presents some important differences when compared to second language acquisition because the previous experience of acquiring a language other than the first language and the results of this experience, bilingualism, can influence the process of acquiring an additional language.

Multilingual education is also different from bilingual education. In both bi- and multilingual education more than one language is used as the medium of instruction, but multilingual education can present additional challenges because it is more ambitious. By multilingual education, we mean educational programmes that use languages other than the first languages as media of instruction (although some teach additional languages as school subjects) and they aim for communicative proficiency in more than two languages. Accomplishing this calls for complex educational planning in order to accommodate multiple linguistic aims, curricular materials, and teaching strategies within the framework of limited school schedules. Multilingual education, like bilingual education, can take different forms because it is necessarily linked to the sociolinguistic context in which it takes place and has to take into account the relative status and use of the languages involved.

The chapters in this book examine multilingualism and multilingual education – that is the development of multilingual competence with the help of the educational system. Multilingual education is not an easy enterprise and, thus, this book aims to provide information and insights that can respond to the increasing demand for multilingualism and for educational programmes that prepare students for a multilingual world. The book also aims to provide theoretical, empirical and practical bases for planning and implementing multilingual education. Specifically, it addresses issues that are relevant to multilingual acquisition and multilingual education – for example, the role of bilingualism in multilingual acquisition, the integration of content in multilingual instruction, appropriate teacher education, and the role of culture in multilingual schools, among others. It also presents examples of multilingual school programmes and bilingual programmes in multilingual contexts in different parts of the world in order to better illustrate not only the achievements of multilingual education but also the challenges it poses. Although some of the chapters in the book are not about multilingualism, they provide insights on issues relevant to multilingual education. This book can be used as a textbook or a resource book and it may be of interest to researchers working on bilingualism and multilingualism, teacher educators and teachers who work or plan to work in bi/multilingual programmes, and language policy planners.

It is divided into three parts. The first part, 'Multidisciplinary Perspectives on Multilingual Education', presents general perspectives on multilingualism and multilingual education and focuses on sociodemographic and psycholinguistic aspects of multilingualism. In the opening chapter, G. Richard Tucker describes a number of multilingual communities and offers a worldwide view of multilingualism that illustrates the need for multilingual education. Jasone Cenoz and Fred Genesee's chapter reviews extant psycholinguistic research on multilingual acquisition and considers its implications for multilingual education.

The second part, 'Educating Towards Multilingualism', includes four chapters concerned with a number of specific pedagogical matters. Chapter 3, by Myriam Met, critically examines issues in content-based language instruction and its relevance to multilingual education; Met also suggests some important factors to consider when planning content-based language instruction. The chapter by Roy Lyster discusses the role of specific instructional strategies for language teaching in immersion classrooms and their relevance to multilingual education. In Chapter 5, Michael Byram explores another crucial area of multilingual education by examining the role of culture in multilingual classrooms. Nunan and Lam provide an overview of different models of teacher education in Chapter 6, and they offer useful guidelines for teacher education in multilingual contexts.

The third part, 'Case Studies in Multilingual Education', includes six examples of bi/multilingual education from different parts of the world. These are not the only examples of multilingual education, but they have been selected to represent different regions of the world and different sociolinguistic contexts. Some of these case studies focus on community contexts and government policies that can affect the type and form of multilingualism and multilingual education; for example, the cases of Luxembourg, Bolivia, Peru, the Philippines and Eritrea. The case studies from Canada, Europe and the Basque Country describe specific multilingual schools and provide information about important programmatic aspects of the schools and about the results of evaluations of the schools. The case studies presented here represent different stages of implementation of multilingual education. The European, Luxembourg and Canadian multilingual schools, for example, have existed for some time and thus are examples of *established* multilingual education. In contrast, while the Basque Country has an established bilingual education system, it has only recently taken its first steps towards establishing multilingual schools. Likewise, Eritrea is taking its first steps to establishing multilingual schools using a variety of local languages. Some of these case studies, such as the Philippines, Eritrea and Bolivia, describe multilingual contexts in which bilingual education is being implemented; they have been included nevertheless because they have important lessons to share with educators interested in multilingual programmes. The Philippines and Bolivia cases, for example, illustrate the challenges of developing multilingual schools using indigenous languages that have not previously been used for educational purposes. The authors of each chapter in this section have provided a critical analysis of the successes and challenges of their respective cases. Collectively, all the chapters in this book are intended to broaden our understanding of the unique characteristics of multilingualism and multilingual education and to provide theoretically and empirically based insights that can guide the implementation of multilingual education programmes elsewhere. There is clearly much that remains to be done to develop a full understanding of multilingual education.

References

Edwards, J. (1994) *Multilingualism*. London and New York: Routledge.

The Contributors

Michael Byram, Professor of Education at the University of Durham, has been involved in teaching foreign languages in Britain and other countries for more than twenty years. He is interested in the relationship of language learning and cultural learning in foreign language courses, and has published several books on the subject, including *Investigating Cultural Studies in Foreign Language Teaching* (Multilingual Matters, 1991) and *Teaching-and-Learning Language-and-Culture* (Multilingual Matters, 1994).

Jasone Cenoz is Associate Professor of English Linguistics at the University of the Basque Country (Spain) where she teaches linguistics and psycholinguistics. Her publications are in the fields of second language acquisition, bilingualism, multilingualism and interlanguage pragmatics. She is currently conducting a research project on the acquisition of English as a third language by Basque-Spanish bilingual children.

Nadine Dutcher is an education specialist working now mainly on language issues in education. With support from the Summer Institute of Linguistics and the Ministry of Education in Eritrea, she evaluated the mother tongue language programmes in Eritrea. For the World Bank she has evaluated bilingual education programmes in Guatemala, Papua New Guinea, Paraguay, Peru and Vanuatu. She has published two papers for the World Bank: 'The Use of First and Second Languages in Education: A Review of International Experience (1994) and 'The Use of First and Second Languages in Primary Education: Selected Case Studies' (1982). She has two masters degrees: one in primary education from Teachers College, Columbia University, New York and another in applied linguistics from Georgetown University, Washington, DC.

Fred Genesee (Professor, Psychology Department, McGill University) has conducted extensive research on alternative forms of bilingual and immersion education. He is the author of *Learning Through Two Languages: Studies of Immersion and Bilingual Education; Educating*

Second Language Children and *Classroom-based Evaluation in Second Language Education* (with J. Upshur). He is currently co-authoring a teachers' guide on enriched language and cultural education with Else Hamayan and Nancy Cloud.

Andrew Gonzalez, FSC is a member of the La Salle Brothers of the Philippines (*Fratrum Scholarum Christianarum*), a fraternity of religious educators, and is currently the Secretary of Education, Culture and Sports of the Republic of the Philippines. He holds a doctorate in linguistics from the University of California at Berkeley and was a member of the *Komisyon sa Wikang Filipino* (Commission on the Filipino Language). He has published extensively in the fields of language planning, national language development and applied linguistics. He is also a member of the editorial or advisory board of the *Annual Review of Applied Linguistics, Journal of Translation and Textlinguistics*, and *Second Language Instruction/Acquisition Abstracts*, and was editor of the *Philippine Journal of Linguistics* for more than twenty years.

Charlotte Hoffmann grew up in a bilingual family and has herself experience of raising children to become trilingual. She was trained in languages and linguistics first in Germany and then in England, where she lives. She is currently Senior Lecturer at the University of Salford, where she teaches German language and lectures in Sociolinguistics and Bilingualism, and she is also Associate Director of the European Studies Research Institute. She is interested in a variety of aspects of individual and societal multilingualism. Her publications are in the fields of child bilingualism and trilingualism, trilingual competence, and multilingualism in Europe, specially with regard to language contact, maintenance and shift, and language planning in Spanish- and German-speaking areas.

Nancy H. Hornberger is Goldie Anna Professor and Director of the Educational Linguistics Programs at the Graduate School of Education, University of Pennsylvania, Philadelphia, USA. She specialises in sociolinguistics, bilingualism, biliteracy, and language planning with a focus on educational policies and programmes for indigenous and immigrant language minority populations in South America and the United States. Her recent publications include *Indigenous Literacies in the Americas: Language Planning from the Bottom Up* (Mouton, 1996), *Sociolinguistics and Language Teaching* (Cambridge University Press, 1996), and *Research Methods in Language and Education* (Kluwer Press, 1997).

Born in Hong Kong, **Agnes Lam** left home to study at the University of Singapore in 1973. In 1984, she completed a PhD in linguistics and a

TESOL Certificate at the University of Pittsburgh. She then taught at the National University of Singapore until 1990. She is now an associate professor and the associate director of the English Centre, University of Hong Kong. A holder of several visitorships, she has also worked briefly at other universities such as Tsinghua University in Beijing and the University of Cambridge. Her research interests include psycholinguistics and language education. She is also a poet.

Luis Enrique Lopez is Director of PROEIBAndes, the Graduate Program in Bilingual Intercultural Education for the Andean Countries, at the University of San Simon in Cochabamba, Bolivia. He specialises in bilingualism and language and educational planning for indigenous populations. He has served as general advisor to the Bolivian Education Reform and as technical expert to the Experimental Bilingual Education Project of Puno, Peru, and to other projects and indigenous organisations in Bolivia, Ecuador, Guatemala, Nicaragua and Paraguay. He has published various books and articles on multilingualism, interculturalism and bilingual education and also helped produce educational materials in various Amerindian languages.

Roy Lyster (PhD, University of Toronto) is Associate Professor in the Department of Second Language Education at McGill University in Montreal and co-convener of the Scientific Commission on Immersion Education for the International Association of Applied Linguistics (AILA). His research investigates the characteristics and effects of language instruction and corrective feedback in immersion classrooms and includes analyses of teacher–student discourse and the negotiation of form. Results of his research have appeared in *Applied Linguistics, Language Learning, Studies in Second Language Acquisition, The Canadian Modern Language Review,* and *The Modern Language Journal.*

Myriam Met is Coordinator of Foreign Languages for Montgomery County Public Schools in Maryland where she is responsible for curriculum development and implementation of immersion programmes and foreign language instruction at the secondary level with a foreign language enrolment over 30,000 students. Prior to joining MCPS, she was with Cincinnati Public Schools for ten years, where she served as a coordinating teacher and then supervisor of foreign languages, ESL and bilingual education, K-12. Dr Met has consulted on programme development and curriculum and has been involved with teacher training at all levels of instruction in the US, Europe, and Japan. She has published in journals and professional books on topics related to second language instruction.

David Nunan is Professor of Applied Linguistics and Director of the English Centre at the University of Hong Kong. He is also Dean, Graduate School of Education, Newport Asia-Pacific University, and President-elect of TESOL. He held teaching, researching and consulting positions in Thailand, Singapore, the United States, Britain, Japan and the Middle East. David Nunam has published over 100 books and articles in the areas of curriculum and materials development, classroom-based research, and discourse analysis. His recent publications include _Second Language Teaching and Learning_ (Heinle/Newbury House), _The Self-Directed Teacher_ (Cambridge University Press), and _Voices from the Language Classroom_ (with Kathleen M. Bailey) Cambridge University Press). His most recent textbooks project are _ATLAS: Learning Centered Communication_ (Heinle & Heinle/International Thomson Publishing), _Listen In_ (International Thomson Publishing), and _Go For It!_ (Heinle & Heinle).

G. Richard Tucker (PhD, McGill University) is Professor and Head of the Department of Modern Languages at Carnegie Mellon University. Prior to joining CMU, he served as President of the Center for Applied Linguistics (1978–1991), and as Professor of Psychology at McGill University (1969–1978). He has published more than 175 books, articles, or reviews concerning diverse aspects of second language learning and teaching. In addition to his work in North America, he has spent a number of years living and working as a language education advisor for the International Division of the Ford Foundation in Southeast Asia and in the Middle East and North Africa.

Part 1

Multidisciplinary Perspectives on Multilingual Education

Chapter 1

A Global Perspective on Multilingualism and Multilingual Education

G. RICHARD TUCKER

The World's Language Demography

Despite pressures and influences toward commonality from a seemingly pervasive mass media, the residents of the world continue to speak an amazing array of mutually unintelligible languages (see, for example, Bright, 1992; Cheshire, 1991; Comrie, 1987; Edwards, 1994). These languages vary in typological characteristics, geographical spread, and number of native speakers. If written, they also vary in terms of the type of system that is used to record them (e.g. alphabetic, logographic, syllabic-alphabetic).

Incidence of multilingualism

The number of languages spoken throughout the world is estimated to be approximately 6000 (Grimes, 1992). Although people frequently observe that a small number of languages such as Arabic, Bengali, English, French, Hindi, Malay, Mandarin, Portuguese, Russian and Spanish serve as important link languages or languages of wider communication around the world, these are very often spoken as second, third, fourth or later-acquired languages by their speakers (see, for example, Cheshire, 1991; Comrie, 1987; Edwards, 1994). The available evidence seems to indicate that governments in many countries deliberately present a somewhat skewed picture of monolingualism as normative by the explicit or implicit language policies that they adopt and promulgate (Crystal, 1987). Thus, fewer than 25% of the world's approximately 200 countries recognise two or more official languages, with a mere handful recognising *more than*

3

two (e.g. India, Luxembourg, Nigeria, etc.) Despite these conservative government policies, available data indicate that there are many more bilingual or multilingual individuals in the world than there are monolingual. In addition, many more children throughout the world have been, and continue to be, educated via a second or a later-acquired language – at least for some portion of their formal education – than the number of children educated exclusively via first language. In many parts of the world, bilingualism or multilingualism and innovative approaches to education which involve the use of two or more languages constitute the normal everyday experience (see, for example Dutcher, 1994; World Bank, 1995, Dutcher, Chapter 12 this volume).

Multiple languages in education

The use of multiple languages in education may be attributed to, or be a reflection of, numerous factors such as the linguistic heterogeneity of a country or region (e.g. Luxembourg or Singapore); specific social or religious attitudes (e.g. the addition of Sanskrit to mark Hinduism or Pali to mark Buddhism); or the desire to promote national identity (e.g. in India, Nigeria, the Philippines). In addition, innovative language education programmes are often implemented to promote proficiency in international language(s) of wider communication together with proficiency in national and regional languages (see Cenoz, Chapter 8 this volume). The composite portrait of language education policies and practices throughout the world is exceedingly complex – and simultaneously fascinating. In Oceania, for example, linguists estimate that a mere 4% of the world's population speaks approximately 20% of the world's 6000 languages. In Papua New Guinea, a country which has a population of approximately 3,000,000, linguists have described more than 870 languages. Here it is common for a child to grow up speaking one local indigenous language at home, another in the market place, adding Tok Pisin to her repertoire as a lingua franca, and English if she continues her schooling. Analogous situations recur in many parts of the world, such as India which has declared 15 of its approximately 1650 indigenous languages to be 'official'; or Guatemala, or Nigeria, or South Africa, to name but a few countries in which multilingualism predominates, and in which children are frequently exposed to numerous languages as they move from their homes into their communities and eventually through the formal educational system.

Several Illustrative National Profiles

Let me turn now to a very brief consideration of several illustrative language education profiles. No attempt is made to provide an exhaustive treatment of worldwide language education policies and practices (see instead Dickson & Cumming, 1996); rather, several examples have been chosen from southeast Asia, Africa, Latin America, and Europe to illustrate the breadth and the richness of national policies and practices across countries. Some of these situations are fully described in the case study chapters presented in Part 3 of this volume along with other equally interesting situations.

The Philippines

The Philippines is an archipelago which comprises some 7000 islands. Approximately 150 mutually unintelligible languages are spoken throughout the country. The official languages are Filipino (formerly called Pilipino, based upon Tagalog the language of the metropolitan Manila region) and English. The country has a 50-year history of thorough, longitudinal evaluation of various educational alternatives (see, for example, Gonzalez & Sibayan, 1988). After more than a decade of experimenting with diverse approaches to language education and as a result of a nationwide language policy survey undertaken during 1967 and 1968, policy makers in the Philippines adopted a novel approach to bilingual education in 1974 (see Gonzalez, Chapter 9 this volume). The plan involves language by subject-matter specificity throughout the primary and secondary levels of education. Under this policy, English is used as the medium of instruction for English language arts, science and mathematics; Filipino is used for Filipino language arts and for the remainder of the content areas. In regions of the country where Filipino is not spoken natively, bilingual education is not sufficient and multilingual education is provided through the addition of a third language. Thus, for example, in certain areas of the country, the local indigenous language (Cebuano, Hiligaynon, Ilokano, etc.) is used as the initial medium of instruction in the first two primary grades with a gradual introduction of both Filipino and English to the curriculum as well. In addition, in many areas Spanish is introduced at the secondary level as a 'foreign' language.

The results of a comprehensive qualitative and quantitative summative evaluation of the bilingual education programme revealed that there was a positive relationship between academic performance in

English and in Filipino; that competence in English predicted success more than competence in Filipino, even for subjects taught in Filipino; that socioeconomic status was the major predictor of academic achievement; that teacher subject-matter proficiency was an important predictor of student proficiency; and that the provision of competent teachers and adequate materials were essential for academic success (see Gonzalez, Chapter 9 this volume). Ironically, given the tremendous attention and care devoted to the teaching of English as a second language in the Philippines, educators there bemoan the paucity of attention paid to the teaching of Filipino in non-Tagalog areas.

Unfortunately, there seem to be no extant studies from the Philippines which specifically compare the results of innovative educational programmes in trilingual settings as compared to those in bilingual settings. In principle, some data would be available for secondary analysis from the research cited above although no assessments of children's development in languages other than Filipino or English were conducted. Given the complex and interesting language demography of the Philippines such studies would be exceedingly interesting and potentially valuable from a policy standpoint.

Brunei Darussalam

A language education 'experiment' somewhat similar to that in the Philippines is currently under way in Brunei. There the government has recently implemented a policy of *dwibahasa* in which English and Bahasa Malay are used (roughly for educational purposes equivalent to English and Filipino in the Philippines) namely English for language arts, science and mathematics, and Bahasa Malay for language arts and the other content subjects. The two situations are somewhat analogous to that alluded to above in trilingual settings in the Philippines since virtually no child enters school in Brunei speaking English or standard Malay as the first language. Thus for many children it appears as though English and Malay are superimposed upon the child's indigenous language. However, from a policy perspective, it seems that there is a good deal of controversy over the existence and the potential use of non-mainstream varieties of Malay for formal education (see, for example, Martin, 1995).

Although this educational experiment is only in its formative stages, there has already been some exciting international discussion of the work (see, for example Tucker, 1996; and the entire two-volume special issue of the *Journal of Multilingual and Multicultural Development*). Since those associated with the *dwibahasa* initiative have indicated their intention to pursue a longitudinal qualitative and quantitative programme of research, the results of this educational intervention will certainly bear watching.

Guatemala

Approximately 40% of Guatemala's citizens are Indians, and about 60% are 'Ladinos', a mixture of the Mayans and the Spaniards who conquered the area in the sixteenth century. Government and private estimates (Grimes, 1992) indicate that anywhere from 25 to 50 mutually unintelligible languages are spoken throughout the country. Spanish is the official language, but is spoken as a first language by less than half of the population. The other half speak mainly Mayan languages with approximately 75% of these speaking one of four languages – Kaqchikel, Q'eqchi', Mam, and K'iche'. Beginning in 1980, the government, with international assistance, has undertaken a very interesting series of projects on bilingual education in the rural areas of the country (the National Programme for Bilingual Education is known by the Spanish acronym PRONEBI). This programme has been the object of intensive external evaluation (for a summary, see Dutcher, 1994). The work undertaken as part of PRONEBI seems to have culminated in a rather remarkable reform in the educational system of Guatemala – helping to focus the attention of the Ministry of Education on issues of the quality and relevance of rural education. The succession of projects has served to legitimise the use of the first language for teaching students who are not native speakers of the official or dominant language. An important lesson drawn from the Guatemalan experience is that children can ultimately learn the language of wider communication well (in this case Spanish) if they begin their education, including the development of literacy, in their first language (see also Hornberger & López's Chapter 10 this volume, on Peru and Bolivia). They will remain in school longer, and attain higher levels of subject matter achievement than their counterparts who are submerged exclusively in Spanish. For purposes of this chapter it is important to note that students who succeed in elementary school and proceed to secondary school add a third language to their repertoire – in this case English which is important for economic and social reasons as well as for ensuring access to a variety of post-secondary educational options.

Namibia

Language education policy and planning activities within Namibia are well under way. Namibia, located in southwest Africa, represents a country richly endowed with multiple languages and cultures as well as one with a history of politicisation attributable to the country's colonial past and the policies of apartheid. Since independence in 1990, the official language of Namibia has been English with the African languages indigenous to Namibia (Khoekhoegowab, Oshikwanyama, Oshindonga, Otjiherero, Rugciriku, Rukwangali, Setswana, Silozi, Thimbukushu, and Ju|'hôa), as well as Lozi from Zambia and Afrikaans and German being recognised as local 'national' languages (see Haacke, 1994). The language policy articulated by the Ministry of Education calls for the local 'national' language to be used as the medium of instruction at least through Grades 1–3 with continuing study of that local language through secondary school. At some point within the primary cycle of education, there is to be a transition to English as the major medium of instruction with the introduction of another language as a 'foreign' language at the secondary level (in addition to German, this might include either French or Latin at the present time). The official policy of the country is one which encourages multilingualism (see also Dutcher's Chapter 12 this volume, on Eritrea). Although there is no indication at present that materials are being developed for the teaching of African languages as second languages within Namibia, there is active discussion of the topic. Clearly, the development of language education policy and practice in this linguistically complex, recently independent nation will be fascinating to follow.

Luxembourg

The Grand Duchy of Luxembourg is a fascinating example of a small European country (with a population of approximately 395,000 according to the 1990 census) in which the *entire* school-aged population follows a trilingual education system using Luxemburger, French and German (see Hoffmann, Chapter 7 this volume). The policy of trilingual education was designed and implemented to achieve the goals of educating children in Luxemburger for purposes of facilitating national identity and integration while simultaneously developing the highest possible degree of proficiency in two languages of major economic, occupational and strategic importance – German and French. As a general principle, students begin their primary education in Luxemburger with the early introduction of German and French as subjects for study. By the end of the primary cycle, most content classes are taught via German although Luxemburger and French continue to be taught as subjects. At the secondary level, German is used to teach a majority of the content subjects with the exception of mathematics which is taught via French. According to Lebrun and Baetens Beardsmore (1993), this educational 'innovation' seems to result in multilingual proficiency for a majority of the youngsters – an outcome which they attribute to a fortuitous coincidence of curricular and extra-curricular conditions.

The major reason for presenting these five examples is to illustrate the breadth and complexity of language education policies and practices throughout the world and to indicate the myriad factors (e.g. fostering national identity, facilitating heritage language or religious tradition maintenance, promoting occupational or social mobility, etc.) that play a role in causing groups to develop and institutionalise programmes to promote multiple language proficiency.

Prevalent Educational Myths

Against this backdrop of worldwide linguistic complexity and a growing need for multilingual education, a variety of myths appear to be relatively firmly entrenched in the minds of many parents, educators and policy makers. In my own work during the past 30 years in various parts of the world, I have found the following to be among the more common, and the more serious, with respect to the implementation of innovative language education programmes:

- If the major goal is to develop the highest degree of proficiency and subject-matter mastery via *language X*, the more time spent educating the child via that language, the better.
- Anyone who can speak a language can teach successfully via that language.
- Pidgins are not real languages; their speakers are incapable of logical or complex thought; therefore pidgins cannot be used as media of instruction.
- There is one, and only one, 'correct solution' to the choice and sequencing of language(s) for purposes of initial literacy training and content instruction for all multilingual countries.
- In multilingual countries, it is too expensive to develop materials and to train teachers in a number of different languages.

In reality, conclusions based upon the available research literature suggest that these statements are indeed myths (see, for example Dutcher, 1994; Summer Institute of Linguistics, 1995; Tucker, 1991), and that quite a different set of inferences should be drawn by educators and policy makers. Children can, and should, initially be introduced to literacy training and to educational programmes in their first language. Furthermore, the cost of producing materials in languages with relatively few speakers is not prohibitive. Pidgins and Creoles possess the properties of all so-called natural languages and are perfectly appropriate vehicles for instruction in areas where they are widely spoken. And finally, regardless of which language or languages are being considered for inclusion in educational pro-grammes, it is critical that teachers be professionally trained. Let me turn now to the results of a study that Nadine Dutcher (1994) and I have recently completed for the World Bank.

Conditions for Successful Multilingual Education

In our survey of the use of first and second languages in education, we examined the publicly available literature from research con-ducted in three different types of countries: (1) those with no (or few) first language speakers of the language of wider communication (e.g. Haiti, Nigeria, the Philippines); (2) those with some first language speakers of the language of wider communication (e.g. Guatemala); and (3) those with many first language speakers of the language of wider communication (e.g. Canada, New Zealand, the United States). For the purposes of this present introduction, I will summarise what I hope are a few of the familiar highlights of this review. Dutcher and I noted that even though there are a number of models available for implementation, the following common threads cut across *all* successful programmes which have as one of their goals providing students with multiple language proficiency and with access to academic content material:

- Parental and community support and involvement are essential.
- Development of the child's first language is encouraged to ensure cognitive development and to facilitate the acquisition of second and third languages.
- Development of the child's first language, with its related cognitive development, is more important in promoting second and third language development than mere length of exposure to these later acquired languages.
- Children learn a second, or later, language in different ways

depending upon their cultural background and their individual personality.

- Cognitive/academic language skills, once developed and content-subject material, once acquired, transfer readily.
- Teachers must be able to understand, speak and use the language of instruction proficiently whether it is their first or second language.

The results from the available published, longitudinal and critical research undertaken in varied settings throughout the world indicate clearly that the development of multiple language proficiency is possible, and indeed that it is viewed as desirable by educators, policy makers and parents in many countries. Furthermore, Dutcher and I were intrigued to find that:

- recurrent costs for innovative programmes are about the same as they are for 'traditional' programmes (although there may be additional one-time start-up costs); and that
- cost-benefit calculations can typically be estimated in terms of the cost savings to the education system, improvements in years of schooling, and enhanced earning potential for students with multiple language proficiency.

Thus, the data available to us suggested strongly that economic considerations should not be a barrier to the implementation of innovative language education programmes.

Implications of Extant Research for Educational Reform

In this section, I propose to identify and comment briefly on two cross-cutting themes which seem to me to be critical linchpins in moving forward policy or planning discussions within the domain of language education reform: (1) the critical role of the child's first language in initial literacy attainment and content-subject mastery and the subsequent transfer of skills across languages; and (2) the natural tension between importing a model versus importing a 'cycle of discovery' (see Johnson, 1996; Swain, 1996; Tucker & Donato, 1995). With regard to the first issue, despite decades of sound educational research, there still remains a belief in many quarters that somehow when an additional language is introduced into a curriculum, the child must go back and relearn all over again concepts already mastered. Although there remains much to be learned about the contexts and strategies that facilitate transfer across languages, the fact that such transfer occurs should not be a topic for debate. The work of Hakuta (1986) and his colleagues provides clear evidence that a child who acquires her basic literacy or numeracy concepts in one language can transfer these concepts and knowledge easily to her second or third or other later-acquired languages. The existence of this phenomenon is not in question; rather we should continue to seek strategies and contexts that facilitate or optimise maximal cross-language transfer.

Likewise, in many settings, there is a tendency to review positive research findings from a particular local situation (let us say for argument sake, those with French immersion programmes in Quebec; see Genesee, 1987; Lambert & Tucker, 1972), and to conclude that the educational model *per se* can be imported wholesale into a new and very different sociolinguistic context. In fact, the inference to be drawn is quite different – what can and should be imported is a cycle of discovery, the continual process of evaluation, theory building, generation of hypotheses, experimentation and further evaluation. Multilingual education is a challenging undertaking which necessitates attending to a complex set of interacting educational, sociolinguistic, economic, and political factors – these vary situation by situation, and must remain the object of continual formative, and ultimately summative, evaluation.

Key Issues Warranting Further Attention

Based upon a review of available literature, it also seems possible to identify four relatively neglected areas which deserve additional future attention. These are the:

- need for additional sociolinguistic research throughout the world;
- need for more thorough examination of the concept and parameters of transfer;
- need for materials development, reproduction and distribution in the so-called truly less commonly spoken languages (e.g. the majority of the African languages spoken in Namibia; the majority of the languages in Papua New Guinea, etc.); and the
- need for developing a cadre of trained teachers who are proficient speakers of these languages.

Despite several decades of rather extensive sociolinguistic fieldwork in many areas, there remains much to be done to describe the language situation in many parts of the world (for example, the World Bank is currently engaged in a preliminary educational mission in Guinea Bissau but relatively little is known about the distribution and status of languages and their speakers throughout the country, which makes sound educational planning problematic). Many of the world's languages have yet to be written, codified or elaborated. Furthermore, there are no materials available for initial literacy training or for advanced education; nor are there teachers who have been trained to teach via many of the world's languages. These are issues that have been identified as crucial by the World Bank in their most recent report of priorities and strategies for enhancing educational development in the twenty-first century (World Bank, 1995) – and they are issues which must be dealt with effectively before systemic reform which will encourage multilingual proficiency can be widely implemented.

Conclusions

By way of summary, let me identify a number of important questions that I think must be addressed whenever parents, educators and administrators discuss the prospects of multilingual education for their communities:

- What are the explicit or implicit goals for formal education in the region?
- Is there general satisfaction throughout the region with the level of educational attainment by all participants (both those who terminate their education relatively early and those who wish to go on to tertiary studies)?
- Is the region relatively homogeneous or is it heterogeneous linguistically and culturally and how would multilingual education complement the linguistic and cultural characteristics of the community?
- Does the region have an explicit or implicit policy with respect to the role of language in education, and how would multi-lingual education fit or not fit with existing policy? Is this policy based upon tradition or the result of language (education) planning?
- What priorities are accorded to goals such as the development of broadly based permanent functional literacy, the value of education for those who may permanently interrupt their schooling at an early age, and the power of language to foster national identity and cohesiveness?

- Are the language(s) selected for instruction written, codified, standardised, and elaborated?
- Is there a well-developed curriculum for the various levels/ stages of formal education (i.e. a framework which specifies fairly explicitly a set of language, content, cognitive and affective objectives that are then tied to or illustrated by exemplary techniques, activities, and supported by written materials)?
- Are sufficient core *and* reference materials available for teachers and for students in the language(s) of instruction? If not, are there trained individuals available who can prepare such materials?
- Are there a sufficient number of trained and experienced teachers who are fluent speakers of the language(s) of instruction *and* who are trained to teach via that language(s)?

Questions such as these are ones that must be considered by community leaders as they consider the implementation of any innovative language education programme.

References

Bright, W. (ed.) (1992) *International Encyclopedia of Languages.* New York: Oxford University Press.

Cheshire, J. (ed.) (1991) *English Around the World: Sociolinguistic Perspectives.* Cambridge: Cambridge University Press.

Comrie, B. (ed.) (1987) *The World's Major Languages.* New York: Oxford University Press.

Crystal, D. (1987) *The Cambridge Encyclopedia of Language.* Cambridge: Cambridge University Press.

Dickson, P. and Cumming, A. (eds) (1996) *Profiles of Language Education in 25 Countries.* Slough, UK: National Foundation for Educational Research.

Dutcher, N. in collaboration with G.R. Tucker (1994) The use of first and second languages in education: A review of educational experience. World Bank, East Asia and the Pacific Region, Country Department III. Washington, DC.

Edwards, J. (1994) *Multilingualism.* London: Routledge.

Genesee, F. (1987) *Learning Through Two Languages.* Cambridge, MA: Newbury House.

Gonzalez, A. and Sibayan, B.P. (1988) *Evaluating Bilingual Education in the Philippines (1974–1985).* Manila: Linguistic Society of the Philippines.

Grimes, B.F. (1992) *Ethnologue: Languages of the World.* Dallas: Summer Institute of Linguistics.

Haacke, W. (1994) Language policy and planning in Namibia. In W. Grabe (ed.) *Annual Review of Applied Linguistics: 1993/94* (pp. 240–53). New York: Cambridge University Press.

Hakuta, K. (1986) *Mirror of Language: The Debate on Bilingualism.* New York: Basic Books.

Johnson, K. (1996) Response to M. Swain: Discovering successful second language teaching strategies and practices: From program evaluation to classroom experimentation. *Journal of Multilingual and Multicultural Development* 17, 105–13.

Lambert, W.E. and Tucker, G.R. (1972) *The Bilingual Education of Children.* Rowley, MA: Newbury House.

Lebrun, N. and Baetens Beardsmore, H. (1993) Trilingual education in the Grand Duchy of Luxembourg. In H. Baetens Beardsmore (ed.) *European Models of Bilingual Education* (pp. 101–20) Clevedon: Multilingual Matters.

Martin, P.W. (1995) Whither the indigenous language of Brunei Darussalam? *Oceanic Linguistics* 34, 27–43.

Summer Institute of Linguistics of Papua New Guinea (1995) *A Survey of Vernacular Education Programming at the Provincial Level within Papua New Guinea.* Ukarumpa, Papua New Guinea: Summer Institute of Linguistics.

Swain, M. (1996) Discovering successful second language teaching strategies and practices: From program evaluation to classroom experimentation. *Journal of Multilingual and Multicultural Development* 17, 89–104.

Tucker, G.R. (1991) Developing a language-competent American society: The role of language planning. In A.G. Reynolds (ed.) *Bilingualism, Multiculturalism, and Second Language Learning* (pp. 65–79). Hillsdale, NJ: Lawrence Erlbaum.

Tucker, G.R. (1996) Some thoughts concerning innovative language education programs. *Journal of Multilingual and Multicultural Development* 17, 315–20.

Tucker, G.R. and Donato, R. (1995) Developing a second language research component within a teacher education program. In J.E. Alatis (ed.) *Georgetown University Round Table on Languages and Linguistics: 1995* (pp. 453–70). Washington, DC: Georgetown University Press.

World Bank (1995) Priorities and strategies for education. Washington, DC: The International Bank for Reconstruction and Development/The World Bank.

Chapter 2

Psycholinguistic Perspectives on Multilingualism and Multilingual Education

JASONE CENOZ and FRED GENESEE

Multilingualism and multilingual acquisition are widespread, not only in officially recognised bilingual and multilingual communities but all over the world. Despite this, the process of acquiring several non-native languages (i.e. multilingual acquisition) and the final result of this process (multilingualism) have received relatively little attention in scientific research in comparison to second language acquisition and bilingualism. Indeed, multilingualism and multi-lingual acquisition are often considered as simply variations on bilingualism and second language acquisition, and 'second language acquisition' (SLA) is often used as a cover term to refer to any language other than the first language irrespective of the type of learning environment and the number of other non-native languages known by the learner (Sharwood Smith 1994: 7).

Multilingual acquisition and multilingualism are complex phenomena. They implicate all the factors and processes associated with second language acquisition and bilingualism as well as unique and potentially more complex factors and effects associated with the interactions that are possible among the multiple languages being learned and in the processes of learning them. Like bilingual acquisition and bilingualism, multilingual acquisition and multi-lingualism are complex because they can occur simultaneously or successively, formally (through instruction) or naturally (outside school), and in childhood, adolescence, or adulthood. The sociocultural status of each language along with the languages' respective roles and functions in society can contribute additional complexities. Moreover, multilingualism can characterise individuals or whole societies. Societal multilingualism does not necessarily imply individual multilingualism – for example, individual multilingualism has often been encouraged among elite members of society even in officially 'monolingual' communities 'as a marker of high status' (Edwards, 1994). Individual and societal multilingualism pose different scientific and practical questions that lead to different kinds of knowledge.

In this chapter we focus on individual multilingualism – the individual's acquisition of multilingual competence, some tentative explanations for additive multilingualism, and implications for multilingual education. Even though there are a number of studies on simultaneous trilingual acquisition in pre-school children (Hoffmann, 1985), in this chapter we focus on the psycholinguistic aspects of multilingual acquisition in school settings. Simplistically, multilingual competence in individuals can be understood as the capacity to use several languages appropriately and effectively for communication in oral or written language. But, we shall see in the next section that such a definition is problematic and overly simplistic (see also Byram, Chapter 5 this volume).

Defining Multilingual Competence

Communicative competence is generally regarded by most contemporary educators as an essential goal of second language acquisition. The concept of communicative competence was originally proposed by Hymes (1972) who emphasised the importance of the ability to use language effectively and appropriately in social context. Most current models of communicative competence have built on Hymes' original conceptualisation which has been expanded to include a number of different components, such as sociolinguistic, pragmatic (or actional), discourse, and strategic competence (Bachman, 1990; Canale & Swain, 1980; Celce-Murcia *et al.*, 1995).

What is multilingual competence? Is it the same as monolingual competence in several languages? The idea that second language competence is comparable to monolingual competence has been seriously challenged in recent years. Although most of the challenges have been raised in discussions of second language acquisition and bilingualism, they are equally germane to discussions of multi-lingualism and multilingual acquisition. Cook (1992, 1993, 1995); Grosjean (1989, 1992), and others, have criticised what they call 'monolingual prejudice' or 'the monolingual view of bilingualism' according to which the proficiency that second language learners should aim for is 'native-like,' where native-like is defined in terms of monolingual language proficiency.

Indeed, bilinguals, in and outside school, are usually evaluated according to their 'monolingual' competence in their non-native languages. In other words, the exalted ideal speaker-listener of theoretical linguistics is held up as the model of competence for all language users. However, as Edwards (1994) points out, a perfectly balanced bilingual or multilingual is exceptional. Thus, since second language learners seldom acquire completely native-like monolingual competence and rarely become balanced bilinguals, it is not uncommon to talk about failure in second language acquisition. As a result, according to Grosjean (1989), the proficiency of second language learners is often considered deficient and is not judged on its own merits relative to the learners' real needs and use.

In comparison to this 'fractional' view of an idealised form of bilingualism, Grosjean (1992) has proposed a holistic view. He argues that bilinguals are fully proficient speakers who have specific configurations of linguistic competencies that reflect, in part, unique interactions of the languages they know. Bilinguals seldom have balanced proficiency because they have developed communicative competencies in two languages according to the specific contexts in which they learn to use them. The language competence of bilinguals should not be regarded as simply the sum of two monolingual competencies, but rather should be judged in conjunction with the users' total linguistic repertoire.

In a similar vein, Cook (1992) has proposed the notion of 'multicompetence' to designate a unique form of language competence that is not necessarily comparable to that of monolinguals. According to Cook, second language users should not be viewed as imitation monolinguals in a second language, but rather they should be seen to possess unique forms of competence, or competencies, in their own right (Cook, 1993: 270). Jessner (1997) also adopts a holistic view of bilingualism and emphasises the fact that multilingual competence is dynamic rather than static and notes further that language proficiency changes as a result of adjustments to the interacting linguistic subsystems that reflect the user's communicative needs.

These alternative views of bilingualism are particularly interesting when applied to multilingualism and multilingual acquisition. If we go beyond bilingualism, we are even less likely to find balanced multilinguals because the multilingual speaker has a larger linguistic repertoire than monolinguals but usually the same range of situations in which to use that repertoire. Thus, multilingual speakers will have more specific distributions of functions and uses for each of their languages and, therefore, they should not be measured against the yardstick of a monolingual speaker who uses the same language in all contexts. From a psycholinguistic perspective, this view also implies that multilinguals possess a configuration of linguistic competencies that is distinct from that of bilinguals and monolinguals. This perspective has important implications for multilingual education as it challenges 'ideal native competence' as the only goal for language learners.

Thus, although all of the components that are generally regarded as part of communicative competence among monolinguals may be necessary for effective communication in multiple languages, multilingual competence presents specific characteristics that distinguish it from monolingual competence. More specifically, multilingual speakers tend to use different languages in different situations for different purposes. Therefore, while they may need all the components of communicative competence in total, they do not necessarily and often do not need to develop all competencies to the same extent in each language. In fact, schools that aim for multilingualism are likely to set different goals for each language according to the learners' specific communicative needs in each language. For example, if there are native-speakers of the target languages in the community, then students in multilingual schools would probably be expected to acquire competence using the target languages in informal as well as formal day-to-day situations. In comparison, if one of the target languages is the primary language used in higher education (university) but is not spoken in the community at large, then students might be expected to acquire competence in the target language for academic purposes only.

Multilingual Acquisition

It is commonly believed that learning an additional language is easier for those who already know a second language than for monolinguals; in other words, there is positive transfer from second language learning to learning additional languages. In this section, we review research that addresses this possibility. Studies on this issue have used different approaches – some have examined the effects of bilingualism on the acquisition of general proficiency in additional languages, while others have examined specific aspects of proficiency, such as listening comprehension or lexical acquisition. Table 2.1 summarises published research on multilingual acquisition.

The studies listed in Table 2.1 have been carried out with different

Table 2.1 Studies in multilingual acquisition

	Country	L1–L2	L3	Tests
Thomas (1988)	US, N = 26	English–Spanish	French	Grammar, vocabulary, writing
Bild & Swain (1989)	Canada, N=47	Italian and non-Romance/English	French	Cloze test, oral story telling
Jaspaert & Lemmens (1990)	Belgium N=12/66	French/Italian	Dutch	Grammar, vocabulary, reading, writing
Zobl (1993)	US, N=33	German, Chinese, Arabic, etc.	English	Grammar
Cenoz & Valencia (1994)	Basque Country, N=321	Spanish, Basque	English	Grammar, vocabulary, reading, writing, speaking, listening
Klein (1995)	US, N=32	Hebrew, Italian, Polish, Russian, etc.	English	Lexis, syntax

language combinations and in different learning contexts; they also differ greatly with respect to research methodologies and testing procedures. These studies have something in common: they all analyse multilingual acquisition in formal contexts. Moreover, in all cases, they involve bilingual students who are proficient in at least one minority language (for example, Spanish in the US, Italian in Belgium, Basque in the Basque Country), and this may be either their first or their second language.

Overall, the findings from these studies indicate that bilingualism does not hinder the acquisition of an additional language and, to the contrary, in most cases bilingualism favours the acquisition of third languages (see Bild & Swain, 1989; Cenoz & Valencia, 1994; Klein, 1995; Thomas, 1988; also cf. Jaspaert & Lemmens, 1990; Zobl, 1993). For example, research on the acquisition of French as a third language in Canadian immersion programmes has noted advantages among third language learners in comparison to monolinguals (see Bild & Swain, 1989; Genesee, 1983, and Chapter 11 this volume; Gulutsan, 1976; Hurd, 1993). Advantages that have been found with respect to general language proficiency have also been noted in studies that have examined specific language-related domains – such as perceptual discrimination (Cohen *et al.*, 1967; Davine *et al.*, 1971; Enomoto, 1994) and listening comprehension in a third language (Edwards *et al.*, 1977; Wightman, 1981).

Not all studies report positive effects of bilingualism on third language acquisition. Jaspaert and Lemmens (1990) and Zobl (1993) reported no significant differences between second and multilingual language acquisition. Nevertheless, in both studies, the authors regarded multilingual acquisition as an additive process. Jaspaert and Lemmens (1990) consider that 'the results of the analysis of the data certainly warrant a positive evaluation of the acquisition of Dutch' (pp. 53–4) by bilingual children since, in fact, Italian immigrants in the trilingual Foyer project under investigation in their study achieved high levels of proficiency in Dutch as a third language. In addition, even though Zobl (1993) found no significant differences between monolingual and multilingual subjects in the performance of a grammaticality judgement task, he noted that the multilingual subjects' responses suggested that they had formulated 'wider grammars', arguably because they knew more languages. Zobl argued that these findings are compatible with the hypothesis that multilinguals are advantaged in learning additional languages. Mägiste (1984) obtained significantly lower scores for a group of bilingual immigrant students in comparison to monolingual students on a number of tests of English proficiency. One cannot rule out the possibility in this case that there were mitigating factors, of a sociolinguistic nature related to the learners' immigrant status, for example, at play in these results.

Transfer and Multilingual Acquisition

Research on multilingual acquisition has shown that the magnitude of the transfer between languages can be affected by the linguistic distance among the languages involved (Bild & Swain, 1989). There is evidence for cross-linguistic transfer in multilingual acquisition when the languages involved are similar with respect to phonetic structure, vocabulary and syntax (Möhle, 1989; Singleton,

1987). For example, learners of French and English who have already acquired a non-Indo-European first language tend to transfer vocabulary and structures from other Indo-European languages they know rather than from their first language (Ahukanna _et al._, 1981; Bartelt, 1989; Ringbom, 1987; Singh & Carroll, 1979).

It has also been suggested that transfer is more likely from the first language than from later-learned languages so that learners are more likely to transfer from their first languages (Ringbom, 1987). However, such effects are less potent than typological similarity between the languages regardless of when they are learned, as noted above. At the same time, there is considerable evidence which indicates that there is a positive and significant relationship between students' first language development, especially their development of literacy skills, and their second language development; Cummins has dubbed this the 'developmental interdependence hypothesis' (see Cummins, 1981). These findings have been found particularly in the case of students who speak a minority group language. While the precise mechanisms underlying this developmental relationship have not been specified with precision, a type of transfer of some general sort is generally thought to be at play. Moreover, although direct empirical evidence concerning the relationship between first language development and multilingualism is lacking at present, it seems likely that a similar relationship might hold in the case of multilingual acquisition. Thus, it seems reasonable to expect that multilingual education, like bilingual education, is most likely to succeed in settings where the students' first language is given every opportunity to develop fully. This is especially likely to be true in the case of learners whose first language is a minority language and, therefore, susceptible to neglect in formal education. However, this is an empirical question.

There is some, although conflicting, evidence concerning the effect of context of learning on transfer. On the one hand, some research suggests more positive transfer in language learning in formal settings. Thomas (1988), for example, not only found that bilinguals (English–Spanish) outperformed monolinguals (English) when learning French as a third language, but also that those bilinguals who had received formal training in Spanish obtained higher scores on a grammar test in French as a third language than bilinguals who had had exposure to Spanish in non-school settings. These findings are supported by research which indicates that literacy skills in the first language can enhance third/multilingual acquisition under the assumption that there is a common underlying proficiency when it comes to the development of literacy skills (Cummins, 1981). Swain _et_ *al.* (1990) found that bilingual students who were literate in their first *and* second languages demonstrated advantages in third language acquisition over bilingual students who were literate in only their second language.

On the other hand, however, positive cross-linguistic influences have also been found in the case of oral language skills acquired in informal settings. Hammarberg and Williams (1993) conducted a longitudinal study of the acquisition of Swedish as a third language by a native speaker of English who was also proficient in German and could speak some French. They observed cross-linguistic influence from English, German and French when acquiring Swedish without formal instruction. Clearly, our understanding of the effects of language learning in formal (i.e. school settings) versus naturalistic settings on multilingual acquisition are at best preliminary and do not provide sufficient evidence at this point to support the differential effects of either setting with any certainty.

In sum, the extant evidence points toward a form of additive multilingualism; that is, in general, bilingualism has a positive effect on the acquisition of additional languages and this can be facilitated by factors related to typological similarity and perhaps context of acquisition. At the same time, it must be admitted that we still know very little about the conditions in which multilingual acquisition is additive or, alternatively, subtractive. Many specific questions remain to be answered. Is multilingual acquisition facilitated by the simultaneous acquisition of several languages or by consecutive acquisition? Is there an optimal age for the introduction of third and additional languages? Is transfer more likely at different stages of multilingual acquisition? Are the effects different or more pronounced in formal versus naturalistic contexts? Does level of proficiency in the first and second languages play a role in facilitating multilingual acquisition? Why does bilingualism positively affect the acquisition of additional languages?

Additive Multilingualism: Possible Explanations

In this section, we examine possible explanations for the additive multilingual effects noted in the previous section. The explanations of additive multilingualism that we present are derived from our understanding of current theory and extant empirical evidence concerning ways in which *bilingualism* might positively affect cognitive development which in turn might facilitate multilingual acquisition. Our explanations for additive multilingualism are necessarily conjectural because we currently lack direct evidence for our arguments.

Numerous studies have reported that bilingualism can have positive effects on cognitive development. This has been demonstrated on tasks of concept formation, creativity, visual-spatial abilities, and metalinguistic awareness (see Bialystok, 1991; Cummins, 1993; Cummins & Swain, 1986, for reviews), and it has been noted in a wide variety of language situations with learners of different ages and levels of proficiency (Diaz & Kingler, 1991). Extrapolating these findings to multilingual acquisition raises at least two related possibilities: (1) The putative cognitive advantages of bilingualism might facilitate the acquisition of additional languages; in other words, multilingual acquisition is enhanced by the greater cognitive flexibility and metalinguistic awareness that is reported to develop as a consequence of bilingualism. (2) The experience of acquiring a second language optimises the development of specific processing strategies that can enhance multilingual acquisition.

Before exploring these possibilities further, we must keep in mind that not all bilinguals demonstrate cognitive and linguistic advantages. In this regard, Lambert (1974) was the first to distinguish between additive and subtractive forms of bilingualism. Additive bilingualism tends to occur in situations where the first language is valued and acquisition of a second language does not replace the first language. In comparison, subtractive bilingualism tends to occur in situations where there is pressure to replace a socially non-dominant first language with a second, more socially dominant language. Additive bilingual contexts are associated with positive cognitive outcomes while subtractive bilingual contexts are often associated with negative cognitive consequences. When this distinction is applied to multilingual acquisition, it might be expected that additive bilingualism, but not subtractive bilingualism, would be associated with additive multilingualism and the benefits of additive bilingualism might, in turn, facilitate the acquisition of additional languages.

Cummins' threshold hypothesis provides a possible explanation for the differential consequences of bilingualism noted above (Cummins, 1976). According to the threshold hypothesis, the cognitive effects of bilingualism are dependent on the bilingual's degree of proficiency in his or her two languages. High levels of proficiency in two languages (upper threshold) are associated with positive cognitive consequences while low levels of proficiency (lower threshold) with negative cognitive effects. According to Cummins

(1979), the level of linguistic proficiency is a factor that mediates the effects of bilingualism on cognitive development because different levels of proficiency determine the quality of the interaction that school children have in educational contexts. Applying this hypothesis to multilingual acquisition, the following might be expected: attaining an upper threshold of bilingual proficiency leads to cognitive advantages which in turn benefit third language acquisition. The following formula illustrates this multilingual acquisition hypothesis according to which the cognitive outcomes of bilingualism mediate the relationship between bilingualism and multilingualism:

| additive bilingualism or upper threshold | $\rightarrow$ | cognitive advantages | $\rightarrow$ | benefits in multilingual acquisition |

Several studies of multilingual acquisition are compatible with the extended threshold hypothesis. In particular, in a comparison of monolinguals and bilinguals learning English as a third language, Cenoz (1992) found that the bilinguals outperformed the mono-linguals on a number of English language tests; she attributed the bilinguals' advantage to the cognitive advantages associated with their bilingualism. The Basque–Spanish bilinguals in this study were students who spoke either Basque or Spanish as a first language; all had Basque as a language of instruction. All the subjects also studied Spanish at school and used Spanish 'on the street' since it is the dominant language in most communities. This is an additive bilingual situation because the second language does not replace the first language. The findings of this study are compatible with Cummins' threshold hypothesis because the students who had Basque as a language of instruction can be presumed to have attained an upper threshold of proficiency in Spanish (the dominant community language) and Basque and, thus, to have benefited from cognitive advantages.

Other studies have reported that the use of minority languages as languages of instruction leads to beneficial effects. For example, the use of Italian for instructional purposes in the Foyer project (Jaspaert & Lemmens, 1990) was associated with positive effects on multilingual acquisition (Italian-French-Dutch) in the case of Italian immigrants in Belgium. Formal instruction (Thomas, 1988) or the acquisition of literacy in a minority language have also been associated with additive multilingualism in the United States and Canada (Swain *et al.*, 1990).

Other researchers have reported advantages among multilinguals with respect to their use of specific processing strategies. For example, McLaughlin and Nayak (1989) have suggested that 'expert' language learners use a wider variety of learning strategies and are more vigilant with respect to the effectiveness of different strategies than 'novice' learners. Similarly, Genesee (Chapter 11 this volume) suggests that double immersion (or trilingual education) for English-speaking children in Canada may enhance the development of language learning strategies. In a series of comparisons of monolinguals and multilinguals learning artificial linguistic systems, Nation and McLaughlin (1986); McLaughlin and Nayak (1989); and Nayak *et al.* (1990) found that multilingual subjects were superior to monolinguals in a number of ways: (1) they demonstrated greater flexibility in switching strategies according to the demand characteristics of the task – for example, they preferred mnemonic strategies for a memory task and linguistic strategies for a rule-discovery task; (2) they were more likely to modify strategies that were not effective in language learning; and (3) they were more effective using implicit learning strategies (see also, Hurd, 1993). Their superiority in these domains was attributed to their enriched experience as language learners which arguably helped them choose more appropriate strategies and use a variety of different strategies for learning the experimental artificial language.

Apart from cognitive advantages, bilingualism has also been related to increased communicative competence. Ben-Zeev (1977) and Genesee *et al.* (1975) argue that bilingual children are more sensitive and responsive to the needs of their interlocutors than monolingual children. In a similar vein, Thomas (1992) found that bilinguals who were learning a third language used more communication strategies in comparison with monolinguals who were more worried with grammar and vocabulary. The fact that bilinguals have to switch languages according to situational demands could enhance their sensitivity to the functions of language for social communication. Although research in this area is limited, Baker (1993) highlights its importance because it connects cognition with the bilinguals' social skills. In fact, further research in this area could provide an additional explanation of additive multilingualism by attributing advantages in multilingual education to the bilinguals' highly developed communicative sensitivity.

Implications for Multilingual Education

It has become customary to distinguish between additive and substractive bilingualism, following Lambert's usage (Lambert, 1974). As we note in this chapter, a similar distinction may be useful with regards to multilingualism and multilingual education so that educators and policy makers seek those conditions that are optimal for multilingual development. Multilingual education must be 'additive' if it is to lead to the positive outcomes that educators aim for and that have been documented systematically in the case of bilingualism and some forms of bilingual education. An important goal of future research on multilingualism should be to discover those conditions that promote additive multilingual education. At present, we have some indications of what these conditions are, but there is much that remains to be discovered.

Whether or not multilingual education is deemed successful may depend to a large extent on the definition or goals of multilingualism that underlie it. Following Grosjean, Cook, and others, it is recommended that multilingual competence not be viewed as simply the sum total of several monolingual competencies; that is to say, the aim of multilingual education is not to approximate the ideal monolingual speaker-listener of traditional linguistic theory. Rather, a more realistic definition would refer to the unique set of communication skills needed by specific groups of multilingual learners as reflected in their day-to-day lives. To expect and aim for the same levels and kinds of proficiency as for monolinguals could engender a false feeling of underachievement since, as was pointed out earlier, multilinguals may not need the same levels of proficiency in all of their languages in all of the same discourse domains as monolinguals.

While our review of available research indicates that there are many lacunae concerning additive multilingualism, direct and indirect indications of the conditions that might be important for creating additive multilingual educational programmes emerged. There is some evidence for the importance of linguistic distance – typological similarity has been found by a number of researchers to facilitate the acquisition of additional languages. Likewise, the well documented advantage that some bilinguals demonstrate in using alternative strategies for language processing, and other kinds of learning, is a potentially facilitating factor in multilingual acquisition. Multilingual education could capitalise on the putative cognitive benefits of bilingualism by designing curricula and instructional activities that help multilingual learners use their previous linguistic knowledge and strategies to learn additional languages. Instruction that calls on bilinguals' putatively more advanced metalinguistic awareness could also be beneficial in this regard.

Research indicates that under certain circumstances *second* language acquisition is positively dependent on the level and nature of the learners' proficiency in their first language (see Cummins, 1981). A similar developmental relationship might be expected to hold in the case of multilingual acquisition although direct evidence of this is lacking. In other words, additive multilingual education, like additive bilingual education, may be more likely to occur in settings where the students' first language is fully developed. This is especially likely to be true in the case of learners whose first language is a minority language and, therefore, susceptible to neglect in formal education (see Cenoz, Chapter 8; Gonzalez, Chapter 9; Hornberger & López, Chapter 10 this volume). Moreover, promoting literacy in the first and second languages may be particularly important in order to promote third language acquisition.

Another factor that may have important implications for multilingual education but has not received direct attention is age. There has been a great deal of empirical investigation on the effects of age on second language acquisition (see Long, 1990; Singleton, 1989, for example). The effectiveness of early introduction of second languages as media of instruction has been mixed, with some studies reporting no differences between younger and older learners and others reporting advantages for older relative to younger learners (see Genesee, 1987, and Chapter 11 this volume). It follows from these mixed results, however, that a case could be made for introducing second and third languages into multilingual school programmes progressively in order to optimise the differential advantages that younger and older learners bring to the task of language learning. That is to say, second and third languages might best be introduced in succession so that learners are able to consolidate skills in their first and second languages, respectively, before taking on third or additional languages. More systematic research is needed to examine the specific effects of early versus delayed instruction in and through third languages. In a related vein, research on the consequences of consecutive versus simultaneous second and third language learning is also needed.

Research on multilingual acquisition and multilingualism is in its infancy. In this chapter, we have summarised and interpreted the scant evidence that is available. As well, we have drawn heavily on research concerning bilingualism and second language acquisition to compensate for the lack of direct evidence concerning multilingualism and multilingual acquisition. While, in principle, our understanding of multilingualism can be informed by research on second language acquisition and bilingualism, these sources of information can never be a totally adequate substitute for specially designed studies of multilingualism and multilingual acquisition. Multilingualism and multilingual education are complex, and it is to be expected that they will be influenced by a great number of individual and contextual variables and interaction effects. Many of these factors may be the same as those that affect bilingualism and second language acquisition. If we are to acquire a thorough understanding of this complexity of multilingualism and multilingual education and to develop effective multilingual education programmes in a variety of settings, we will need the benefits of more systematic and careful research.

References

Ahukanna, J.G.W., Lund, N.J. and Gentile, J.R. (1981) Inter- and Intra-Lingual Interference effects in learning a third language. *Modern Language Journal* 65, 281–7.

Bachman, L.F. (1990) *Fundamental Considerations in Language Testing*. Oxford: Oxford University Press.

Baker, C. (1993) *Foundations of Bilingual Education and Bilingualism*. Clevedon: Multilingual Matters.

Bartelt, G. (1989) The interaction of multilingual constraints. In H.W. Dechert and M. Raupach (eds) *Interlingual Processes* (pp. 151–77). Tübingen: Gunter Narr.

Ben-Zeev, S. (1977) The effects of bilingualism in children from Spanish-English low economic neighborhoods on cognitive development and cognitive strategy. *Working Papers in Bilingualism* 14, 83–122.

Bialystok, E. (1991) Metalinguistic dimensions of biligual language proficiency. In E. Bialystok (ed.) *Language Processing in Bilingual Children* (pp. 113–40). Cambridge: Cambridge University Press.

Bild, E.R and Swain, M. (1989) Minority language students in a French immersion programme: Their French proficiency. *Journal of Multilingual and Multicultural Development* 10, 255–74.

Canale, M. and Swain, M. (1980) Theoretical basis of communicative approaches to second language teaching and testing. *Applied Linguistics* 1, 1–47.

Celce-Murcia, M., Dörnyei, Z. and Thurrell, S. (1995) Communicative competence: A pedagogically motivated framework with content specifications. *Issues in Applied Linguistics* 6, 5–35.

Cenoz, J. (1992) Enseñanza-aprendizaje del inglés como L2 o L3. Leioa (Spain) Universidad del País Vasco-Euskal Herriko Unibertsitatea.

Cenoz, J. and Valencia, J.F. (1994) Additive trilingualism: Evidence from the Basque Country. *Applied Psycholinguistics* 15, 195–207.

Cohen, S.P., Tucker, R. and Lambert, W.E. (1967) The comparative skills of monolinguals and bilinguals in perceiving phoneme sequences. *Language and Speech* 10, 159–68.

Cook, V. (1992) Evidence for multi-competence. *Language Learning* 42, 557–91.

Cook, V. (1993) *Linguistics and Second Language Acquisition.* London: Macmillan.

Cook, V. (1995) Multi-competence and the learning of many languages. *Language, Culture and Curriculum* 8, 93–8.

Cummins, J. (1976) The influence of bilingualism on cognitive growth: A synthesis of research findings and explanatory hypotheses. *Working Papers on Bilingualism* 9, 1–43.

Cummins, J. (1979) Linguistic interdependence and the educational development of bilingual children. *Review of Educational Research* 49, 222–51.

Cummins, J. (1981) The role of primary language development in promoting educational success for language minority children. In California State Department of Education (eds) *Schooling and Language Minority Students: A Theoretical Framework* (pp. 3–49). Los Angeles: Evaluation, Dissemination and Assessment Center.

Cummins, J. (1993) Bilingualism and second language learning. *Annual Review of Applied Linguistics* 13, 51–70.

Cummins, J. and Swain, M. (1986) *Bilingualism and Education.* London: Longman.

Davine, M., Tucker, R. and Lambert, W.E. (1971) The perception of phoneme sequences by monolingual and bilingual elementary school children. *Canadian Journal of Behavioural Science* 3, 72–6.

Diaz, R.M. and Kingler, C. (1991) Towards an explanatory model of the interaction between bilingualism and cognitive development. In E. Bialystok (ed.) *Language Processing in Bilingual Children* (pp. 167–92). Cambridge: Cambridge University Press.

Edwards, J. (1994) *Multilingualism.* London: Routledge.

Edwards, H.P., Doutriaux, C.W., McCarrey, H. and Fu, L. (1977) *Evaluation of the Federally and Provincially Funded Extensions of the Second Language Programs in the Schools of the Ottawa Roman Catholic Separate School Board.* Ottawa: Ottawa Roman Catholic Separate School Board.

Enomoto, K. (1994) L2 perceptual acquisition: The effect of multilingual linguistic experience on the perception of a 'less novel' contrast. *Edinburgh Working Papers in Applied Linguistics* 5, 15–29.

Genesee, F. (1983) Bilingual education of majority language children: The immersion experiments in review. *Applied Psycholinguistics* 4, 1–46.

Genesee, F. (1987) *Learning Through Two Languages.* Cambridge, MA: Newbury House.

Genesee, F., Tucker, R. and Lambert, W. (1975) Communication skills in bilingual children. *Child Development* 46, 1010–14.

Grosjean, F. (1989) Neurolinguists, beware! The bilingual is not two monolinguals in one person. *Brain and Language* 36, 3–15.

Grosjean, F. (1992) Another view of bilingualism. In R.J. Harris (ed.) *Cognitive Processing in Bilinguals* (pp. 51–62). Amsterdam: North Holland.

Gulutsan, M. (1976) Third language learning. *Canadian Modern Language Review* 32, 309–15.

Hammarberg, B. and Williams, S. (1993) A study of third language acquisition. In B. Hammarberg (ed.) *Problem, Process, Product in Language Learning* (pp. 60–70). Stockholm: Stockholm University.

Hoffmann, C. (1985) Language acquisition in two trilingual children. *Journal of Multilingual and Multicultural Development* 6, 479–95.

Hurd, M. (1993) Minority language children and French immersion: Additive multilingualism or subtractive semi-lingualism? *Canadian Modern Language Review* 49, 514–25.

Hymes, D. (1972) On communicative competence. In J.B. Pride and J. Holmes (eds) *Sociolinguistics* (pp. 269–85). Harmondsworth: Penguin.

Jaspaert, K. and Lemmens, G. (1990) Linguistic evaluation of Dutch as a third language. In M. Byram and J. Leman (eds) *Bicultural and Trilingual Education: The Foyer Model in Brussels* (pp. 30–56). Clevedon: Multilingual Matters.

Jessner, U. (1997) Towards a dynamic view of multilingualism. In M. Pütz (ed.) *Language Choices? Conditions, Constraints and Consequences* (pp. 17–30). Amsterdam: Benjamins.

Klein, E.C. (1995) Second versus third language acquisition: Is there a different? *Language Learning* 45, 419–65.

Lambert, W.E. (1974) Culture and language as factors in learning and education. In F.E. Abour and R.D. Meade (eds) *Cultural Factors in Learning and Education* (pp. 91–122). Bellingham, Washington: 5th Western Washington Symposium on Learning.

Long, M. (1990) Maturational constraints on language development. *Studies in Second Language Acquisition* 12, 251–86.

Mägiste, E. (1984) Learning a third language. *Journal of Multilingual and Multicultural Development* 5, 415–21.

McLaughlin, B. and Nayak, N. (1989) Processing a new language: Does knowing other languages make a difference? In H.W. Dechert and M. Raupach (eds) *Interlingual Processes* (pp. 5–16). Tübingen: Gunter Narr.

Möhle, D. (1989) Multilingual interaction in foreign language production. In H.W. Dechert and M. Raupach (eds) *Interlingual Processes* (pp. 179–94). Tübingen: Gunter Narr.

Nation, R. and McLaughlin, B. (1986) Novices and experts: An information processing approach to the 'good language learner' problem. *Applied Psycholinguistics* 7, 41–56.

Nayak, N., Hansen, N., Krueger, N. and McLaughlin, B. (1990) Language-learning strategies in monolingual and multilingual adults. *Language Learning* 40, 221–44.

Ringbom, H. (1987) *The Role of the First Language in Foreign Language Learning.* Clevedon: Multilingual Matters.

Sharwood Smith, M. (1994) *Second Language Learning: Theoretical Foundations.* London: Longman.

Singh, R. and Carroll, S. (1979) L1, L2 and L3. *Indian Journal of Applied Linguistics* 5, 51–63.

Singleton, D. (1987) Mother and other tongue influence on learner French. *Studies in Second Language Acquisition* 9, 327–46.

Singleton, D. (1989) *Language Acquisition: The Age Factor.* Clevedon: Multilingual Matters.

Swain, M., Lapkin, S., Rowen, N. and Hart, D. (1990) The role of mother tongue literacy in third language learning. *Language, Culture and Curriculum* 3, 65–81.

Thomas, J. (1988) The role played by metalinguistic awareness in second and third language learning. *Journal of Multilingual and Multicultural Development* 9, 235–46.

Thomas, J. (1992) Metalinguistic awareness in second- and third-language learning. In R.J. Harris (ed.) *Cognitive Processing in Bilinguals* (pp. 531–45). Amsterdam: North Holland.

Wightman, M. (1981) *The French Listening Comprehension Skills of Grade-Six English Program Students; Second Year of Testing.* Ottawa: Research Centre/ Centre de Recherches. Ottawa Board of Education.

Zobl, H. (1993) Prior linguistic knowledge and the conservation of the learning procedure: Grammaticality judgments of unilingual and multilingual learners. In S.M. Gass and L. Selinker (eds) *Language Transfer in Language Learning* (pp. 176–96). Amsterdam: Benjamins.

Part 2
Educating Towards Multilingualism

Chapter 3

Curriculum Decision-making in Content-based Language Teaching

MYRIAM MET

Content-based language teaching is an approach to second language instruction that involves the use of a second language to learn or practise content. In most instances, content is defined as material that is generally outside the realm of the traditional course material of language programmes. As such, many content-based courses or programmes use the second language as the medium for learning the content of specific courses (such as mathematics, science, art, or social sciences), shifting the focus from language as course content to language as the medium of instruction.

In this chapter, a variety of approaches to the integration of language and content are examined. Designing content-based second/ foreign language curriculum involves a number of key decisions. These decisions influence not only the nature and extent of content learning, but also the nature and extent of language learning. These key decisions are explored in the following sections, as we examine these topics:

- Rationale for integrating language and content.
- Models of integrating language and content.
- Making decisions about language and content.
- Content and the attainment of cultural objectives.
- The role of explicit language instruction.
- Teacher preparation and teacher planning.

Rationale for Integrating Language and Content

Content-based courses or programmes of language instruction are a natural concomitant of communicative approaches to second/foreign language instruction that emphasise the use of language to interpret, express, and negotiate meaning (Savignon, 1991). Using language for meaningful communication in authentic interactions with others (whether orally or through print) has resulted in a radical revision of how classroom language practice and tasks are designed. Communicative classrooms are characterised by activities and tasks that have a purpose and require an authentic exchange of meaning. Many of these purposes reflect the real-life needs of students who must be able to function in a variety of survival (or more sophisticated) situations in the target culture. In the early stages of language development, these situations include curriculum content that may be relatively egocentric (e.g. exchanging information about personal needs, wants, and preferences). Beyond such personal topics, other purposes of communicative language tasks may reflect students' needs or desire to talk about the world around them, the world of ideas. As such, using language to communicate about content is both consistent with and supportive of communicative language teaching.

Teaching language through content has been shown to be effective. Studies of students in immersion programmes, where content is learned through the medium of a new language, have shown that students develop high levels of language proficiency and meet (or exceed) expectations for content learning as well (Genesee, 1987; Hoffmann, Chapter 7; Cenoz, Chapter 8; Genesee, Chapter 11, this volume). Learning language through content provides students with opportunities to use language as it functions in the real world: to communicate authentic meanings, for authentic purposes, and to accomplish authentic tasks. It can also be time efficient: by combining language and content instruction, time set aside in the school day for learning language(s) as a separate subject may be reduced substantially. The latter may be an important consideration in educational settings where students are expected to learn one, two (or more) non-native languages over the course of their compulsory school years. Time is a particularly important issue in multilingual programmes where teachers may be concerned that there is more material for students to learn than usual, but not enough time to cover it all.

A constructivist rationale for content-based language teaching

In recent years, constructivist theory has helped shape curriculum decisions in many disciplines. It provides a strong rationale for content-based language curricula. Constructivist theory is holistically oriented and meaning-based. That is, learning takes place through experiences provided in meaningful contexts. Thus, knowledge is rooted in context and the 'parts' of learning make sense when seen within the context of the 'whole'. Unlike more traditional models of learning, in which teachers transmit bits of information which students are expected eventually to integrate into an understanding of the whole, holistic approaches allow students to see how the parts fit into the whole right from the start. The holistic perspective is based in part on research which suggests that the brain stores information in networks (Caine & Caine, 1991). The greater the number of connections and the stronger the connections among bits of information or the networks themselves, the deeper and more powerful the learning.

The importance of context to learning is reflected in a constructivist emphasis on authentic situations, experiences, and tasks. In constructivist classrooms, curriculum and instructional practices are designed to provide real or simulated real-life tasks for students to perform or problems to solve. And, because real-life tasks often call upon both declarative and procedural knowledge from a variety of disciplines, schools have placed greater emphasis than ever on interdisciplinary curriculum, and thematic approaches to curriculum organisation. In these approaches, learning outcomes and the experiences that lead to them are integrated across disciplines. This is because, from a constructivist perspective, learning is strengthened when students can perceive the connections among the many concepts and facts they are learning; when they can see how the parts both fit in the whole and relate to one another. Through thematic/topical/problem-solving approaches to curriculum design, students are enabled to see how what they are learning in one subject relates to what they are learning in others. For language educators, this can imply that the content to be integrated with language be the content students are engaged with in the rest of their school day.

Constructivist perspectives and language teaching

Many contemporary approaches to language teaching and learning, and in particular content-based instruction, are consistent with the constructivist approaches in the broader field of education described above. Given the importance of context, meaning and the connections among the information to be learned, a constructivist (and communicative) approach to language curriculum design would suggest that vocabulary and grammar be taught in clusters related to given contexts or topics, as opposed to lists of vocabulary or isolated rules of grammar divorced from how they are used in authentic communicative interactions. Constructivist approaches also suggest that the learning problems or tasks students engage in should have an authentic purpose. Authentic purposes tend to be more cognitively engaging than are those perceived by students as contrived or irrelevant. Students are most likely to be successful learners if the tasks they engage in require attention to meaning. As noted earlier, a major premise of communicative language teaching is that the purpose of language is for use in authentic spoken or written interactions – authentic being defined as real-life interactions that involve real-life meanings exchanged for real-life purposes. This means that decontextualised drill and practice in which form, but not meaning, is the focus is less helpful to students than tasks that are purposeful and require serious attention to meaning. Certainly, in schools, learning subject matter in a second language has real purposes and involves real meanings.

In content-based instruction, meaning is always the focus of instruction, learning experiences, and tasks. Students need to communicate with the teacher, one another, or texts, in order to access or apply content. In so doing, the cognitive demand of tasks requires students to call upon their existing knowledge, concepts, skills and strategies. This strengthens the connections between the elements of language being practised/learned and previous knowledge. As we have seen, research indicates that strengthening and making connections among concepts and knowledge increases learning and retention. For example, determining the kinds of housing most appropriate to different climates requires students to describe weather and houses for a task that is significantly more cognitively demanding than simply looking out the window to describe today's weather or describing one's ideal house. The relationships among cognitive engagement, cognitive demands, meaning and context in language practice are perhaps among the strongest arguments for content-based language instruction.

Content-based curriculum decision-making

Given the potential of using content to promote language development, it is not surprising to find increasing attention being given by curriculum developers to integrating language and content instruction. Decisions about whether content is to be integrated into language education programmes and how it will be done are made by curriculum developers (both administrators and teachers) who are charged with determining what students learn and how they should learn it. Decisions about the content of the language curriculum and instructional delivery require thoughtful reflection on the purposes of language education, the desired outcomes of the language programme, and the types of instructional experiences that will help students to attain those outcomes.

In multilingual settings, the kinds of curriculum decisions educators must make may be complex. Often, students may be expected to learn more than one new language at school, and they may be expected to perform at high levels in these languages in different contexts and settings both within and outside the school. For example, in many countries, students may be educated in a national language that differs from their home language for part or all of the school curriculum. Many of these students may expect to use the language of schooling throughout their academic careers. For these students, passing external examinations and subsequently attaining acceptance into advanced institutions of learning or jobs will be dependent upon their ability to deal with both academic and social language in sophisticated ways. Some of these students (and their families) may be long-time residents of their country, but represent a linguistic or ethnic minority. Others may be immigrants for whom effective participation in the civic and social life of their communities depends upon proficiency in the language of the school. In addition to the home and national languages, students may be expected to function in yet a third language, such as English, for international communication. In such places, decisions about the integration of language and content teaching need to reflect the purposes and settings of language use beyond the classroom. The following section describes various approaches to integrating language and content and proposes a model for classifying them along a continuum that reflects the relative emphasis given to content in language in a programme's instructional design.

Models of Language/Content Integration

In recent decades, there has been a number of approaches to integrating language and content. In this chapter I will use the term 'content-based' to describe a range of language education programmes that integrate content. Content-based instruction may be found at all levels of the educational system and around the globe. Immersion programmes, for example, may be found in elementary and secondary schools, and there are immersion programmes worldwide (Johnson & Swain, 1997): in Australia, Hong Kong, North and South America, and Europe. In addition to immersion, there are other approaches to content-based language teaching as well.

The varied approaches to integrating language and content reflect a continuum that allows for a range of models for integrating language and content. At one end of the continuum are *content-driven language programmes* (see Figure 3.1). In these programmes, content is taught primarily or exclusively through the medium of the second language, and student mastery of content may share equal importance with the development of language proficiency. Content-driven language programmes are perhaps best reflected by immersion programme models. In immersion programmes, students learn the curriculum in a second language for 50% or more of the school day. In total immersion, the school curriculum is taught entirely through the medium of a language that is new to the student, although after several years the use of target language may be gradually reduced to 50% of the school day. Partial immersion programmes provide half the school day in the first language, and half in the second language from the outset. Less time-intensive models of content-driven language instruction are programmes in which one (or more) subjects may be taught exclusively through the foreign language. For example, in some programmes, students learn science only in the foreign language, and, conversely, the language curriculum consists solely of teaching the second language through science. Towards the middle of the continuum are programme models that combine content courses with language courses. For example, students may learn one or two subjects in the target language, in addition to a more traditional language class. At the other end of the continuum of content-based language programmes are *language-driven content programmes*. In these programmes, students learn language as a subject at designated times devoted to language instruction (typically several hours per week). In these courses, content serves as an effective vehicle for communicative language experiences. Language skills may be practised through

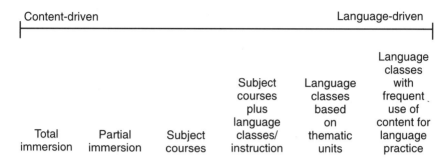

Figure 3.1 Content-based language teaching: A continuum of content and language integration

activities drawn from subject matter or other content, enriching or extending concepts already taught in the first language or second language. Students may study history or geography, mathematics, or art in the second language.

How curriculum developers make decisions about content and language outcomes depends upon whether a programme is primarily content-driven or language-driven, as we shall see in the discussions that follow. Although all programmes on the content-based continuum integrate the teaching of language and content, the role that content plays in relation to language development and the amount of explicit language instruction students receive may vary substantially. Most importantly for programme planners, decisions about selecting content, decisions about how content should be integrated with language, and the resulting language skills students acquire are directly linked to the way in which the relationship between content and language is designed. These decisions are critical in ensuring that students achieve the objectives of the language education programme.

Making Decisions about Content and Language

In designing curriculum for content-based language programmes, language educators must select the content to be taught through the target language. Two major factors can affect the efficacy of their decisions: the language proficiency of the learner and the fit between the desired language outcomes and the content selected. We will consider each of these factors below.

How language proficiency influences the selection of content

It is stating the obvious to note that when content material is abstract and conceptually challenging (such as a subject like philosophy) and students have minimal language proficiency, it is difficult to teach content in a way that preserves the academic integrity of the discipline. This can be a significant issue in content-driven programmes, particularly those in bilingual and multilingual societies, where students are often expected to acquire advanced levels of academic language proficiency in a non-native language. These programmes may place equal importance on student attainment of content outcomes and attainment of language outcomes, so that content-based second language teaching must allow these students to develop and/or apply concepts and understandings that are in keeping with general curriculum expectations. To do less is to shortchange students' intellectual development. For students whose principal schooling is conducted in a second language, mastery of curriculum expectations is critical for school (and later) success. Since most schooling learning is heavily dependent on language skills, there is a strong interaction between content and language growth.

In content-driven programmes where there is also language instruction that is complementary to content instruction, the language curriculum can support content learning. This curriculum will be determined by the language demands of the academic curriculum. Because there is a strong interaction between cognition and the ability to verbalise thought, complementary language/content teaching has a dual benefit for students being schooled in a second language: as students grow in their ability to verbalise in second language their conceptual understandings, they both strengthen their conceptual understanding and grow in their language proficiency.

In language-driven courses and programmes, students learn a second language or third language as a subject, not as the principal vehicle for schooling. Students' language proficiency is an important consideration in choosing content to be integrated with language. For students with limited second language/third language skills, it is helpful to choose content that lends itself to concrete experience. Content that relies heavily on visuals or hands-on experiences is not only easier to learn, but it also promotes language development. This is because visuals and concrete experience make input comprehensible: students are able to relate the language they hear (or read) to its referents, matching meaning with experience. Some aspects of the physical, natural and biological sciences can be learned in the second language/third language with the aid of visuals (such as pictures or video); they may be learned through observing an experiment as it is described and then carrying it under the direction of the teacher. Contemporary approaches to mathematics instruction often emphasise hands-on learning such as use of mathematics manipulatives and other forms of physical engagement to promote concept development.

For young students (who are usually novice language learners), content-based language learning through concrete experiences is facilitated because the school curriculum for young students is by its very nature concrete. In fact, for very young students, such as kindergarteners and first graders, the content of the school curriculum is not very different from the language curriculum. Young children learn to count from 1 to 10 (or higher), learn the names of the colours, days of the week, months of the year. They learn about families, homes (for people and animals), community workers. Many of these same topics are introduced in the first stages of the second language programme.

Another factor to consider when choosing content is the relationship between the language proficiency of the students and their cognitive maturity/age. Content-based teaching can be challenging when the growth of students' language proficiency is dramatically outpaced by their conceptual development. For example, teaching world history to US high school students can be difficult. Most US students do not attain high levels of foreign language proficiency in school because they do not begin language study before age 14. They have limited exposure to the language both in and outside school. As a result, even after several years of language study, content learning in the second language can be quite a challenge.

As we have seen, the language proficiency of students influences curriculum decision-making. Curriculum developers will find it helpful to select content that has the potential for successful student learning. In all content-based language programmes – whether content-driven or language driven – careful attention must be paid to ensure that students gain the language proficiencies needed to meet the demands of the content. In immersion-type programmes, teachers must be assiduous about enabling students to develop the requisite language skills, and must plan as conscientiously for students' language growth as they do for content. And, in other types of content-based courses, language teachers whose students have even less proficiency than do students who are schooled in their second language must be judicious in selecting content topics and activities that are within the range of students' linguistic capabilities.

Language outcomes and content learning: Making the fit

All language education programmes should be guided by a clear notion of long-term goals and specific learning outcomes that students are expected to attain. Making decisions about content requires careful consideration of what students will be expected to be able to do in the second language, and how content teaching can contribute to helping students achieve the goals of the language programme.

Today, most language education programmes aim to prepare students to use their new language skills for the purposes and in the situations they are most likely to encounter outside the classroom. In primarily monolingual settings (such as the US) these purposes and situations may be difficult to anticipate for many students. In contrast, in bilingual or multilingual societies, the personal, social, and professional needs of language learners may be more easily predicted. In some countries, some or all of students' schooling is in a second language. That language may be required for academic success, and for effective participation in the civic and economic life of the community. In monolingual, bilingual and multilingual countries, the uses to which students will put their skills in a given language (such as English) may be more predictable, yet relatively broad in scope. In addition, national curricula, along with formal examinations, may require high levels of performance in both content taught in a second language as well as in the second language (or third language) itself. For these reasons, selecting the content to be taught in a language programme is a very important decision.

In content-driven programmes, such as partial immersion, or other programmes in which students learn one or more subjects through the medium of a second language or third language, language educators must decide *which* subjects are to be taught in the target language. In many of these programmes, there may be limited or no explicit language instruction in addition to the subjects taught in the content. As we will see, the language proficiencies students develop will clearly reflect the academic language (lexicon, functions, discourse style) of the subjects they study. The selection of content is therefore a vitally important decision for language educators, because their decisions will need to consider the desired language outcomes that students are expected to achieve. In the discussion that follows we will see how content influences the language skills students will develop.

As a case in point, let us consider a programme for young children in which all science instruction is in Spanish (a programme that may be found in a few places in the US). In addition, there is very little time devoted to explicit language development, nor is there a curriculum that specifies second language outcomes. The language skills developed in this type of programme are tied to the nature of the discipline studied – science. Some of the language skills developed through learning science in a second language may be useful beyond the science classroom, and others restricted to it. Certain functions and lexical domains may be learned and others may not. Students who learn a second language/third language through the study of science will likely be able to use language for hypothesising, describing cause and effect relationships, or describing objects and their properties. Their vocabulary may be extensive when asked to describe the life cycle of a moth, explain the difference between cumulus and nimbus clouds, or describe the operation of a simple pulley. However, they may not be able to engage in a casual conversation with a peer.

A similar point could be made about the language proficiencies that result from learning mathematics in a second language. Mathematics is often favoured as a subject to be taught in a new language, and in many respects (as we will see later) mathematics is ideal content for teaching language. In other respects, however, mathematics can be limiting as well, particularly in the areas of reading and writing. Although students may first encounter orally new mathematical concepts linked to concrete, hands-on experiences, eventually students are also expected to read mathematics texts and be able to explain in writing their understanding. Many educators now also expect students to develop skills in communicating about mathematics, and some assessment measures of mathematics performance require students to write an explanation of how they derived a solution to the problem or task.

Reading mathematics texts is significantly different from reading other kinds of texts, such as magazines, newspapers, or narratives. Most language learners are expected to gain skill in reading narrative or expository second language texts. But the kinds of strategies and skills that lead to the successful construction of meaning of those kinds of texts may differ from those required for reading mathematics. Reehm and Long (1996) cite studies that have shown that the 'structure and language of mathematics texts are unique in regard to directionality, parallel examples, and a heavy reliance on symbols' (p. 35). For example, while it is often helpful to students to identify the main idea of a paragraph or other text segment, in mathematics 'the main idea may be in words, in symbols or left unstated for the student to construct' (p. 37). Because symbols are frequent and significant in mathematics texts, they represent a special challenge. Unlike alphabet-based reading, symbols cannot be decoded through phonemic relationship between sound and symbol. Symbols thus constitute a sight vocabulary for mathematics readers. Reading mathematics texts also differs from reading narrative texts in that pre-reading strategies such as skimming may be counterproductive, since mathematics texts must be read carefully and thoroughly (Reehm & Long, 1996).

For older students, mathematics not only becomes more conceptually abstract, that is, more difficult to access through concrete, hands-on experiences, but also more specialised in vocabulary and rhetorical features. Algebra has a distinct terminology (e.g. *knowns, unknowns*) and rhetorical style in the statement of problems. Its language may be limited in usefulness to students beyond the classroom, and may not, therefore, be a suitable choice of a language course taught primarily through content.

The context of the language programme may also influence the degree to which mathematics as content limits or shapes the language proficiencies of students. For example, novice learners of French in the US learning through mathematics will have limited opportunities to expand their range of communicative abilities in French beyond the language of the mathematics classroom. Their ability to communicate in a range of situations, about a range of topics, or express a range of language functions may be limited to those encountered through study of mathematics. In contrast, novice learners of English in Europe, who may have multiple opportunities (and motivation) to use English outside the mathematics classroom, may not be equally constrained in their language development.

While the selection of science or mathematics may, in some ways, constrain the development of diverse language functions or discourse styles, learning a second/foreign language through the social sciences may allow students to develop a wider range of language functions, structures, vocabulary, and rhetorical styles. For this reason, the content of many elementary and middle school social studies classes (civics, history, geography, economics) may have appeal to language educators. Unfortunately, this strength is also a great drawback: to access the concepts in depth and with rigour, students need to be well beyond even the intermediate stages of language development by age 10 or so. At this age, for example, US students are expected to be able to explain (i.e. talk or write about) the motivations of the Europeans who first explored and then settled in the Americas. A year or so later students can be expected to debate the merits and shortcomings of various forms of government (democracy, monarchy, oligarchy and totalitarianism, to name a few). To do so both requires and promotes language growth. But without a sufficient language base, students may develop an incomplete understanding of the concepts.

It should be clear from the preceding discussion that the content taught shapes the language that is learned, and that language proficiency affects the content that can be learned. Therefore, selecting which content, and how much content, is taught, is an important curriculum decision. When selecting content, language educators may find it useful to consider the following factors:

- *The degree to which learning the content is important.* If second language content instruction substitutes for instruction in first language, and content learning is important, educators need to select content that is accessible in light of the language proficiencies of students. Often, learning of content has equal importance with the learning of language, and students will be expected to function academically and/or professionally in a national or official language that is not their first language.
- *The degree to which content-driven instruction is the sole or primary vehicle for the development of language skills.* If the content is the major source of language development, it is important to select subject matter that will provide students with an opportunity to attain the range of language proficiencies they are expected to develop.
- *The extent of content-based instruction.* The more subjects – and the greater the amount of time – spent learning content in the second language/third language, the greater the likelihood that a wider range of language skills (including social language) will develop over time. For example, in immersion programmes sufficient interactions between teachers and students (and among the students) provide for the development of language functions and vocabulary beyond those encountered in content itself.
- *The proficiency of students upon entry into the course or programme*

When students enter with some degree of language proficiency, and/or have sources of language input either in other language classes or outside the classroom, then concerns about the constraints of certain subjects may be addressed. In second language content courses that presuppose intermediate or higher levels of proficiency prior to course enrolment, students will have had previous exposure and opportunities to develop language skills. Those gained through study of course content will complement the language skills already developed.

In the following section I will examine the implications of language courses where content-based teaching is supplementary to explicit language instruction, and the criteria by which choice of content/subject to teach may be made.

Putting language outcomes first

As noted at the opening of this section, content-based language teaching should enable students to attain the goals and language learning outcomes of the language education programme. Programmes are usually driven by stated curricular objectives, expected outcomes that describe what students should know and be able to do with language. These outcomes determine what teachers teach and, quite often, *how* they teach.

When language outcomes drive teacher decisions about what students will learn and how, content-based teaching takes on a different dimension. In these language-driven content courses, such as content-based third language courses, content is used as a vehicle to provide meaningful, purposeful language experiences that are cognitively engaging and demanding. The primary purpose of classroom activities is to enhance language performance. Content serves as a powerful mechanism for promoting communication in the new language. Thus, language is the driving force in decision-making, and teachers select content that allows them to achieve the desired language outcomes. Content may be taught through integrated units that draw upon many disciplines; or, teachers may design entire language instruction units drawn from a single discipline; or, individual content lessons may be used whenever these lessons can support language units. In these approaches to language-driven content teaching, then, content drawn from other subjects or disciplines is part of, but not the whole, language course. In these courses, content instruction is in addition to/complementary to language instruction. Often, the subjects taught in the second language/third language are also learned by students in their first language. (Indeed, ensuring content mastery is not the responsibility of the language teacher in these courses.) Selecting content in language-driven content courses is based on very different criteria from those used in content-driven language courses; the roles of learner's language proficiency and ultimate language proficiency differ as well. And, success is gauged not by the students' mastery of non-language content, but by their ability to use the language proficiently.

Choosing content that supports language outcomes is an attractive option for teachers whose language curriculum is a primary force in instructional decision-making, and whose students demonstrate limited language proficiency. In this approach, content is secondary to language development; it is selected to reflect the potential of content to promote language growth. Often, it is drawn from the school curriculum to strengthen the position of language education within the general school programme and to provide for cognitively engaging and demanding language practice activities. Language-driven content teaching represents an effective means of structuring classes that require authentic communication, that focus on communicative purposes that are meaningful and engaging to students, and that provide for deeper learning of both language and content.

In selecting content for language-driven courses, language educators may find it helpful to consider a number of factors.

- *The fit with specified language objectives.* The content should be an effective means of enabling students to attain the objectives of the language curriculum. The content selected should allow students to develop and practise targeted language skills (including reading and writing), and allow sufficient opportunities for students to communicate in the language.
- *The fit with students' current language proficiency.* Teachers will find it helpful to look for content vehicles (units, experiences, tasks, or activities) that are commensurate with the current language proficiency of their students, yet that also provide extensive opportunities for students to stretch, expand, and refine their skills.
- *The degree of cognitive engagement and demand.* Teachers will need to consider the degree to which the lesson/unit will be cognitively engaging to students. In some places, it may be

expected that the content will both connect to subject matter taught at that grade level, and that content-based language instruction will maintain the rigour and integrity of the discipline.

Applying the criteria to mathematics

Mathematics provides a good example of a content that addresses the factors described above, particularly for students in the early years of schooling (i.e. ages five to 12).

Fit with language objectives. The mathematics curriculum lends itself exceedingly well to second language instruction because many of the objectives of entry-level language classes can be taught through basic concepts in mathematics. Mathematics concepts must be applied to real-life contexts. One cannot simply measure – one must measure something. Novice language learners who may be expected to learn about classroom objects, parts of the body, or clothing, can apply their mathematics skills to measuring and reporting the size and weight of objects in the classroom, the ratios among the measurements of given parts of the body, or the relative weights of types of footwear. Similarly, language learners may learn to express food preferences, describe their family, identify leisure time activities, while in mathematics they learn to make and interpret graphs. Students can make graphs that depict food preferences, family size, books read per month.

Fit with students' language proficiency. Mathematics concepts can be taught through hands-on activities and the use of concrete materials. This means that students can access the concepts even when they are functioning at novice or intermediate skill levels. The accessibility of mathematics to students with limited language proficiency is considerably greater than is the accessibility of subjects such as history. History, and other subjects, are often taught through discussion, lecture, or extensive reading, requiring high levels of language proficiency.

Cognitive engagement and demand. For young students learning mathematics through a second language is inherently engaging and demanding. But even older students will find mathematics-based activities a motivating approach to language practice. Few older students can sustain interest in reciting numbers from 1–100. In contrast, practising numbers can be both cognitively engaging and demanding if students are required to complete number patterns (e.g. 1, 2, 5, 14, 41, . . .) or to estimate, then calculate, how many grapes equal the weight of an apple.

Applying the criteria to other content domains

We have seen the criteria on p. 49 applied to mathematics. The second language/third language teacher looking to apply these criteria to other potential content vehicles for language practice will find that not all topics in all disciplines will be equally useful. For example, a primary grades science unit on rocks may not have a good fit with the objectives of the language curriculum, as it may involve the development of specialised vocabulary (e.g. igneous rocks) of minimal communicative usefulness outside class. Further, it may not provide sufficient opportunities for language development (oral interaction, writing, etc.).

On the other hand, content vehicles that work well with the language curriculum may not be obvious at first glance, particularly when teachers try to connect with the rest of the school currriculum. Sometimes it takes a great deal of thought and ingenuity to design content-based experiences that meet the criteria on p. 49 and thus serve the language curriculum. One language teacher demonstrated her creativity in a unit that compared the countries of Ghana and Mexico. Her eight-year-old students of Chinese made Venn diagrams to compare animals found in one or more of these countries, combining a second language unit on animals with a social science unit. Other creative ways of using content to enhance language skills have included asking 12-year-olds who were studying the geography of Africa to learn and apply the language of comparatives and superlatives as they discussed regions with greater/lesser population density, distances between cities and countries, and the extent of natural resources in selected countries. A lesson on density allowed students to develop vocabulary for fruits, as they predicted, then observed, which fruits float or sink in a tub of water. (More sophisticated vocabulary can be developed by experimenting with liquids of differing viscosities or with different objects.) Students can be stretched grammatically, expanding their ability to describe cause and effect relationships ('The orange floats in water because . . .' versus 'When an object is placed in a liquid that is denser than . . .') Novice level language learners can learn about the properties of surface tension (and can practise counting) as they predict, then experiment with, the number of drops of water that will fit on a coin when dropped one-by-one from an eye dropper.

Summary

The preceding discussion has outlined the implications of decisions about the nature and selection of content for language teaching. In addition, it should be clear that content-driven language courses in which content learning is as important, or almost as important as language learning, may yield different results from language courses that simply use content learning as a convenient and effective vehicle for achieving language outcomes.

In content-driven programmes, selecting content to be taught in the second language may be relatively straightforward. In multilingual educational settings, students frequently are schooled in their second language in immersion or immersion-type programmes. However, in other types of content-driven programmes (such as partial immersion or a third language content-based course), decisions about which content to teach through the second language or third language may be facilitated by considering the issues discussed in this section.

- How important is the learning of specific content in relation to the language? If content is very important, then students must have, or must quickly acquire, sufficient language proficiency to ensure that the rigour of course content is not diminished. This also implies that sufficient time must be available for students to gain the necessary language/content skills.
- Will the course content provide sufficient exposure to the range of language skills students require to meet their communicative needs and purposes? If not, can complementary/supplementary language instruction be made available?
- Do students need the kinds of language proficiencies that this content will provide (e.g. will learning to explain and describe the human digestive system address the communicative needs of the learner?)?

In contrast, in language-driven courses curriculum designers may begin by determining the communicative language outcomes of the course, and then identifying which types of content (or content experiences) can facilitate language development. In this approach, content-based courses are primarily language courses. They may be interdisciplinary in the selection and utilisation of content from a variety of content areas and experiences. In addition, they may enrich or expand content already learned in first language. When language learning is the more important course/programme goal, curriculum decisions may be based upon

- the suitability of the content to the desired language outcomes;
- the accessibility of the content to the students' current language proficiency; and
- the degree of interest and academic rigour the content provides.

Culture in the Content-based Language Programme

In many places, culture learning is becoming an increasingly important aspect of the foreign/second language programme. Culture learning involves learning information, acquiring skills of observation and analysis that facilitate cross-cultural encounters and future learning, learning to interact successfully with culture bearers, and gaining insight into one's own culture. Culture learning may be particularly important in places where more than one language is used regularly in the schools and the community. In multilingual contexts, students may be expected to interact appropriately in diverse situations that may include participants from their own native language/culture as well as those from others. Further, students who expect to use their language beyond the borders of their community or country will need to know a great deal about interacting appropriately (including language use) as well as about other aspects of the lives of the people whose language they are learning. In the US, the National Standards in Foreign Language Education acknowledge the vital role that culture plays in allowing for effective communicative interactions. Students not only need to know about other cultures, they need to know how to behave (both verbally and non-verbally) in them, that is, they need to be biculturally competent (see Byram, Chapter 5, this volume). Increasing attention to the role of culture in language education is also a feature of the work of the Council of Europe (Byram & Zarate, 1994).

Deciding what to teach about other cultures, and how to prepare students to be effective participants in them, is a challenge to most language teachers. This challenge may be heightened in the content-based language programme, particularly when content is the primary focus. In teaching science or mathematics in the second language, there may not be a natural avenue for including culture learning in the curriculum – teaching students cultural information may not naturally occur in a discussion of the evaporation/condensation cycle. Similarly, teaching students the subtleties of courtesy in the second language culture, or aspects of register may be difficult to weave into a lesson on graphing. Further, in some instances, teaching content in the second language is difficult to achieve within the constraints of time allotted. Teachers in all disciplines often report that it is difficult to cover course material in the time available. It may be even more difficult in second language content courses leaving little 'extra' time for culture learning. Informal observations of the teaching of culture in immersion programmes suggest a similar phenomenon: the school day is packed full of material for students to master. Adding explicit second language language or culture instruction to an already full schedule is difficult.

One area in which culture can be naturally integrated with content is in teaching the social sciences. Here aspects of cultural information can be integrated into teaching about the history, geography, or economics of students' own or other countries. For example, a French immersion teacher found that she could integrate information about Paris, the capital of France, into a unit on the student's own capital city of Washington, DC. Similarly, a geography lesson on Africa can be used to compare and contrast topographical features of selected countries in Africa with features in countries where German is spoken. Content-teachers must be mindful that planning for the teaching of culture outcomes must be as conscientiously and carefully addressed as content and language outcomes.

In content-based programmes where the language curriculum is the driving force, integrating culture learning can be more easily achieved because the language/culture curriculum is the primary focus of instruction. It is desirable, however, for culture learning to be integrated into content teaching to the fullest extent possible. It is useful for teachers to remember that culture learning, like language and content, is more easily learned and retained when it is embedded in authentic contexts, purposes and meanings, and when learning is cognitively engaging and demanding.

The Role of Explicit Language Instruction

Because language proficiency is often the ultimate goal of content-based courses, explicit language instruction may be desirable (see Lyster, Chapter 4 this volume, for a fuller discussion). Extensive studies of the language proficiency of immersion students (who, of course, are enrolled in intensive and extensive content-based language programmes) indicate that even after many years of participation, immersion students are not native-like in their expressive skills. They do not speak or write as natives do, and they demonstrate only partial control of the grammatical system. A number of immersion educators have begun to examine the role that explicit language instruction can play in improving the proficiency of immersion students (Day & Shapson, 1991; Harley, 1989; Lyster, 1994).

The implications of the outcomes of immersion programmes would suggest that other forms of content-based second language instruction can benefit from explicit language instruction. As indicated earlier, students who participate in second language content courses may have restricted opportunities to develop a broad range of language competencies. Supplementary language courses, classes, or lessons can complement the language developed through content. Such considerations are of primary importance when working with students with limited proficiency in the second language, or with students who may have limited access to the second language outside the school setting, and for whom content teaching represents their major access to the language. In contrast, when the language curriculum drives decisions about the role and extent of content in instruction (as is often the case in third language courses), the opportunities for direct, explicit instruction in language remain. Content then becomes the vehicle for language use and application.

Explicit language instruction may be part of the content course or complementary to it. Where courses are complementary, it is most helpful to ensure that the second language/third language content course provides experiences that reinforce the desired language outcomes. Language outcomes may be functions, vocabulary, grammar, discourse skills, etc. For example, grammar may be taught explicitly and practised through content. Students may learn and apply the forms of the past tense by discussing historical events, by describing the steps previously followed in a science experiment, or by explaining how they arrived at the solution to a mathematics problem. Students' discourse skills can be enhanced and expanded by role playing imagined encounters between famous persons (e.g. Mahatma Gandhi and Nelson Mandela, Galileo and Albert Einstein). Where content-driven courses (such as algebra or biology) provide limited opportunities for the development of social language, complementary language courses can provide instruction in the social vocabulary and communicative functions needed by students. Similarly, opportunities to read narrative and expository second language texts will be important for the development of learner strategies needed for encountering a wide range of unfamiliar texts in the second language, particularly if the second language content course provides for encounters with a narrow range of texts and text types.

Teacher Preparation and Teacher Planning

Teaching content through the medium of a language new to students requires specialised professional knowledge, skills and abilities. In this section, we will examine what content-based language teachers need to know and be able to do (see Met, 1994 for a fuller discussion; see also Lyster, Chapter 4; Nunan & Lam, Chapter 6; Gonzalez, Chapter 9 this volume).

Content knowledge and pedagogy

Perhaps the most obvious demand of content-based language teaching is that teachers know the content well. Indeed, informal reports of attempts to institute content-based language programmes indicate that second language teachers are often concerned that their knowledge base in the subjects they are asked to teach is inadequate. Most second language teachers are professionally prepared as language specialists. Just as mathematics teachers are not usually specialists in second language development, so too second language teachers are usually not specialists in mathematics. Subject-matter knowledge is particularly important in content-driven programmes in which the second language teacher may be solely or primarily responsible for the teaching of content. While many teachers may have sufficient content knowledge to teach in the primary grades, more advanced courses can be a challenge. In addition to content knowledge, it is important for teachers to be skilled in content pedagogy. They should be well-informed of effective instructional practices and current approaches in the discipline. For example, in the US major reforms in the teaching of mathematics and science have been implemented in the last decade. Second language teachers who teach these subjects will be more effective content teachers if they are knowledgeable and skilled in the new pedagogical practices.

Second language acquisition and language pedagogy

Second language content teachers are language teachers. Like all language teachers, they must understand how language develops and be familiar with current pedagogical practices in language education. We know more today than ever before about how students develop skills in non-native languages, particularly in school settings. This growing body of knowledge is increasingly part of language teacher preparation programmes and is reflected in classroom practice. In content-based language programmes, where teachers may be content specialists with proficiency in the second language, it will be important that they understand and be able to apply the strategies of effective language instruction. Teaching content in a language in which students have limited proficiency differs significantly from teaching that same content in a student's first language (Met & Lorenz, 1997; Met & Lorenz,1993; Snow, 1987) and teachers will need a repertoire of strategies to ensure that students develop both content and language skills.

Planning for instruction

In addition to requiring a broader repertoire of professional preparation in terms of knowledge and skills, second language content teachers may also carry out their responsibilities differently from other content teachers or other second language teachers. Perhaps most salient among the differences is in planning for instruction.

All effective teachers plan for instruction, but second language content teachers have additional factors to consider: the language proficiency of students, the language objectives for the unit of instruction, the interaction between the language and content objectives, and how objectives will be assessed. Although these factors will be discussed in order below, it is important to recognise that the decisions teachers make in planning are interdependent and interact with one another.

Planning for content

Planning begins with identifying what students will learn. What should they know and be able to do as a result of instruction? Once content units or objectives have been identified, teachers may want to gauge the degree of language proficiency required to attain content objectives. Where feasible, content objectives may be sequenced so that those that demand greater language proficiency come later in the instructional programme. This can allow time for teachers to build the required language skills over the course of the unit or year (we will return to this idea shortly). For example, the year-long social science course objectives for a class of eight-year-olds include study of the culture, geography, and climate of three world regions. Teachers might decide to teach the geography of a given region before teaching about its culture, because many of the geography objectives can be taught through use of visuals and hands-on experiences. In contrast, many aspects of culture are more abstract and are taught primarily through classroom discussions or reading. Teachers might also choose a world region about which students already have some information, because background knowledge and existing schemata provide context and anchors that facilitate learning. In turn, as students begin to gain skills in the content to be taught – and the language related to this content – learning about the geography, climate, and cultures of other regions will be facilitated.

Just as course content can be sequenced to reflect the language proficiency required, it is also useful to sequence activities within a unit or lesson. Activities that move from the concrete to the abstract allow students to develop the requisite language skills for content by providing comprehensible input – students can match what they hear with what they see or experience. For example, a group of elementary school students is learning about closed circuits and circuit interruptors. The teacher could allow students to experiment on their own with materials that conduct electricity and can complete a circuit and then conduct a lesson that systematically examines the conductivity of the materials used. But since this is a second language content class the teacher is concerned that students may not be able to name the various materials or explain their reasons. As a result, the first activity the teacher designs is prediction: as the teacher shows each object she thinks aloud, naming the object and some of its properties. She then asks students to raise their hands if they think it can conduct electricity and therefore complete the circuit. To reinforce and support language, the teacher has provided a worksheet with pictures and labels. Students will circle the objects that they predict will conduct electricity. By selecting this activity as first in the lesson, the teacher ensures that students have been provided the language supports needed to carry out their task.

Planning for instruction includes selection of instructional materials. In addition to hands-on materials, students will need print materials to support both content learning and language growth. Often, materials written for native speakers are inaccessible to second language learners. Teachers need to select existing materials or develop their own that allow students to develop content knowledge and concepts but that are within the range of their language competence. Further, because reading can be a powerful tool in providing comprehensible input and in promoting language growth, teachers need to be sure that materials selected are well designed. They should be well organised, so that headings and sub-headings provide advance organisers and allow students to anticipate meaning. Illustrations should be clear and useful; text or captions should relate directly to illustrations so that the meanings of unknown language may be reasonably deduced. Key vocabulary should be highlighted in some way so that it is salient to students, and definition through illustrations, paraphrase, or example should allow students access to meaning.

Planning for language growth

Every second language content teacher is a language teacher. Every second language content lesson should result in language growth. Whether they teach in content-driven programmes, such as immersion, or in language-driven content programmes, it is important for second language content teachers to consider carefully language outcomes for every lesson.

Snow *et al.,* (1989) have identified two types of language objectives in content lessons: content-obligatory and content-compatible. Content-obligatory objectives are easily identified – students simply cannot learn the content without them. For example, it would be difficult to discuss the causes of pollution in the environment without knowing certain vocabulary (e.g. *pollution, environment*) and ways to describe cause-and-effect relationships (e.g. *because, when. . . . then . . .*). This type of language is so necessary for the learning of content that few teachers have trouble identifying the content-obligatory language for a unit.

Content-compatible language objectives are sometimes more challenging for teachers to identify. Content-compatible language objectives are those language skills that *might be taught* within the context of a given content lesson, but are *not required* for content mastery. For example, in a content-based language lesson on calculating percents, a teacher might have students calculate the percent of reduction on the price of clothing items. But students could also calculate the percent of students in their class that would like to travel to Alaska, read more than two books per week, or like certain flavours of ice cream. While the content (calculating percents) has some obligatory language, the choice of topic is open.

To determine content-compatible language objectives teachers turn to three sources:

(1) *The language curriculum.* Teachers may consult the language objectives of the curriculum to identify areas where students need instruction and practice. For example, if the language curriculum specifies that students will use comparatives and superlatives, a second language content teacher in the lesson on percents described above might ask students to make comparisons about the relative costs of clothing items or the preferences of students.

(2) *Teacher observation/analysis of student needs.* Teachers are good judges of areas where students need further instruction and support, so that their knowledge of student needs is an important source of content-compatible language objectives. For example, a teacher notes that students have difficulty with the third person singular form of verbs. To provide meaningful practice, the teacher incorporates this grammar point in a content lesson on percents. Students calculate the amount of time a partner spends on five daily routines (attending class, doing homework, playing sports, watching TV, sleeping, etc.). Students then report what they have learned about their partner (David studies at home for 10% of the day. He sleeps . . . etc.)

(3) *Content-obligatory language for future content lessons.* It was noted above that all content requires certain language skills for successful content mastery. Teachers can anticipate the demands of future content lessons, and build into their lesson planning the development of needed language. For example, a primary grades teacher knows that students will soon study their local community. One aspect of their community that they will learn about is modes of transportation. Therefore, the teacher decides to incorporate the transportation vocabulary students will be needing into current lessons: she has students make bar graphs that depict how members of their family get to work each day. By building vocabulary for a future unit into current instruction, this teacher decreases the amount of new language students will need for success in a future unit.

Second language content teachers can ensure that students develop language skills by planning as thoughtfully for language growth as they do for content mastery. This is particularly critical for teachers in content-driven language programmes, where opportunities to incorporate content-compatible language objectives may be easily overlooked. For teachers in language-driven content programmes, where the primary focus is language and content is the vehicle for language growth, most lesson planning involves planning for content-compatible language objectives.

Planning for assessment

Since second language content teaching integrates language and content outcomes, teachers will need to consider how students will be assessed. If content mastery is important, as in content-driven language programmes, teachers will need to decide the degree to which language and content are assessed independently of one another. Effective content teachers use a number of instructional strategies that allow students to access content despite limited language proficiency. As a result, students may acquire concepts yet be unable to verbalise their understanding well. On the other hand, the ability to verbalise understanding of new concepts reflects a higher level of attainment. Students who can explain or discuss concepts thus demonstrate a higher level of content mastery and language proficiency. In some places, students may be expected to take external content examinations in first language or second language, and teacher decisions about integrating the assessment of language and content may thus reflect prevailing circumstances beyond the classroom walls. In content-based programmes where language is of primary importance, content mastery may not be considered significant when assessing students, particularly if the second language content teacher is not responsible for ensuring that students master content. Nonetheless, since equitable assessment requires that teachers assess students in ways consistent with how students were taught, language assessment should reflect the content vehicles used for instruction.

Many teachers find it helpful to design a draft of their assessment instrument (such as a test) when planning their unit of instruction. Drafting the assessment prior to instruction assists teachers in identifying: what should students know and be able to do as a result of instruction? How important is content mastery? What are the language outcomes students should attain? How will I recognise acceptable (or better) performance when I see it? What kinds of instructional experiences do I need to provide to ensure that students are enabled to attain unit objectives? How will my assessment measure ensure consistency with my instructional programme?

Conclusion

In the decades between the explosive growth of immersion programmes in North America (beginning in the mid-1960s) and the present, there has been considerable growth in the use of content-based language teaching. As we have seen, content-based teaching can substitute for or supplement content taught in first language, as well as substitute for or complement language-only courses. In the last three decades, language educators have had opportunities to observe, experience and explore the ramifications of content-based language programmes for the development of second or third language proficiency. This chapter has attempted to draw attention to some of the issues related to designing curriculum for content-based programmes or courses of study. These issues are related to definitions of content, the interactions between language learning and content learning, the implications of content teaching for culture learning, and the implications for teacher preparation and planning.

While much has been done, much remains before us. Experience has provided language educators with information about content-based language instruction, but information derived from research studies is limited. Experience and common sense, rather than an established research base, currently help guide decisions about which courses are most effective for second language instruction.

We need to know a great deal more about the relationship between content-based teaching and other variables related to students (age, cognitive maturity, motivation for language learning); programme models and design (partial/total immersion; single courses); teacher skills and content knowledge; and materials available and/or used for content instruction. In particular, the role of explicit language instruction needs to be explored: not *whether* there should be direct language instruction, but rather what kind, how much, and when? Lastly, second language educators need to determine effective ways of ensuring that content-based language programmes prepare students to communicate in culturally appropriate ways in the various contexts which they are likely to encounter.

References

Byram, M. and Zarate, G. (1994) *A Common European Framework for Language Teaching and Learning. Definitions, Objectives and Assessment of Socio-Cultural Competence.* Strasbourg: Council of Europe.

Caine, R.N. and Caine G. (1991) *Making Connections.* Alexandria, VA:

Assocation for Supervision and Curriculum Development.

Day, E. and Shapson, S. (1991) Integrating formal and functional approaches to language teaching in French immersion: An experimental study. *Language Learning* 41, 25–58.

Genesee, F. (1987) *Learning Through Two Languages*. Rowley, MA: Newbury House.

Harley, B. (1989) Functional grammar in French immersion: A classroom experiment. *Applied Linguistics* 10, 331–59.

Johnson, K. and Swain, M. (1997) *Immersion Education: International Perspectives*. Cambridge: Cambridge University Press.

Lyster, R. (1994) The effect of functional-analytic teaching on aspects of French immersion students' sociolinguistic competence. *Applied Linguistics* 15, 263–387.

Met, M. (1994) Teaching content through a second language. In F. Genesee (ed.) *Educating Second Language Children* (pp. 159–82). Cambridge: Cambridge University Press.

Met, M. and Lorenz, E. (1993) Preparing global citizens: A foreign language program for all students. In *Curriculum Handbook* (pp. 11.211–11.240). Alexandria, VA: Association for Supervision and Curriculum Development.

Met, M. and Lorenz, E. (1997) Lessons from US immersion programs: Two decades of experience. In K. Johnson and M. Swain (eds) *Immersion Education: International Perspectives* (pp. 243–64). Cambridge: Cambridge University Press.

Reehm, S.P. and Long, S.A. (1996) Reading in the mathematics classroom. *Middle School Journal* 27, 35–41.

Savignon, S.J. (1991) Communicative language teaching: State of the art. *TESOL Quarterly* 25, 261–77.

Snow, M. (1987) *Immersion Teacher Handbook*. Los Angeles, CA: Center for Language Education and Research, University of California.

Snow, A., Met, M. and Genesee, F. (1989) A conceptual framework for the integration of language and content in second/foreign language programs. *TESOL Quarterly* 23, 201–17.

Chapter 4

Immersion Pedagogy and Implications for Language Teaching

ROY LYSTER

Since its inception in Canada in 1965, French immersion has been the subject of a vast number of research studies. The majority of these studies were initially programme evaluations, assessing linguistic outcomes in English and French as well as learning outcomes in subjects other than French (Genesee, 1987; Lambert & Tucker, 1972; Swain & Lapkin, 1982). Such studies generally confirmed the communicative strengths of immersion students, particularly their almost native-like comprehension skills as well as their fluency and confidence in second language production, albeit less native-like in terms of accuracy. Subsequent studies pointed more specifically to weaknesses in grammatical, lexical and sociolinguistic development (Harley *et al.*, 1987, 1990), and re-searchers suggested that such weaknesses may result from at least two discrepancies inherent in initial concepualisations of immersion pedagogy. First, Swain (1985) proposed that comprehensible input alone is not sufficient for successful second language learning; comprehensible output is also required, involving, on the one hand, ample opportunities for student output, and, on the other, the provision of useful and consistent feedback from teachers and peers (see also Allen *et al.*, 1990). Second, Swain (1988) argued that subject-matter teaching does not on its own provide adequate language teaching; language used to convey subject matter needs to be highlighted in ways which make certain features more salient for L2 learners (see also Allen *et al.*, 1990; Harley, 1993, 1994a; Met, Chapter 3 this volume). These two important arguments – that immersion cannot rely exclusively on comprehensible input nor on content teaching to ensure successful language learning – have changed the ways in which researchers and educators conceptualise immersion pedagogy.

Language immersion has generally been defined as a programme in which the second language is not learned through language instruction but rather through subjects such as science and geography taught in the second language. Accordingly, immersion pedagogy has relied extensively on the use of comprehensible input and negotiation of meaning to convey subject matter. For example, based on a survey of experienced immersion teachers, Snow (1987) presented 10 core instructional strategies in effective immersion pedagogy. Several served primarily to assist comprehension: extensive use of body language, realia, visuals, and manipulatives, in addition to predictability in routines and redundancy in lessons. Similarly, in immersion kindergarten classrooms (with students about age five), Tardif (1991) observed teachers drawing on a considerable number of paralinguistic elements. Immersion teachers referred to context three times as often as teachers in the English kindergarten, and they often asked students to respond to them physically by manipulating concrete objects or by performing actions (raise hands, become small, curl up, etc.).

While such techniques clearly benefit the development of comprehension skills, particularly in early stages, their contribution to production skills over time is now considered less certain. For example, based on data from a study of classroom processes in 23 Grade 1, 2 and 3 French immersion classrooms (with students between ages six and nine), Netten (1991) concluded that teachers should not rely on non-verbal depictions of meaning to facilitate communication, but should instead develop as many verbal connections as possible. Hullen and Lentz (1991) suggested that the use of comprehensible input as a key strategy in immersion needs to be developed beyond mere language comprehension so as to include an explicit focus on the interpretation and critical analysis of multiple discourse types and genres. Swain (1985, 1995) proposed that the emphasis on comprehension in immersion classrooms allows learners to process language semantically but not syntactically; that immersion students are not more 'pushed' to process language syntactically provides a further explanation for gaps in their interlanguage development. As a result, researchers have begun to characterise features of immersion pedagogy that entail a language focus; the move is toward 'a more language oriented second language classroom' (Netten, 1991).

To consider pedagogical options in language classrooms, Stern's

(1990, 1992) characterisation of the analytic-experiential dimension in second language pedagogy has been adopted. Analytic teaching strategies are those that emphasise accuracy and involve the study and practice of specific second language items and skills related to pronunciation, grammar, functions, discourse and sociolinguistics. Experiential teaching strategies focus on content, aim to engage students in purposeful activities, and emphasise fluency over accuracy and the use of language for meaningful communication. Stern does not present analytic and experiential teaching strategies as dichotomies, however, and instead advocates their integration in variable proportions in relation to learners' needs and programme objectives. It thus provides a framework for conceptualising diverse pedagogical options that permit teachers to integrate language and content, to encourage extensive interaction among classroom participants, and, at the same time, to implement a systematic focus on language development.

Key questions in immersion pedagogy are concerned with the ways in which and the extent to which analytic teaching strategies may be combined with more experiential ones in order to provide optimal conditions for second language learning. These issues, however, are not restricted to immersion contexts and are the subject of a growing body of research concerned with the role of focus on form in second language learning in general (e.g. Doughty & Williams, 1998; Lightbown & Spada, 1990; Long, 1991, 1996). Immersion contexts lend themselves well to such research for two reasons: first, their predominant focus is on meaning, and second, the persistence of non-target-like forms in immersion students' interlanguage development points to the need for novel ways of focusing on form in these highly experiential contexts. Because key questions in multilingual education are also concerned with the role of direct language instruction as well as with the integration of language and content instruction, current research on immersion pedagogy can inform multilingual programmes on these timely issues (Met, Chapter 3 this volume).

Genesee (1991: 198) proposed that there are at least three lessons from immersion that are relevant to other school settings where second languages are taught: namely, that an effective second language programme; (1) integrates content and language instruction; (2) encourages extensive interaction; and (3) incorporates explicit and systematic planning for language development. Accordingly, the key features of immersion pedagogy to be characterised in this chapter may be adapted to other school settings, including multilingual contexts. Indeed, the characteristics of immersion pedagogy to be featured herein emerge from the interplay of the three 'lessons' delineated by Genesee, giving rise to the following question: *When a second language is learned through content-based instruction and communicative interaction, what characterises the pedagogical intervention that results from explicit and systematic planning for second language development?* This chapter aims to explore this question by first examining features of teacher-student interaction in immersion contexts and then features of planned language instruction in these same contexts. Following Rebuffot and Lyster (1996), a relatively unplanned focus on language occurring during content-related interaction will be referred to as a *reactive* approach, whereas communicatively based instruction planned from a language perspective will be referred to as a *proactive* approach to language teaching (cf. Doughty & Williams, 1998).

Reactive Approach

This section will consider specific features of a reactive approach to language teaching, which includes teachers' use of corrective feedback during communicative interaction in addition to other attempts to draw learners' attention to language features as opportunities arise during content-based lessons.[1] The first part of this section is concerned with different types of negative and positive feedback in immersion classrooms, and the second part concerns the *negotiation of form* as it pertains to immersion pedagogy. Both sections present interactional data from an observation study of four immersion classrooms in the Montreal area: one Grade 4 class in an early total immersion programme and two Grade 4 and one split Grade 4/5 class from a middle immersion programme beginning in Grade 4. The students in this sample are between the ages of nine and 11.[2]

Teacher feedback

In Lyster and Ranta (1997), we reported on analyses of 18.3 hours of transcribed interaction recorded during 13 French language arts lessons and 14 subject-matter lessons including science, social studies, and mathematics. Our primary research question aimed to address how teachers and students engage in error treatment during communicative interaction, namely, during subject-matter lessons as well as during French language arts lessons with a thematic focus. Consequently, lessons selected for analysis excluded formal grammar and spelling lessons.

Six feedback types were discerned in the data:

(1) **Explicit correction** refers to the explicit provision of the correct form. As the teacher provides the correct form, he or she clearly indicates that what the student had said was incorrect (e.g. 'Oh, you mean . . .,' 'You should say . . .').

(2) **Recasts** involve the teacher's reformulation of all or part of a student's utterance, minus the error. Recasts are implicit in that they are not introduced by phrases such as, 'You mean . . .,' 'Use this word,' 'You should say . . .,' etc. Recasts also include translations in response to a student's use of L1.

(3) **Clarification requests** indicate to students either that their message has not been understood by the teacher or that the utterance is ill-formed in some way, and that a repetition or a reformulation is required. This is thus a feedback type that can refer to problems in either comprehensibility or accuracy, or both; however, we coded feedback as clarification requests only when these moves followed a student error. A clarification request includes phrases such as 'Pardon me,' and in French, 'Hein?' It may also include a repetition of the error as in 'What do you mean by X?'

(4) **Metalinguistic clues** include either comments, information, or questions related to the well-formedness of the student's utterance, without explicitly providing the correct form. Metalinguistic comments generally indicate that there is an error somewhere (e.g. 'Il y a une erreur', 'Can you find your error?', 'Ça se dit pas en français', 'Non, pas ça', 'No, not X', or even just 'No'.). Metalinguistic information generally provides either some grammatical metalanguage which refers to the nature of the error (e.g. 'It's masculine') or a word definition in the case of lexical errors. Metalinguistic questions also point to the nature of the error but attempt to elicit the information from the student (e.g. 'Is it feminine?').

(5) **Elicitation** refers to at least three techniques that teachers use to elicit directly the correct form from the student. First, teachers use various questions to elicit correct forms (e.g. 'Comment on dit ça?' 'Comment ça s'appelle?' 'How do we say X in French?'). Second, teachers elicit completion of their own utterance by strategically pausing to allow students to 'fill in the blank' (e.g. 'It's called a . . .'). Such moves may be preceded by some metalinguistic comment such as 'No, not that. It's a . . . ' Third, teachers occasionally ask students to reformulate their utterance (e.g. 'Reformule cette phrase-là').

(6) **Repetition** refers to the teacher's repetition, in isolation, of the student's erroneous utterance. In most cases, teachers adjust their intonation so as to highlight the error.

Of the 3268 student turns in the total database, only 34% contained an error (or unsolicited uses of L1). Of these errors, 62% received some kind of feedback from the teacher. Of the 686 teacher turns with feedback, the distribution of the different feedback types was as follows: recasts 55%, elicitation 14%, clarification requests 11%, metalinguistic clues 8%, explicit correction 7%, and repetition of error 5%. Recasts were by far the most widely used technique.

We examined not only the distribution of different feedback types, but also the ways in which learners reacted to the different types of feedback in turns immediately following teacher feedback. We referred to such reactions as *uptake* and classified these utterances as either *repair* or *needs-repair*. Repair referred to the correct reformulation of an error as uttered in a single student turn and not to the sequence of turns resulting in the correct reformulation; nor did it refer to unprompted self-initiated repair. Four types of other-initiated repair (cf. Schegloff *et al.*, 1977) occurred in the database, including either the student's (a) repetition or (b) incorporation of the teacher's reformulation, or student-generated repairs in the form of (c) peer- and (d) self-repair. The needs-repair category included student utterances coded as acknowledgments (such as 'yes' or 'no' in response to teacher feedback), hesitations, same or different errors, partial repairs, or 'off-target'.

The findings revealed that the recast, the most popular feedback technique, was the least likely to lead to uptake: Only 31% of the recasts led to uptake, with a fairly even distribution between repair and needs-repair. Explicit correction led to uptake only 50% of the time, although it was more than twice as likely to lead to repair as needs-repair. Clarification requests, metalinguistic clues, and repetition were similar in that they were effective at eliciting uptake from the student (88%, 86%, and 78%, respectively), although metalinguistic clues were more successful at eliciting repair (45%) than either clarification requests (28%) or repetition (31%). Of all six feedback types, the most successful for eliciting uptake was elicitation: All learner utterances following elicitation involved uptake with an almost even distribution between repair and needs-repair.

Finally, repair was examined more closely by distinguishing learner repetitions and incorporations from student-generated repair (i.e. peer- and self-repair). Recasts and explicit correction accounted for no peer- and self-repairs, of course, because both (by definition) provide correct forms to students, so students can only repeat. Conversely, elicitation, clarification requests, metalinguistic clues, and teacher repetition of error, lead only to peer- and self-repair since none of these provides learners with the correct forms, only signals or clues. Elicitation proved to be particularly powerful, accounting for 43% of all student-generated repairs. Metalinguistic clues accounted for 26%; clarification requests, 20%; and repetition of error, 11%.

In a follow-up study reported in Lyster (1998a), further analyses of the same transcripts revealed at least two potential sources of ambiguity from the learner's perspective. First, teachers used a great deal of *non-corrective repetition*; that is, they often repeated students' well-formed utterances. There were almost twice as many non-corrective repetitions as corrective recasts: 18% of all student utterances were followed by a non-corrective repetition while 11% were followed by a recast (that is, almost 30% of all student utterances in the database were followed by either a repetition or a recast). The discourse functions of these non-corrective repetitions proved to be identical to those of recasts: interrogative ones served either as confirmation checks or as requests for additional information, and declarative ones served either to consolidate what students had said or to provide additional information. Furthermore, these functions occurred in identical proportions across recasts and non-corrective repetitions, no doubt making it difficult for learners to distinguish the corrective function of recasts from the non-corrective function of repetitions and, concomitantly, difficult for them to notice the difference between their non-target utterance and the teacher's reformulation. There was therefore considerable ambiguity in these classrooms as students had to sort out whether the teacher's intentions were concerned with form or meaning. Such ambiguity may indeed be an inevitable characteristic of immersion classrooms where the emphasis is placed on meaning and where language is learned through content.

The second source of ambiguity was found in the teacher's use of positive feedback coded as signs of approval (including affirmations such as *oui, OK, bien sûr, c'est ça, d'accord*, praise markers such as *très bien, excellent, bravo*, as well as repetition of the student's repair). As expected, many signs of approval (34%) occurred immediately after a student's repair. Surprisingly, however, 47% of all signs of approval occurred immediately after errors; this included 32% after errors when teachers provided no corrective feedback (teacher ignores error and acknowledges content before proceeding) and 15% after errors just before the teacher's feedback (teacher acknowledges content then reformulates student's utterance into a correct one). The other 19% were signs of approval that occurred immediately after the teacher's feedback (teacher reformulates student's utterance then acknowledges content).

To determine whether teachers expressed approval more often in response to well-formed utterances than to ill-formed utterances, the co-occurrence of signs of approval was examined with recasts, with non-corrective repetition, and with teacher topic continuation after errors when teachers provided no corrective feedback. Surprisingly, signs of approval occurred in equal proportions across the three types of teacher responses: Approval accompanied 27% of all recasts, 26% of all non-corrective repetitions, and 29% of all teacher topic-continuation moves immediately following errors. This finding clearly indicates that teachers use signs of approval to reinforce messages related to content, irrespective of language form, and reveals a dilemma for teachers whose mandate is to teach both language and content: How can teachers reinforce the substantive content of students' utterances while giving them clear messages about language?

Negotiation of form

In Lyster and Ranta (1997), we proposed that 'negotiation of form' has the potential to minimise ambiguity in communicative classrooms given the way that it focuses learners' attention on form during meaningful interaction (see also Lyster, 1994a, 1998a,b). We characterised the negotiation of form as feedback that allows for peer- and self-repair, including elicitation, metalinguistic clues, clarification requests, and repetition of learner error. These four interactional moves are distinguished from recasts and explicit correction in that they provide learners with signals that facilitate peer- and self-repair rather than with mere rephrasings of their utterances. We speculated that the negotiation of form may benefit L2 learning by drawing learners' attention to form during communicative interaction in ways that allow them to re-analyse and modify their non-target output as they test new hypotheses about the target language (Pica *et al.*, 1989; Swain, 1993, 1995). That is, providing learners with signals that facilitate peer- and self-repair may draw their attention to target–non-target mismatches more effectively than mere suppliance of target forms in the input, at least in content-based classrooms where interactional exchanges are motivated by a variety of purposes and foci (Lyster, 1998a,b).

The term 'negotiation of form' was considered to capture more accurately than 'negotiation of meaning' the ways in which teachers focused on form during meaningful interaction. In contrast to the latter's primarily conversational function, which aims 'to resolve communication breakdowns and to work toward mutual comprehension' (Pica *et al.*, 1989: 65), we attributed to the negotiation of form a more didactic function: namely, 'the provision of corrective feedback that encourages self-repair involving accuracy and precision and not merely comprehensibility' (Lyster & Ranta, 1997: 42). The negotiation of form maintains the mutuality inherent in negotiation by returning the floor to students along with cues to draw on their own linguistic resources. Conversely, there appeared to be little to negotiate between teacher and student when either recasts or explicit corrections were provided.

The aim of the remainder of this section is to broaden the scope of the negotiation of form so as to include not only its corrective function but also its function of providing or eliciting relevant information about language during interaction related to content. Whereas the need to systematically integrate language and content in immersion classrooms has been clearly proposed (e.g. Met, 1994, Chapter 3 this volume; Snow *et al.*, 1989; Swain, 1996), other classroom observation studies have revealed that immersion teachers tend to separate content lessons from language lessons and teach grammar in isolation of meaningful contexts (Swain, 1988; Swain & Carroll, 1987). However, Rachelle, one of the teachers participating in the classroom studies described above, was particularly adept at focusing on language features during the presentation of content lessons or in language arts with a thematic focus. This section presents examples of this integration as reported in Lyster (1995).

Rachelle's first language is French. She had taught for 21 years: 14 years at the secondary level teaching French as a first language, and seven years in French immersion at the elementary level. She was teaching Grade 4 in the total immersion programme where the students' school day was all in French except for about one hour of English. The home language of her students varied: 12 of her 30 students spoke English at home, six spoke French, four Arabic, three Chinese, three Spanish, one Greek, and one Polish. Perhaps due to her experience as a French first language teacher at the secondary level, Rachelle demonstrated high standards concerning language form and was a good example of a teacher who pushes students in their output.

Analyses presented in Lyster and Ranta (1997) indicated that she recast considerably less than the other three teachers and drew more on negotiation techniques: 70% of her feedback turns led to student uptake whereas the other three teachers varied from 43% to 50%. Rachelle had an extremely interactive and enthusiastic classroom. Her negotiation techniques clearly did not stifle communication, as she effectively integrated a focus on form into meaningful contexts.

We will spend a morning, as it were, with Rachelle and her students, as we examine four different extracts recorded on 16 January, 1995. We first look at two extracts from a science lesson on how mammals adapt to their environment for protection. We then look at an extract from a discussion about meteorology as a pre-reading activity in the French language arts class. The final extract is an explicit lesson on grammatical gender. A focus on grammatical gender was one of Rachelle's objectives throughout the morning, and arose in various contexts. The extracts have been translated from French to English. The original French versions appear in the Appendix.[3]

Extract 1: Well-adapted mammals

R: OK, today we're going to talk about mammals, well-adapted mammals. What does that mean? What does that word mean, mammals that are well-adapted? What word does 'adapted' come from?

St: A . . . ad . . ., ada . . ., well it's because . . .

R: It looks like adopted, doesn't it?

St: Yes.

R: Well, it's not 'adopted', it's 'adapted'. 'Adapt' comes from what word, Liz? What other word could we make with 'adapt'? Adapt . . .

St: Adoption.

R: Eh?

St: Adaption?

R: No, not adoption.

St: Adaptation.

R: Bravo, adaptation. What does that mean? What does 'adaptation' mean? [. . .] Animals that are well-adapted? Adaptation? . . .

St: Accustomed? [*habitué*]

R: He says it would be 'accustomed'. Is that right?

Sts: Yes.

R: So another word. We'll see. Accustomed [*Ha - bi - tu - é*] So they're mammals that are well accustomed. Another word, what do you say?

St: They're ready, like in summer they know that winter's coming so they're ready.

R: They're animals that are ready. How do we spell 'ready' [*prêt*]?

Sts: %*P, R, E, accent grave, S*%?

R: *P, R, E, accent grave, S*. Is that right?

Sts: %Yes%.

Sts: %No%

R: Who agrees with that word?

St: %One T.%

St: %Two T's.%

R: Who doesn't agree? You don't agree?

St: Because *près* like that means you're near [*proche*].

R: *Près* like that means you're near [*proche*] . . . Do we mean animals that are near?

Sts: No.

R: No! One T. Animals that are: *P, R, E, accent circonflexe, T* . . . ?%

St: %*Accent grave?*%

R: What is it in the feminine?

Sts: *Prête.*

R: *Prête.* Are the girls ready [*prêtes*]? Are the boys ready [*prêts*]?

Sts: Yes.

R: Are the mammals ready [*prêts*]?

St: Yes.

R: Mammals that are ready, that are accustomed, that are adapted. Is there another word? [. . .]

Rachelle begins this interaction by focusing on meaning and form: she asks what *adapté* ('adapted') means but also from what word it derives. The students try out different hypotheses (*adoption*, *adaption*) until they find the right word, *adaptation*, which allows Rachelle to return to meaning. The students then propose words they believe to be semantically associated with *adapté*: *habitué* ('accustomed') and *prêt* ('ready'). Rachelle focuses on the form of *prêt* by asking the students how to spell it. They propose different spellings which allows Rachelle to make a distinction between *prêt* and its homonym *près* ('near') and to negotiate these forms with the students ('Who agrees with that word?'). Rachelle then successfully elicits the feminine form of the word *prêt* and proceeds to model explicitly the masculine/feminine distinction before recontextualising the word *prêt* in relation to well-adapted animals: *Est-ce que les filles sont prêtes? Est-ce que les garçons sont prêts?* [. . .] *Est-ce que les mammifères sont prêts?* She then reiterates the synonyms that the students have proposed before eliciting other meanings of the word *adapté*.

Extract 2: Skunks

R: Now there's the skunk, my friends. What do skunks do? Skunks? How do we spell 'skunk' [*mouffette*]?

Sts: <Everyone answers something different at the same time>

R: Two F's ... and two T's. Good. Does *professeur* take two F's and two S's?

Sts: No.

R: What does it take?

St: %One F.%

StD: %Two S's.%

R: Two S's and ...?

St: One F.

R: One F. Gotta be careful. So, skunks, what do they do? Nancy?

St: Well, there's a stream of perfume that doesn't smell very good [*un jet de parfum qui sent pas très bon ...*]

R: So, '*un jet de parfum*'. We'll call that a ...?

Sts: ... liquid.

R: Liquid. A liquid ...

StD: ... that stinks [*puant*].

R: A stinking liquid, well, we can also call that, a liquid that doesn't have a good odour, how do we call that? A liquid that doesn't have a good odour? When it's a good odour? *C'est o ...*?

Sts: *Odoreux?*

R: *O ... do ...?*

Sts: *Odorant?*

R: What?

Sts: *Odorant.* ['sweet-smelling'; 'fragrant']

R: *Odorant.* And if it's ...

Sts: *Désodorant.*

R: What?

Sts: *Désodorant.*

R: *Désodorant.* [laughs]

St: *Désodorance?*

StD: *Indodorance?*

R: *In-, in-,* that's not a bad idea! *In-* means 'not'. *Inodoran ...*?

St: %ce.%

R: % the word is: %, **mal***odorant.* ['foul-smelling']

St: Oh yeah.

Rachelle's initial focus is again on content ('What do skunks do?') although she immediately refers to form ('How do we spell *mouffette?*'). This leads her to introduce a side sequence in which she elicits the spelling of *professeur* since she knows that her students often spell it with two 'f's' instead of one. Returning to the topic of the skunk's defences, Rachelle elicits *un jet de parfum* although she prefers the next student's contribution, *un liquide puant*. In search of a more sophisticated term than *puant*, Rachelle elicits from the students the word *odorant* in order to allow them to discover its opposite, *malodorant*. Although it is she who finally provides the word *malodorant*, in the process the students propose the prefixes *dé-* and *in-*. Rachelle points out that *in-* is a particularly good idea since it means 'not'. This short sequence on prefixes, integrated into a lively discussion about skunks, is particularly interesting in that we know from research that immersion teachers tend not to focus on structural information about vocabulary outside of separate grammar lessons (Allen *et al.*, 1990) and that immersion students are limited in their productive use of such derivational morphology (Harley, 1992; Harley & King, 1989).

The next sequence has been extracted from a pre-reading discussion about a story entitled '*La météorologie en folie.*' Prior to the extract, Rachelle focuses on form as she elicits the grammatical gender of *météorologie* as well as its pronunciation and spelling (many students omit the *-ro-* and pronounce it as *météologie*). She then focuses on meaning as she elicits definitions of meteorology and has the students brainstorm to enumerate various atmospheric phenomena. She continues her focus on meaning as she asks the students, 'What does a meteorologist do?'

Extract 3: What does a meteorologist do?

R:　Now, what does a meteorologist do?

St:　Um, it says what it's gonna be like . . .

R:　It says? Who's it?

St:　It explains . . .

R:　Who's it? Tell me who **it** is.

St:　It's persons . . .

R:　Ah! It's a person! It's a person here.

StD:　A person who . . . who says um . . . if it's gonna rain, if it's gonna be sunny, if . . .

StD:　It's the /weatherman/ [in English].

R:　Who says . . .?

St:　Who says the weather.

R:　Who says the weather?

StD: Who announces the weather.
R: Who announces! Who announces the weather. Does he only announce the weather that we're going to have today, now?
Sts: No.
R: What else does he announce?
St: Tomorrow, eh . . .
R: Tomorrow. So, he, also, he . . . tomorrow he . . .?
St: He warns/informs [*prévient*].
R: What?
St: Warns/informs [*prévient*]?
R: He warns/informs us. He forecasts [*prévoit*].
St: He warns that there will be . . .
R: He warns us. He forecasts in advance. He forecasts in advance.
St: There's another word too.

This extract reveals how Rachelle has her students focus on the meaning of *météorologiste* and at the same time pushes them to refine their vocabulary use. In describing what a meteorologist does, the students are led along a continuum from general all-purpose verbs to more specific ones: *dire* → *expliquer* → *annoncer* → *prévenir* → *prévoir*.

The final utterance in this extract is interesting in that it is a student-initiated one that leads to lengthy discussion about grammatical gender. After saying, 'There's another word too', the student introduces a synonym of *météorologiste*, namely, *météorologue*. Rachelle immediately asks what its gender is, and the students agree that both *météorologiste* and *météorologue* can be either masculine or feminine with no inflectional changes (i.e. *un* or *une météorologiste*; *un* or *une météorologue*). She then asks them if they know of other names of occupations whose forms do not change according to gender. After considerable brainstorming, they have proposed the following words: *vétérinaire, dentiste, secrétaire, concièrge, élève, thérapeute, linguiste*. During their search for these words, the students were able to experiment with several phonological distinctions (e.g. *directeur-directrice; poète-poétesse; illustrateur-illustratrice; instituteur-institutrice; assistant-assistante*) as well as with pairs whose spelling changes but not the pronunciation (e.g.*professeur/e, auteur/e*).

The preceding digression reveals that Rachelle's students possess considerable knowledge about grammatical gender and are given opportunities to test their hypotheses in meaningful contexts. In contrast to this spontaneous brainstorming, Rachelle's more formal attempt at a lesson on grammatical gender is less successful, as we see in the following extract.

Extract 4: What's the gender?

R: [...] What I'd like to know is the gender. What's the gender of *avant-midi* and *après-midi*?

St: There's gender ...

R: What is the gender?

St: There's gender and there's number.

R: There's gender and there's number. I don't want the number. I want the gender. Yes, Myra?

St: Is <?> the gender?

R: The gender. What is that I want to know? What is it that I'm asking?

StD: <?> it's the difference.

R: The difference. Do I want to know the difference? Eh? Did I ask for a synonym?

St: No.

R: No. I asked for the gender. Gender seems far away! What's the gender?

St: Gender ... [inaudible; lots of noise].

R: No. What's the gender? What is gender, anyway? We'll begin with number first ... What is number?

St: Number is ...

R: How many numbers in French?

Sts: [Students responses vary from *neuf* to *cent*].

R: What?

St: Nine hundred?

R: No. Gender and number, you don't remember that?

Sts: No.

R: Aye-aye-aye. There are two genders and two numbers. Number, what does that mean to you? Yes.

St: Gender, I know. It's ... it's ... [noisy]

R: No. I didn't ask for verbs. I didn't ask for auxiliaries. What is gender? Number. What gender are you? What gender are you, Richard?

St: Euh ...

R: What gender are you?

StD: Masculine?

R: Your gender is masculine. Is that right?

Sts: No. Yes.

R: Yes, of course. And what gender are you?

St: Feminine.

R: Good! [...] Now, number in French. What's number, Stéphanie? Gender is feminine or masculine. What' s number in French? It's ...

St: It's like feminine or masculine?

R: It's like feminine or masculine? No, that's gender! Number is . . .
St: Singular or plural?
R: Bravo!
Sts: Yes.
R: Singular or plural. Oh la-la, you don't remember that? We're
        going to have to do some more, eh? So here I wanted to know the
        gender. What's the gender of these two words? Do we say *une*
        avant-midi or *un avant-midi*?

This rather amusing sequence reveals considerable confusion on the
part of the students as well as the teacher's consequent frustration.
Although these Grade 4 students had demonstrated considerable
knowledge of grammatical gender during the course of the morning,
this explicit lesson obfuscates the issue as students confound
grammatical gender and grammatical number – properties with no
functional links but which may be juxtaposed in grammar books and
grammar lessons. Clearly, the metalanguage used by Rachelle is not
facilitative in this lesson, nor is the decontexualised nature of the
lesson. Given the richness of meaningful contexts provided by subject
matter in immersion classrooms, as evidenced in Rachelle's lessons
prior to this one, one may well wonder about the need and utility of
such a decontexualised grammar lesson for learners of this age.

This observation should not be construed as an argument against
any explicit focus on language features. It does lend support, however,
to the argument against decontextualised grammar teaching as was
observed by Swain and Carroll (1987). In their large-scale observation
study they found that not only did immersion teachers tend to teach
grammar out of context, but that such decontexualised language
teaching is not effective at eradicating the grammatical inaccuracies of
immersion students. Indeed, researchers such as Long (1991, 1996) have
suggested that it may be more efficient for teachers to focus on form
during meaningful interaction. A preference for focusing on form
during meaningful interaction in this way, however, does not preclude
the planning of lessons with a language focus in either the language
arts class or the subject-matter class. Such units planned from a
language perspective are the subject of the next section.

Proactive Approach

Although Rachelle's attempt at an explicit lesson on gender did not
appear as successful as her treatment of gender during more genuine
interaction (including her off-the-cuff lesson on names of occupations

and their gender distinctions), the explicit treatment of many second language features is certainly justified and perhaps necessary. Research has shown that many language features simply do not get noticed by immersion students, given the limits of the classroom and the nature of classroom discourse.

According to Harley (1993), experiential teaching strategies are of prime importance in promoting incidental language learning and creating genuine task demands, but they do not guarantee that students will observe or express specific form-function relationships. Harley proposed that analytic teaching is needed for those features of the second language that (1) differ in non-obvious or unexpected ways from the first language; (2) are irregular, infrequent, or otherwise lacking in perceptual salience in the L2 input; (3) do not carry a heavy communicative load. In view of these criteria, Harley suggested that the following features may not get noticed in the overall experiential context of the French immersion classroom and may require an analytic focus:

- gender distinctions;
- distinctions in the use of *avoir* and *être*;
- various features of the verb system such as the use of the imperfect, conditionals, and third person plural agreement rules in the present tense;
- the *tu/vous* distinction;
- certain vocabulary features (for example, syntactic frames of verbs not congruent with the learner's first language; lexical derivation, i.e. productive use of affixes).

As defined here, a proactive approach involves instruction that has been planned from a language perspective to promote the perception and use of specific language features in a meaningful context. Such planned activities have their place in either a language arts class with a thematic focus, or in the subject-matter class. This approach builds on Harley and Swain's (1984: 310) proposal that there is a twofold need in immersion for:

(1) the provision of more focused L2 input that provides learners with ample *opportunity to observe* the formal and semantic contrasts involved in the relevant target subsystem (this does not necessarily involve explicit grammar teaching); and
(2) increased opportunity for students to be involved in activities requiring *the productive use* of such forms in meaningful situations. (emphasis added)

A series of four experimental studies undertaken in immersion classrooms has suggested that such instruction can benefit students' interlanguage development, in varying degrees, with respect to aspect (Harley, 1989), the conditional mode (Day & Shapson, 1991), sociostylistic variation (Lyster, 1994b), and grammatical gender (Harley, 1994b, 1998). Studies undertaken in other classroom contexts also support such a role for planned language instruction (e.g. Spada & Lightbown, 1993; White, 1991; White *et al.*, 1991, see Spada, 1997, for a review of several studies that support a role for form focused instruction that includes either direct teaching or corrective feedback).

Aspect

Harley (1989) conducted an experimental study in Grade 6 French immersion classrooms (with 11–12-year-old students) in order to determine the effects of instruction on the grammatical competence of immersion students, with respect to their use of the *imparfait* and the *passé composé*. The instructional unit was designed to provide (1) focused target language input to promote the perception and comprehension of the functional contrasts between the two verb tenses, and (2) more opportunities for students to express these functions in the realisation of interesting, motivating tasks. Some of the activities involved reading a legend, playing language games, working in groups to create new legends, and creating albums of childhood memories. The materials were implemented in six experimental classrooms for approximately 12 hours during an eight-week period.

A pre-test, an immediate post-test, and a delayed post-test were administered to the experimental group as well as to a comparison group in order to compare classes on three measures: a cloze test, a composition task and an oral interview. Immediate post-test results revealed benefits on the cloze test and the oral interview for the experimental group, but no statistically significant differences between the experimental and comparison groups on the composition task. Three months later, on the delayed post-test, no significant differences were found between the groups on any of the measures. However, students in the experimental group continued to improve, but so did students in the comparison group. Harley explained that comparison teachers indicated on questionnaires that they too had devoted a considerable amount of time to the teaching of the *passé composé* and the *imparfait*. Furthermore, experimental teachers indicated that although the treatment materials promoted a focus on content more so than on form (even for teachers), many students had not yet mastered the formal aspects of the verb inflections. Finally, Harley concluded that the amount of time devoted to this difficult feature of French grammar was likely not enough to allow for a sustained advantage.

Conditional mode

Day and Shapson (1991; see also 1996) conducted a classroom study in six experimental and six comparison classes at the Grade 7 level (12–13-year-old students). The study was designed to test the effect of instruction on the use of the conditional in hypothetical situations and in polite requests. The thematic context involved the planning of a (hypothetical) space colony and thus integrated concepts from the science class. Some of the major instructional features of the experimental treatment included the use of:

(1) the cooperative-learning approach to maximise student inter- action and use of the conditional in natural, communicative situations;
(2) linguistic games and exercises . . . to reinforce the use of this form in more formal, structured situations; and
(3) group- and self-evaluation procedures to encourage students to develop conscious awareness of their language use. (p. 35)

The teaching unit was implemented in the experimental classes for an average of 17.4 hours during a six-week period. It included the following major group activities: planning a space colony, presen- tation of an oral report describing and justifying the students' plan, making a model of the plan, preparation of a written report describing each part of the colony and its importance, and preparation of a newspaper article describing the life of the space pioneers.

On the immediate post-test, the experimental group made significant gains on the cloze test and the written composition, but not on the oral interview. The experimental group maintained an advantage on the cloze test and the written composition at the time of the delayed post-test 11 weeks later. Progress was clearly made by the experimental classes on the oral interview as well, but these gains were counterbalanced by one particularly strong comparison class, thus precluding statistically significant differences between groups on measures of oral proficiency. As a result of questionnaire data, the authors suggested that the instructional methods used by the teacher of this comparison class was similar to those used by the experimental teachers 'in that grammar was taught through a combination of formal and functional approaches and a great deal of emphasis was placed on oral and written activities' (p. 52). They concluded that the results reinforce the need for the systematic introduction of the kind of instruction and materials used in their study.

Sociostylistic variation

Lyster (1994b) conducted a classroom experiment at the Grade 8 level (with 13–14-year-old students) which aimed to measure the effect of instruction on French immersion students' sociolinguistic competence: that is, their ability to recognise and produce contextually appropriate language. The instructional unit was implemented in three experimental classrooms for an average of 12 hours over five weeks and involved the following types of activities and practice (p. 269):

(1) Explicit comparisons of various speech acts in formal and informal contexts allowed students to perceive language functions and their appropriate forms in a variety of contexts.
(2) Role plays promoted face-to-face interaction and peer correction through opportunities to practise communicative functions within contrived contexts requiring sociostylistic variation (e.g. asking for and giving directions, proposing an activity, accepting and refusing invitations).
(3) Structural exercises highlighted verb inflections resulting from the use of *tu* or *vous*.
(4) Writing activities required the production of letters and invitations using formal and informal registers.
(5) Intensive reading activities focused on the use of *tu* and *vous* in dialogues extracted from a novel written for and about teenagers, and on lexical differences between French in France and Quebec.
(6) Cooperative learning activities allowed students, on the one hand, to discover differences between formal and informal uses of French in a variety of contexts, in addition to differences between oral and written French within these two levels of formality, and on the other, to apply these stylistic differences in projects undertaken in groups, thereby necessitating extensive negotiation among students.

Results comparing the three experimental and two comparison classes on three proficiency measures indicated that instruction had a positive effect on the learning of specific sociolinguistic features such as the use of *vous* in formal contexts (in both written and oral production), the use of polite closings in formal letters, and an increased awareness of sociolinguistic appropriateness as demonstrated by performance on multiple-choice tests. Classroom observations during the treatment led to the recommendation that cooperative learning activities with an analytic focus be further explored since they generated an exemplary integration of analytic and experiential strategies.

Grammatical gender

Harley (1994b, 1998) conducted a study on the teaching of grammatical gender in six French immersion classrooms at the Grade 2 level (7–8-year-old students). This study differed, then, from the other three experimental studies in that the learners were considerably younger. Whereas it has often been suggested that an analytic focus is more suitable for cognitively mature learners, Harley selected Grade 2 for this study owing to the facility young children have in mastering phonological features and due to the fact that grammatical gender is determined in many respects by morphophonological rules. The treatment was designed to be implemented for 20 minutes a day over a five-week period. In addition to the creation of two illustrated dictionaries (one for masculine words and the other for feminine words) and the labelling of different objects in the classroom with grammatical gender clearly marked, the treatment incorporated a series of age-appropriate language games, including the following:

(1) 'I Spy' (e.g. an object in the class beginning with 'X' which is masculine or feminine).
(2) 'Simon Says' (students performed contrasting actions according to the gender of the noun they heard – touch toes for masculine, head for feminine).
(3) 'Concentration' (matching pictures with the same masculine or feminine endings).
(4) 'Bingo' (to win, students had to name the objects, using correct gender, in the row or column they had filled).
(5) 'My Aunt's Suitcase' (each student in turn adds an item to a memorised list of things packed in the aunt's suitcase – items could be all masculine, all feminine, or all with a certain ending).

The study demonstrated that, relative to students in the six comparison classes, students from the experimental classes made significant long-term progress in their ability to identify the gender of familiar words, but were not at the end of the treatment able to apply the morphophonological rules to unknown words.

Conclusion

Swain (1988) described at least three problems which arise at the interface of language and content teaching. First, in meaning-oriented classrooms, students are able to understand messages without necessarily engaging in some sort of form-function analysis. Second, teachers in such contexts frequently provide learners with inconsistent and possibly random feedback concerning their use of the second language. Third, the input available to students in the classroom may be functionally restricted, that is, the full functional range of certain linguistic items is not used or is infrequently used. Consequently, as the title of her article so aptly states, Swain recommended that content teaching needs to be manipulated and complemented in order to maximise second language learning. She concluded with examples of content teaching adapted to the needs of second language learners which derive from two different approaches: one in which the methodology of the content class itself had been modified to incorporate a stronger language focus, and one in which a language arts programme served to complement the content teaching.

This chapter has demonstrated that teachers can draw on both approaches: one that brings language into the content class and another that provides contextualised language support through planned language arts activities. Observations of the classrooms described in Lyster (1998a,b) suggested that these two approaches cannot always be distinguished from one another, at least at the primary level where the teachers that were observed adopted the 'whole language' approach. This approach minimises explicit language instruction and aims instead to integrate language skills across disciplines. Indeed, the teachers were so adept at blurring the borders between language classes and content classes that the investigators often had to inquire as to whether they were observing a language class or a content class.

More recently, Swain (1996) summarised the need for a language focus in immersion pedagogy in the following way:

situations must be contrived to ensure that students both hear and read the language we want them to learn, and to ensure that students are given opportunities to be pushed beyond their current abilities in the target language through the provision of feedback on the accuracy, coherence and appropriateness of the immersion language they use. (p. 544)

This chapter has examined these two features of immersion pedagogy – provision of feedback and contrived situations – under the rubrics of reactive and proactive approaches to language teaching. They have been considered in terms of the analytic-experiential dimension in second language pedagogy, as proposed by Stern (1990, 1992), in order to permit generalisations to other educational contexts, including programmes that aim for the development of multilingual competence. Within such a framework, teachers can incorporate, in varying degrees, analytic and experiential strategies that accommodate a variety of learners and that may provide learners with optimal conditions for classroom learning, more so than the use of only one strategy at the expense of the other.

With respect to a proactive approach, it was demonstrated in this chapter that instructional units, planned from a language perspective and contextualised in relation to language arts (e.g. the reading of legends) or to subject matter (e.g. the planning of a space colony), can benefit second language development in varying degrees. Such units focus on language features that may otherwise go unnoticed by classroom learners and that are thus considered to be prime candidates for an analytic focus (e.g. aspectual, modal, sociostylistic, and gender distinctions; see Harley, 1993). A proactive approach aims to make such features more salient in the input and to provide opportunities for their use in contexts that may be contrived yet meaning-oriented. Some of the studies reviewed did so by promoting the perception or use of specific target features in a variety of genres (e.g. legends, scientific reports, newspaper articles, informal letters, invitations, childhood albums, novels, role-plays, student-made dictionaries) and by implementing cooperative learning activities as well as language games and exercises that also aimed to encourage the perception or use of the target features. Teachers must continue to take into account, however, that not all language features require this kind of attention since a great deal of language is learned experientially when the classroom is communicatively rich. Accordingly, the primary aim of language teachers must be the establishment of communicatively rich contexts with ample opportunities for interaction along with a primary focus on non-language topics related to subject matter or language arts themes.

Within such a context, the negotiation of form, involving the provision of relevant and helpful information about language during substantive interaction, can provide timely language support and reduce ambiguity from the second language learner's perspective. Teachers can adopt this reactive approach by systematically drawing on the four corrective feedback techniques that encourage peer- and self-repair (i.e. elicitation, metalinguistic clues, clarification requests, or repetition of error) or by drawing attention, in other ways, to relevant language features during interaction related to content, as Rachelle did in the lessons about well-adapted mammals, skunks and meteorology: that is, by eliciting synonyms, antonyms, more precise terms, words with similar structural properties, correct spelling, correct pronunciation, etc. By propitiously providing feedback in this way during meaningful interaction in subject-matter lessons or in thematically contextualised language arts lessons, teachers do not undermine the expression of meaning yet provide learners with important opportunities to notice, in unambiguous ways, relevant form-function links in the second language. As students are encouraged to draw actively on their own linguistic resources in this way, they are also likely to be challenged to become more autonomous language learners.

Notes

1. Although student–student interaction during collaborative tasks is an equally important feature of immersion pedagogy (e.g. Kowal & Swain, 1994, 1997; Lyster, 1994a; Swain & Lapkin, in press), the data presented in this section derive from a study that has focused solely on teacher–student interaction in immersion classrooms.
2. This study has been funded through grants awarded to the author, one from the Social Sciences and Humanities Research Council of Canada (410-94-0783), and another from the Fonds pour la formation de chercheurs et l' aide à la recherche (97-NC-1409).
3. The following conventions are used in the extracts: R = Rachelle; St = student; Sts = more than one student; StD = a different student from the previous student turn. Overlapping speech is indicated by %.

Appendix

Extract 1: (Well-adapted mammals)

R: Bon très bien maintenant aujourd'hui nous allons voir des mammifères, des mammifères bien adaptés. Qu'est-ce que ça

veut dire? Qu'est-ce que ça veut dire ça, ce mot-là? Des
mammifères bien adaptés? Ça vient de quel mot, *adapté*? Oui?

St: A … ad …, ada …, ben c'est parce que …

R: Ça resemble à *adopter* hein?

St: Oui.

R: Ben c'est pas *adopter*, c'est *adapter*. Adapter, Liz? Ça vient de quel
mot? Quel autre mot qu'on pourrait faire avec *adapter*? Adapte …

St: Adapter.

R: Une? Une?

St: Adoption.

R: Eh?

St: Adaption?

R: Non, pas une adoption.

St: Une adaptation.

R: Bravo, une adaptation. Qu'est-ce que ça veut dire? Qu'est-ce que
ça veut dire adaptation? [...] Des animaux qui sont bien adaptés?
Une adaptation? …

St: Habitué. [...]

R: Lui dit que ce serait *habitué*. Est-ce que ça se peut?

Sts: Oui.

R: Donc un autre mot. On va voir. Habitué. Ha..bi..tu..é. Ce sont des
animaux, des mammifères bien habitués. Un autre mot, toi, qu'
est-ce que tu dis?

St: Ils sont prêts eux-autres, comme en été ils savent que l'hiver vont
venir, alors ils sont prêts.

R: Ce sont des animaux qui sont bien prêts, qui sont prêts.
Comment on écrit *prêt*?

Sts: %P, R, E, accent grave, S%?

R: P, R, E, accent grave, S. Est-ce que c'est ça?

Sts: %Oui%.

Sts: %Non%

R: C'est ça. Qui est d'accord avec ce mot-là?

St: %Un T.%

St: %Deux T.%

R: Qui n'est pas d'accord? Toi, tu n'es pas d'accord? David non plus?

St: Parce que *près* comme ça, ça veut dire que tu es proche.

R: *Près* comme ça, ça veut dire *proche*. Est-ce que ça veut dire des
animaux qui sont proches?

Sts: Non.

R: Non! Un T. Ce sont des animaux qui sont P, R, E, accent
circonflexe, T …?%

St: %Accent grave?%

St: Oui.

R: Ça fait quoi au féminin?

Sts: Prête.

R: Prête. Est-ce que les filles sont prêtes? Est-ce que les garçons sont prêts?

Sts: Oui.

R: Est-ce que les mammifères sont prêts?

St: Oui.

R: Les mammifères qui sont prêts, qui sont habitués, qui sont adaptés. Est-ce qu'il y aurait un autre mot? [...]

Extract 2: (Skunks)

R: Maintenant, y a la mouffette, les amis. La mouffette, qu'est-ce qu'elle fait, elle, la mouffette? La mouffette? Comment ça s'écrit, *mouffette*?

Sts: <Everyone answers something different at the same time>

R: Deux F ... et deux T. Très bien. Est-ce que *professeur* ça prend deux F et deux S?

Sts: Non.

R: Qu'est-ce que ça prend?

St: %Un F.%

StD: %Deux S.%

R: Deux S et ...?

St: Un F.

R: Un F. Faut faire attention. Alors, la mouffette, qu'est-ce qu'elle fait, elle? Nancy?

St: Eh ... elle je- ... ben y a un jet de parfum qui sent pas très bon ...

R: Alors un jet de parfum. On va appeler ça un ...?

Sts: Liquide.

R: Liquide. Le liquide ...

StD: Puant.

R: Un liquide puant, aussi on appelle ça un liquide qui a pas une bonne odeur comment on appelle ça? Un liquide qui a pas, qui aurait pas une bonne odeur? Quand c'est une bonne odeur, comment on dit ça? C'est o ...?

Sts: Odoreux?

R: O ... do ...?

Sts: Odorant?

R: Hein?

Sts: Odorant.

R: Odorant. Pis si ...

Sts: Désodorant.

R: Hein?
Sts: Désodorant.
R: Désodorant. [laughs]
St: Désodorance?
StD: Indodorance?
R: *In-, in-,* c'est une bonne idée. *In-* ça veut dire *pas.* Inodoran . . .?
St: %ce.%
R: % on va dire%, *mal*odorant.
St: Oh oui.

Extract 3: (What does a meteorologist do?)

R: Maintenant, une météorologiste ou un météorologiste, qu'est-ce que ça fait?
St: Mais, ça dit qu'est-ce qui va faire . . .
R: Ça dit? Qui ça dit?
St: Ça explique . . .
R: Qui, ça? Dis-moi c'est qui, ça?
St: C'est les personnes qui . . .
R: Ah! C'est une personne! C'est une personne ici.
StD: Une personne qui . . . qui dit em . . .s'il va pleuvoir, s'il va faire soleil, si . . .
StD: C'est le /weatherman/
R: Qui dit . . .?
St: Qui dit la météo.
R: Qui dit la météo?
StD: Qui annonce la température.
R: Qui annonce! Qui annonce la température. Est-ce qu'il fait seulement qu'annoncer la température qu'on va avoir aujourd'hui, en ce moment?
Sts: Non.
R: Qu'est-ce qu'il annonce aussi?
St: Demain, eh . . .
R: Demain. Donc, il, aussi, il . . . demain il . . .?
St: Il prévient. [. . .]
R: Il nous prévient. Il prévoit.
St: Il prévient qu'y aura des . . .
R: Il nous prévient. Il prévoit à l'avance, lui. Il prévoit à l'avance.
St: Y a un autre mot aussi.

Extract 4: (What's the gender?)

R: [. . .] Ce que j'aimerais savoir, moi, c'est quel est le genre? Quel est le genre de *avant-midi* et *après-midi*?

St: Y a le genre . . .

R: Quel est le genre?

St: Y a le genre et le nombre.

R: Y a le genre et y a le nombre. Moi j'ne veux pas le nombre. Eh?
[. . . Moi je veux le genre. Oui eh . . . toi Myra?

St: Est-ce que <?> le genre?

R: Le genre. Qu'est-ce que je veux savoir? Qu'est-ce que je demande
là?

StD: <?> c'est la différence.

R: La différence. Est-ce que je veux avoir la différence? Eh? Je, est-ce
que j'ai demandé le synonyme?

St: Non.

R: Non. J'ai demandé le genre. Eh que c'est loin, le genre. Quel est le
genre?

St: Le genre [inaudible; lots of noise].

R: Non. Quel est le genre? Le genre, c'est quoi? Le nom-, d'abord on
va commencer par le nombre. Le nombre, c'est quoi?

St: Le nombre, c'est . . .

R: Combien qu'on a de nombres en français?

Sts: [Students' responses vary from *neuf* to *cent*].

R: Hein?

St: Neuf cents?

R: Non. Le genre et le nombre vous ne souvenez plus de ça?

Sts: Non.

R: Aye-aye-aye. Y a deux genres et y a deux nombres. Le nombre,
qu'est-ce que ça vous dit déjà? Oui.

St: Le genre, je sais. C'est, c'est . . . [too noisy]

R: Non. J'ai pas demandé des verbes. J'ai pas demandé des
auxiliaires. Le genre, c'est quoi? Le nombre. De quel genre es-tu,
toi? De quel genre es-tu, toi, Richard?

St: Eh . . .

R: De quel genre es-tu?

StD: Masculin?

R: Toi, t'es du genre masculin. Est-ce que c'est vrai?

Sts: Non. Oui.

R: Oui, oui, bien sûr. Toi, de quel genre es-tu?

St: Féminin.

R: Bon! Ah!

StD: C'est comme le masculin <?>?

R: Bon, le nombre en français [. . .]. Le nombre maintenant en
français; c'est quoi le nombre, Stéphanie? Le nombre? Le genre,
c'est féminin ou masculin. Le nombre, c'est quoi en français?

C'est quoi le nombre? C'est . . .
St: C'est comme féminin et masculin?
R: C'est comme féminin et masculin? Ben non, ça c'est le genre. Le nombre, c'est . . .
St: Singulier, pluriel?
R: Bravo.
Sts: Oui.
R: Singulier ou pluriel. Ah la-la, vous vous souvenez plus de ça? Il va falloir en faire, hein? Alors ici, j'voulais savoir de quel genre. Quel est le genre de ces deux mots-là? Est-ce qu' on dit *une avant-midi* ou *un avant-midi*?

References

Allen, P., Swain, M., Harley, B. and Cummins, J. (1990) Aspects of classroom treatment: Toward a more comprehensive view of second language education. In B. Harley, P. Allen, J. Cummins and M. Swain (eds) *The Development of Bilingual Proficiency* (pp. 57–81). Cambridge: Cambridge University Press.

Day, E. and Shapson, S. (1991) Integrating formal and functional approaches to language teaching in French immersion: An experimental study. *Language Learning* 41, 25–58.

Day, E. and Shapson, S. (1996) *Studies in Immersion Education.* Clevedon: Multilingual Matters.

Doughty, C. and Williams, J. (1998) Pedagogical choices in focus on form. In C. Doughty and J. Williams (eds) *Focus on Form in Classroom Second Language Acquisition* (pp. 197–261). Cambridge: Cambridge University Press.

Genesee, F. (1987) *Learning Through Two Languages.* Rowley, MA: Newbury House.

Genesee, F. (1991) Second language learning in school settings: Lessons from immersion. In A.G. Reynolds (ed.) *Bilingualism, Multiculturalism, and Second Language Learning* (pp. 183–202). Hillsdale, NJ: Lawrence Erlbaum.

Harley, B. (1989) Functional grammar in French immersion: a classroom experiment. *Applied Linguistics* 10, 331–59.

Harley, B. (1992) Patterns of second language development in French immersion. *Journal of French Language Studies* 2, 159–83.

Harley, B. (1993) Instructional strategies and SLA in early French immersion. *Studies in Second Language Acquisition* 15, 245–60.

Harley, B. (1994a) Appealing to consciousness in the L2 classroom. *AILA Review* 11, 57–68.

Harley, B. (1994b) A focus on grammatical gender in the primary immersion classroom. Paper presented at the Second Language Research Forum, Montréal, October 9.

Harley, B. (1998) The role of form-focused tasks in promoting the second language acquisition of children in Grade 2. In C. Doughty and J. Williams (eds) *Focus on Form in Classroom Second Language Acquisition* (pp. 156–74). Cambridge: Cambridge University Press.

Harley, B. and King, M. (1989) Verb lexis in the written compositions of young L2 learners. *Studies in Second Language Acquisition* 11, 415–39.

Harley, B. and Swain, M. (1984) The interlanguage of immersion students and its implications for second language teaching. In A. Davies, C. Criper and A. Howatt (eds) *Interlanguage* (pp. 291–311). Edinburgh: Edinburgh University Press.

Harley, B., Allen, P., Cummins, J. and Swain, M. (1987) *Development of Bilingual Proficiency. Final report. Volume II: Classroom Treatment.* Toronto: Modern Language Centre, Ontario Institute for Studies in Education.

Harley, B., Allen, P., Cummins, J. and Swain, M. (eds) (1990) *The Development of Second Language Proficiency.* Cambridge: Cambridge University Press.

Hullen, J. and Lentz, F. (1991) Pour une rentabilisation des pratiques pédagogiques en immersion. *Études de Linguistique Appliquée* 82, 63–76.

Kowal, M. and Swain, M. (1994) Using collaborative language production tasks to promote students' awareness. *Language Awareness* 3, 73–93.

Kowal, M. and Swain, M. (1997) From semantic to syntactic processing: How can we promote metalinguistic awareness in the French immersion classroom? In K. Johnson and M. Swain (eds) *Immersion Education: International Perspectives* (pp. 284–309). Cambridge: Cambridge University Press.

Lambert, W. and Tucker, R. (1972) *The Bilingual Education of Children: The St. Lambert Experiment.* Rowley, MA: Newbury House.

Lightbown, P. and Spada, N. (1990) Focus-on-form and corrective feedback in communicative language teaching: Effects on second language learning. *Studies in Second Language Acquisition* 12, 429–48.

Long, M. (1991) Focus on form: A design feature in language teaching methodology. In K. de Bot, D. Coste, R. Ginsberg and C. Kramsch (eds) *Foreign Language Research in Cross-Cultural Perspective* (pp. 39–52). Amsterdam: Benjamins.

Long, M. (1996) The role of the linguistic environment in second language acquisition. In W.C. Ritchie and T.K. Bhatia (eds), *Handbook of Language Acquisition. Vol. 2: Second Language Acquisition* (pp. 413–68). New York: Academic Press.

Lyster, R. (1994a) La négociation de la forme: stratégie analytique en classe d'immersion. *The Canadian Modern Language Review* 50, 447–65.

Lyster, R. (1994b) The effect of functional-analytic teaching on aspects of French immersion students' sociolinguistic competence. *Applied Linguistics* 15, 263–87.

Lyster, R. (1995) Negotiation of form in communicatively oriented classrooms. Paper presented at the American Association of Applied Linguistics (AAAL) Conference, Long Beach, CA, 26 March.

Lyster, R. (1998a) Recasts, repetition, and ambiguity in L2 classroom discourse. *Studies in Second Language Acquisition* 20, 51–81.

Lyster, R. (1998b) Negotiation of form, recasts, and explicit correction in relation to error types and learner repair in immersion classrooms. *Language Learning* 48, 183–218.

Lyster, R. and Ranta, L. (1997) Corrective feedback and learner uptake: Negotiation of form in communicative classrooms. *Studies in Second Language Acquisition* 19, 37–66.

Met, M. (1994) Teaching content through a second language. In F. Genesee (ed.)

Educating Second Language Children (pp. 159–82). Cambridge: Cambridge University Press.

Netten, J. (1991) Towards a more language oriented second language classroom. In L. Malavé and G. Duquette (eds) _Language, Culture and Cognition_ (pp. 284–304). Clevedon: Multilingual Matters.

Pica, T., Holliday, L., Lewis, N. and Morgenthaler, L. (1989) Comprehensible output as an outcome of linguistic demands on the learner. _Studies in Second Language Acquisition_ 11, 63–90.

Rebuffot, J. and Lyster, R. (1996) L'immersion au Canada: contextes, effets et pédagogie. In J. Erfurt (ed.) _De la Polyphonie à la Symphonie. Méthodes, Théories et Faits de la Recherche Pluridisciplinaire sur le Français au Canada_ (pp. 277–94). Leipzig: Leipziger Universitätsverlag GmbH.

Schegloff, E., Jefferson, G. and Sacks, H. (1977) The preference for self-correction in the organization of repair in conversation. _Language_ 53, 361–82.

Snow, M. (1987) _Immersion Teacher Handbook_. Los Angeles: UCLA.

Snow, M., Met, M. and Genesee, F. (1989) A conceptual framework for the integration of language and content in second/foreign language instruction. _TESOL Quarterly_ 23, 201–17.

Spada, N. (1997) Form-focussed instruction and second language acquisition: A review of classroom and laboratory research. _Language Teaching_ 29, 1–15.

Spada, N. and Lightbown, P. (1993) Instruction and the development of questions in L2 classrooms. _Studies in Second Language Acquisition_ 15, 205–24.

Stern, H.H. (1990) Analysis and experience as variables in second language pedagogy. In B. Harley, P. Allen, J. Cummins and M. Swain (eds) _The Development of Bilingual Proficiency_ (pp. 93–109). Cambridge: Cambridge University Press.

Stern, H.H. (1992) _Issues and Options in Language Teaching_. Edited by P. Allen and B. Harley. Oxford: Oxford University Press.

Swain, M. (1985) Communicative competence: Some roles of comprehensible input and comprehensible output in its development. In S. Gass & C. Madden (eds) _Input in Second Language Acquisition_ (pp. 235–53). Rowley, MA: Newbury House.

Swain, M. (1988) Manipulating and complementing content teaching to maximize second language learning. _TESL Canada Journal_ 6, 68–83.

Swain, M. (1993) The output hypothesis: Just speaking and writing aren't enough. _The Canadian Modern Language Review_ 50, 158–64.

Swain, M. (1995) Three functions of output in second language learning. In G. Cook and B. Seidlhofer (eds), _Principles and Practice in Applied Linguistics: Studies in Honour of H. G. Widdowson_ (pp. 125–44). Oxford: Oxford University Press.

Swain, M. (1996) Integrating language and content in immersion classrooms: Research perspectives. _The Canadian Modern Language Review_ 52, 529–48.

Swain, M. and Carroll, S. (1987) The immersion observation study. In B. Harley, P. Allen, J. Cummins and M. Swain (eds) _Development of Bilingual Proficiency. Final Report. Volume II: Classroom Treatment_. Toronto: Modern Language Centre, Ontario Institute for Studies in Education.

Swain, M. and Lapkin, S. (1982) _Evaluating Bilingual Education: A Canadian Case Study_. Clevedon: Multilingual Matters.

Swain, M. and Lapkin, S. (in press) An anatomy of interaction and second language learning: Two adolescent French immersion students working together. *The Modern Language Journal.*

Tardif, C. (1991) Quelques traits distinctifs de la pédagogie d'immersion. *Études de Linguistique Appliquée* 82, 39–51.

White, L. (1991) Adverb placement in second language acquisition: Some effects of positive and negative evidence in the classroom. *Second Language Research* 7, 133–61.

White, L., Spada, N., Lightbown, P.M. and Ranta, L. (1991) Input enhancement and L2 question formation. *Applied Linguistics* 12, 416–32.

Chapter 5

Cultural Identities in Multilingual Classrooms

MICHAEL BYRAM

There exist many schools throughout the world where more than one language is used as the medium of instruction and where, for some or all of the students involved, the languages are not the one(s) they have acquired in their homes. What may appear to be common features in different schools can have quite different purposes and philosophies. In this chapter, I shall make a broad distinction between multilingual schools where the aims are comparable to those of foreign or second language teaching, i.e. to develop proficiency in more than one language, and those where the issues involved include supporting the existence of different ethnic groups within a state, i.e. where language proficiency is desired not only in itself but as a symbol of identity (see also Hornberger & López, Chapter 10 this volume). I am aware that this categorisation does not cover all cases and that, for example, in the well-known case of Canadian immersion programmes, some programmes might fit into one category, some into the other, and some into both (see Lyster, Chapter 4; Genesee, Chapter 11 this volume). Nonetheless, one of the features of schools for ethnic minorities is that they raise questions about the values, beliefs and practices – the culture – into which young people are socialised through schooling, and I want to suggest that teachers and others involved in programmes where the main purpose is to develop language proficiency need to take these other cultural issues into account too. By considering the difference between these two broad categories of multilingual schools, it will become clear that the 'pure' pursuit of language proficiency through using more than one language as a medium of instruction in fact hides many issues of socialisation and cultural identity.

In order to discuss such issues, I shall perhaps inevitably simplify and generalise, but my main purpose is to identify and describe a number of parameters, a number of concepts, with which teachers can think about their own particular situation. I shall begin with two particular situations presented as classroom vignettes and draw out of them the questions raised by programmes with aims of maintaining multiple ethnic groups in a society. I shall then discuss the concepts involved before returning, in the final part of the chapter, to the specific problems of multilingual classrooms where linguistic proficiency is the main aim. In the two following vignettes, and in places throughout the chapter, I shall describe and discuss 'bilingualism' and 'biculturalism', but this is a shorthand way of saying 'bi- and multi-lingualism and culturalism'. The issues which arise in the case of two languages and cultures are essentially the same for individuals in multilingual schools.

The SESB Project

The first classroom is in Berlin and in a primary school, one of a group of designated 'Staatliche Europaschulen Berlin' (State European Schools in Berlin). The SESB are schools where two languages are used as media of instruction, German and one of five others: English, French, Italian, Russian or Spanish. There are 20 students in the class in their second year of schooling, aged seven to eight. Approximately half of them have German as their first language and half have French. The teacher is French and the subject of the lesson is the organs of the body (respiratory, digestive and urinary systems). In this particular lesson, the teacher introduces a board-game where children in groups have cards on which parts of the three organ systems are drawn. The children throw dice and move a marker round the board. As the marker reaches a space, they have to decide whether the organ on the board corresponds with one of their cards. If so they can place the card on the board and the first to be rid of all their cards wins. As they place the card, however, they also have to say the French word for the organ in question. When a child has a card but cannot remember the word they are often helped by the others, particularly those whose first language is French. They can also consult a large drawing of the human body on which they stuck representations of the organs at the beginning of the lesson under the guidance of the teacher. The teacher speaks only French and the children are expected to speak French too. Cooperation rather than competitiveness is the mood of the game, and the children understand that its purpose is to help them remember the organ systems they have been learning about on previous occasions. The aims of the lesson are: naming of the organs and knowledge of where they are in the body; allocation of the organs to one of the three systems; mastery of the specialist words in French.

On another occasion the group will be separated into those with first language German and those with first language French for lessons in the other language, with native speaker teachers of the 'partner language'. Such lessons will not be foreign language lessons of a familiar kind, where the language is the subject of the lesson, but will have some other subject from the curriculum, taught in the partner language. Here the main emphasis is on the subject matter – for example, categorisation of different kinds of animals in the classroom aquarium – but attention is paid to ensuring that the children learn the specialist words.

The purpose of the SESB is to develop in students of German first language and in students whose first language is one of the other five, a high degree of bilingualism (Doyé, 1996). The SESB system also offers the opportunity for 'intercultural education', where the overall aim is that young people will be able to interact with people of origins different from their own.[1]

The Foyer Project

The second classroom is in Brussels, an officially bilingual city, but with monolingual schools. This school is Flemish and the teacher is certainly speaking Flemish. Some students, aged nine or ten, can be heard to whisper occasionally in French to each other. A few others might even use some Italian. In earlier years the group did not spend all their time together. For some lessons they were divided into two groups, one of which had an Italian-speaking teacher, while the other stayed with a Flemish-speaking teacher. In this school, therefore, both Italian and Flemish are formal media of instruction, especially in the early years of schooling. French is taught as a subject for several lessons per week but is not otherwise part of the school's formal curriculum, administration or means of communication. Nonetheless, French is frequently used by the students, especially outside the classroom, in their recreational time. It is also used between some of the Flemish-speaking teachers and their Italian-speaking colleagues.

This school is part of an experiment to develop a curriculum which will allow students of Italian origin to maintain and develop their relationship with Italy, from which their parents, and in some cases their grandparents, migrated to find work and a new life in Belgium. For most, that 'migration' has become emigration, even though they often talk of returning 'home'. The special arrangements for these students are grafted onto an existing Flemish-speaking school in Brussels. The aim is to offer them a 'bicultural and trilingual' education, through which they will acquire Flemish-Belgian language and culture, Italian language and culture, and French as a means of communication with the French-speaking population of Brussels and Wallonia. The special arrangements are supported – with training for the Italian teachers, teaching materials and so on – by the educational arm of an organisation founded to help immigrants, Foyer. The organisation has established similar programmes for other languages in other Brussels schools, with similar combinations of bicultural and trilingual programmes and aims.[2]

Biculturalism and Interculturalism

These two classrooms have common characteristics as well as many differences. The differences are less visible from immediate observations of the classroom. They are in the aims and purposes of the programmes, in the origins of the students, in the sources of the educational philosophies which underpin them. The common features – classes of students with different first languages, native-speaking teachers from the two language groups, use of both languages as media of instruction – must also be placed in context before any generalisation can be attempted. The immediate context in each case is the expectations held by students and teachers and the formal curriculum of the school. In both cases, the school is attempting to create an education in which students will be introduced to the curriculum found in schools throughout the state. This curriculum, in schools where students are of the same language background, tells them about the history, geography and social structure of the state, introduces them to the dominant culture, and gradually develops in them a loyalty to the state and its culture which is usually described as their 'national identity'.

In the second of our two case studies the situation is made more complex by the aims of the programme and the ethnic identities of the students involved. One of the aims of the Foyer programme is, for immigrant students and their families, 'enhanced opportunities for integration in their country of origin should their parents decide to return' (Leman, 1990: 12). In order to achieve this, the programme not only uses the immigrant language as a medium of instruction in the existing curriculum, but also as the medium through which students learn something about their country of origin, its way of life and aspects of its high culture. The theory underpinning the programme argues that this explicit teaching is complemented by the fact that the teachers are native-speakers and 'bearers' of the culture in question. Through interaction with these teachers, students are exposed to the culture, beliefs, values and practices which the teachers, literally, embody. Thus, unlike a homogeneous class of students of Belgian origin, these students are exposed to two cultures, to two modes of socialisation, to two ethnic/national identities. It is indeed the explicit purpose of the Foyer programme that students should become bicultural and also trilingual, that they should acquire (Flemish) Belgian and Italian culture, and proficiency in Flemish, Italian and French languages.

The situation in our first vignette is different in aims though many of the features of classroom activities are, as indicated in the vignettes, similar. The aims of the SESB programme are to develop proficiency in two languages, which is comparable to the trilingual proficiency of the Foyer programme, and secondly a capacity to interact with people of another culture. There is, however, no explicit aim to develop biculturalism in young people, as it is defined by Foyer, i.e. a sense of belonging to two cultures with some combination of two ethnic/national identities. The fact that students in the SESB programme are taught by native speakers of German and of one of the partner languages means that students with first language German can relate to the former as members of their own ethnic/national group and to the latter as members of another – and vice versa for students whose first language is one of the partner languages. They can relate in the same way to the other students in their class, and the purpose of developing an ability to interact with people of different cultures can be fulfilled in these conditions. Whereas the key word to describe the Foyer programme is 'biculturalism', we might describe the SESB programme with the term 'interculturalism'.

The demands of biculturalism and interculturalism are different. In the Western world, at least, the dominance of people with a monocultural identity which coincides with the national identity of the state in which they live means that they expect everyone living in that state to be like them, to have a simple and single cultural identity. Immigrants are expected to be loyal to the state and nation where they have chosen to live, and monocultural, monolingual people have difficulty in understanding ties with the state and nation of origin. Even in Belgium, where Flemish, Walloon and German identities co-exist within one state, there seems to be little tolerance for other identities. In such situations, the aims of a programme to help students to become bicultural create tensions. Such tensions are widespread in classrooms where more than one language is represented. They are symptoms of other non-linguistic issues which arise in many different kinds of situation.

The presence in the same classroom of students with different languages brought up in families with different practices of socialisation can be due to a wide variety of circumstances, and this applies not just to the more obvious situations of immigration:

- Some education systems tend to separate students of different social class origins speaking different vernaculars, whereas others bring them all together into a 'comprehensive' school.
- The movement of political frontiers creates minorities who are obliged to send their children to schools reflecting the majority's values.
- The migration of great numbers of people looking for work or seeking political asylum creates a different kind of minority which usually hopes to return home some day.
- The creation of new states by colonial powers from another or the same continent obliges people of different ethnic identities to send their children to an education system which those new states hope will create a unified population, after the departure of the colonial powers themselves.

In many such multi-language situations, governments attempt to impose just one language and, more or less explicitly, to suppress others. The notorious case of the suppression of Welsh by the English in the nineteenth and early twentieth centuries can be matched by many other cases throughout the world. In more recent times, governments try to impose an alien language on their own people in order to improve their economic outlook in the post-industrial world-village, as is the case in Singapore. This may however create a threat to loyalty to the state, and even the introduction of another language as a foreign language, let alone as a medium of instruction, can create fears of such threats. For example, there are people in Taiwan who are against the introduction of English as a foreign language in the early years of schooling when 'national identity' is not yet fully formed. It is in the juxtaposition of loyalty to the state and national identity that the non-linguistic, cultural issues of multilingual classrooms begin to surface.

Education and Nationality

The introduction of compulsory schooling coincided in most cases in Europe with the emergence of the nation-state in the nineteenth century. A similar phenomenon took place – and is still taking place – in the twentieth century in other parts of the world, often under the influence of former European colonial governments, but also in the shadow of the new imperialism of the former Soviet Union and the United States. Irrespective of whether the coincidence can be attributed to a third causal factor or is the direct effect of nation formation on education systems, the school is quickly seen to be a locus of control of the emergent social identities of young children. It is seldom stated explicitly, but governments can use schools and their curricula to create the conditions in which children's perceptions of the world are filtered through the cultural artefacts of the dominant social group – the power-holding elite or the socially dominant middle classes – and their ethnocentric vision of their relationships with other countries. In countries where such groups are well-established, the education system is the means of reproducing their position from generation to generation (Bourdieu & Passeron, 1977). In revolutionary situations such as that in the former Soviet Union, the new ruling class used the education system to introduce its own values and philosophy throughout the state (Muckle, 1988).

School curricula introduce students to their local geography, history and identity. The pedagogical justification for this is that young children need to deal with the immediate and the concrete, with the local and the familiar. At the same time this ensures that they identify with that locality as it is portrayed in national terms; their region is not independent but part of a national entity. As they begin to study history, geography, language and literature through the prism of academic disciplines, young people still find themselves reading the national account of international events, history seen from the perspective of their own state not as it was experienced and interpreted by other nation-states. They study the literary icons of their nation, and open geographical atlases in which their own country is the first to be depicted and is in the centre of maps of the world, even though it could equally well be placed at the edge of the page, in purely geographical terms.

The coincidence of 'national' curricula with the interests of a state government and the creation of citizens of a state hides the illogicality of what appears to be a necessary identification of nation with state and state with nation. It is of course possible to define the concept of nation as being dependent on the characteristics of a state. Smith (1991) distinguishes between such an approach which is a 'civic' or Western model and an 'ethnic' and non-Western model. In the former, the components of a nation are 'historic territoriality, legal-political community, legal-political equality of members, and common civic culture and ideology' (1991: 11). In contrast, the ethnic model puts the emphasis on 'community of birth and native culture . . . a community of common descent' (1991: 11). He argues that national identity is separate from any conception of the state:

> The latter refers exclusively to public institutions, differentiated from, and autonomous of, other social institutions and exercising a monopoly of coercion and extraction within a given territory. The nation, on the other hand, signifies a cultural and political bond, uniting in a single political community all who share a historic culture and homeland. (Smith, 1991: 14–15)

Despite some overlap between the two, Smith points to many 'plural' states and to the claim that perhaps only 10% of them could profess to be nation-states.

Yet many governments do act through their education systems as if they were nation-states and deny that nationality and citizenship can be different. The introduction of a National Curriculum in England, while implicitly acknowledging the nationhood of other parts of the United Kingdom, denies nationality to many English children of recent immigrant origin who speak languages other than English in their daily lives. The imposition of one language, one literature, one account of English history, denies these children and their parents the possibility of a distinction between nationality and citizenship. In comparison, the schools of Belgium allow parents of long-established ethnic groups to choose the nationality of their children – as Flemish, French or German – while remaining Belgian citizens, and the Foyer model attempts to build on this situation to offer the children of more recent groups the nationality of their origins within a framework of Flemish nationality and Belgian citizenship. So there are some examples even within a Western concept of nationality where states allow a disjunction between citizenship and nationality, even if other would-be nation-states are much less flexible.

A new dimension has also developed in recent years in Western Europe to challenge the dominance of the nation-state. Those states which belong to the European Union have agreed to introduce into their school curricula the concept of 'the European dimension'. In this case, the suggestion is that governments should, through their curricula, encourage young people to become aware of their belonging to a greater entity than the state. They already have a symbolic designation of this in relation to their citizenship since their passport, though carrying the name of their country, also carries the designation 'European Community'. To what extent this will also lead to the adoption of a European identity together with a national identity – or perhaps, ultimately, instead of a national identity – remains to be seen (Becher, 1996).

However, the nation-state is resistant to change, and despite examples such as the Foyer model, governments in the Western world have resisted as much as they could the demands for curricula which reflect new national identities within the frontiers of the state. Churchill (1986) demonstrates how policies have often been developed to suggest that children of ethnic and national origins different from the origins of the politically dominant group, are deficient and in need of schooling which helps them to conform to the language and culture of the dominant group as quickly as possible. A similar argument could be made with respect to children of a different social class. It is only when minority national groups within a polity acquire power themselves that other policy options to maintain a plural state are adopted. The case of the Foyer programme is an example of this, as is the school system of the German minority in Südtirol, and many other 'old' minorities in Western Europe.

Socialisation and the (hidden) Curriculum

In the relatively simple case of a monolingual child brought up in a family of the dominant social group, the culture acquired in primary socialisation in the home is repeated and developed in the period of secondary socialisation which coincides with schooling. Although the child experiences other social institutions simultaneously, it is the school which provides the major continuity from the culture of the family. This occurs, as suggested above, through the explicit teaching of a curriculum determined by the dominant social group. This is the explicit 'education' which a child receives.

At the same time, but in less explicit ways, the child is exposed to the culture of the hidden curriculum, to the modes of behaving which express beliefs about appropriate human relationships, to the expectations of contributing to the ethos of the school which place value on the child's unconscious understanding of what makes 'a good pupil'. Here too there may be continuity with expectations and relationships experienced in primary socialisation. The child may experience no disjuncture between relationships with parents and with teachers, even though there is a difference in role.

Children whose primary socialisation has taught them different values, beliefs and practices from those of the school and its teachers have a quite different experience of secondary socialisation and the hidden curriculum. This might be evident in differences in such things as dress, and also less evident but equally significant in differences in interpersonal relationships – the amount of physical contact between children or between children and adults, for example. In particular, the language with which they are familiar does not coincide with that of the teachers, even though it appears to be the same. Both student and teacher speak, say, 'German' but one speaks the standard language and the other speaks a non-standard variety, and the non-standard and the standard language of school carry different meanings and connotations. When children speak a 'foreign' language, the difficulties seem to be more obvious and the solution self-evident: they have to acquire the official language of the country used in the school. This simple problem obscures, however, the fact that such children still have the same discontinuities of cultural values, practices and beliefs. These are not overcome by the acquisition of a new code, since they are embodied by the teachers in their unconscious behaviour and in the implicit and taken-for-granted values which underpin the school's practices (Bourdieu, 1977).

If a school wishes to provide continuity between primary and secondary socialisation, it is not enough to use the language of the home as the medium of schooling, for to do so simply encodes the discontinuities in a new and only marginally less accessible way. Since people embody the cultures in which they live, schools need teachers from the same culture as the child new to a school. In the case of the Italian children in the Foyer programme described earlier, the presence of Italian teachers, not Belgian teachers of Italian, was crucial to the bicultural nature of the programme. In addition to speaking Italian as native-speakers, they introduce traditions of education and socialisation which are different from those of the Flemish Belgian school. They teach an explicit curriculum of Italian language and cultural artefacts, history and geography. Less consciously and yet of at least equal significance, they embody different concepts of teacher–pupil relationships, expectations of pupil behaviour and an affective use of Italian which is continuous with that of the home.

It is the hope of the Foyer programme that interaction with Belgian and Italian teachers will help students to become bicultural. Yet, 'bicultural' like 'bilingual' is a sociological rather than a psychological description. It describes someone in terms of their belonging to two social groups, each with its own cultural values, beliefs and practices. It often implies that the normal case is to belong to one such group, and that being bicultural is abnormal. It does not describe the psychological experience of belonging to two groups, and to what extent this is like being two people, two personalities, or to what extent the individual experiences their sense of belonging holistically.

On Being 'Bicultural'

In an article based largely on introspection about her own linguistic and cultural learning, Paulston argues that becoming bicultural is different from becoming bilingual:

> ... becoming bicultural is not just a cognitive process which can be carried out apart from the members of the culture. In this aspect becoming bicultural differs from becoming bilingual. It is perfectly possible to learn a foreign language from non-native speakers. As a matter of fact, I never did have an English teacher who was a native speaker. It is also possible to become bilingual without becoming bicultural, while the reverse is not true. (Paulston, 1992: 120)

She would, on this basis, agree with my earlier point that it is in the hidden curriculum embodied by teachers in their beliefs, values and practices that a second culture can be present in a school. Her account of what it is to be bicultural and not just a speaker with native-like mastery of the linguistic system, is a useful starting point for clarifying the possible consequences of the presence of more than one culture in the classroom and the curriculum. She describes becoming bicultural – and implicitly this also means more than two cultures, and being multicultural, as I said earlier – as acquiring a cultural competence based on two cultural systems. She describes this as 'a chance to pick and choose between two cultural systems ... choose to define some cultural traits as good and some as bad and pick accordingly' (Paulston, 1992: 125).

Although the process of acquiring bi- or multi-cultural competence is not always the conscious process implied in the phrase 'pick and choose', this personal account by an eminent sociolinguist identifies one possible outcome for an individual in the kind of programme represented by the Foyer case. It can also be the outcome for a young person whose home life is lived in one language and culture whereas school life is in another, there being no attempt to represent the home culture in the school. In this perspective, it is not a question of the individual having two separate competencies, but rather a unitary competence from which certain practices are brought into operation in one situation with one kind of interlocutor, and a different selection is made, though not entirely consciously, in another situation.

Competencies need to be distinguished, however, from issues of social identity. An individual who is biculturally competent may identify with only one social group, acknowledging its beliefs, values and practices and not those of another group even though he/she is able to conform to the expectations of the second group. Individual students exposed to more than one culture may thus be competent in more than one linguistic and cultural system but have only one ethnic/national identity. It must also be said that that identity may change with time and place. Children brought up in exogamous marriages – where one parent is from another national group living in relative isolation from their group of origin – without the support of a social group of similar individuals, may identify with the group around them, to which one parent belongs, but identify with the group of the other parent if they move into that group for a longer or shorter period.

The psychological consequences of being exposed to two or more cultures may not however be as easy to handle as Paulston implies was her own case. Research among young people in the German minority in the Italian Südtirol shows that the difference between what they feel and what the societal environment forces them to accept is a source of stress. Egger (1985) interviewed children of mixed marriages between members of the German minority and members of the Italian majority. The children themselves would like to feel they belong to both groups, that indeed they could be 'mediators' between the groups, between which there is often conflict. Yet they are not allowed to do this; they are defined and forced to declare themselves as members of one or the other:

> Eines der fundamentalen Probleme für die Jugendlichen aus zweisprachigen Familien scheint darin zu bestehen, daß die Definition, die sie von sich geben, nicht mit der Definition übereinstimmt, die die Mitglieder der Sprachgruppen über sie abgeben. Kinder aus zweisprachigen Familien möchten sich oft nicht eindeutig für die eine oder andere Sprachgruppe erklären. Die soziale Umwelt scheint aber derart auf die Alternative

'deutsch oder italienisch' eingestellt zu sein, daß auf alle Fälle eine Zuordnung der Personen zu einer der Sprachgruppen erfolgt. Da sich die Jugendlichen selbst nicht entscheiden wollen, werden sie von der unmittelbaren sozialen Umwelt als der 'anderen' Sprachgruppe zugehörig angesehen. So kommt es, daß dieselben Jugendlichen von Deutschsprachigen als Italiener und von Italienschsprachigen als Deutsche angesehen werden.[3] (Egger, 1985: 175)

In the case of the Italians in Belgium, a similar sentiment is expressed as being foreign both in Belgium and in Italy:

- Vous vous sentez belge ou encore italien?
- Ben, disons que c'est difficile. On a pris toutes les habitudes d'ici, mais c'est difficile de dire si on est belge à cause de ça, comme c'est difficile de dire que ... qu'on n'est pas belge, non plus. Puisque tous les enfants sont ici ... alors on est ni l'un ni l'autre. Ici on est étranger, et chez nous on est étranger aussi. Tous les gens de notre âge, toute une génération, sont partis de l'Italie, ... alors si on rentre en Italie on est traité comme des étrangers, puisque la nouvelle génération nous connaît pas. (Byram, 1990: 90)

Being bicultural is thus far more complex than being bilingual. It may be experienced positively as a range of competences, but it can also be experienced negatively as a forced choice of allegiance to one group – to which one parent belongs and not the other, for example – or even as an absence of ethnic and national identity, being a foreigner wherever one is.

Finally, in this attempt to untangle the complexities of being bicultural, there is the question of citizenship. As we have seen, membership in an ethnic group is often but by no means always isomorphic with 'nationality', when the nation is considered to be synonymous with the state. This confusion often leads monolingual and monocultural people to assume that citizenship, in the sense of holding a passport and rights of residence, is or should be synonymous with loyalty to and identification with the dominant culture of the state. Yet it is not infrequent for individuals to have more than one citizenship and passport, but only one national/ethnic identity. The relationship to the state is one of rights and obligations not of loyalty to a particular set of cultural values, beliefs and practices.

It is clear from Webster's definition that citizenship can be acquired at any point and is not dependent on a process of socialisation into and loyalty towards a particular culture, as in the case of a national/ ethnic identity:

> Citizen: (. . .) a member of a state: one who is claimed as a member of a state; a native or naturalised person of either sex who owes allegiance to a government and is entitled to reciprocal protection from it and to enjoyment of the rights of citizenship. (Webster's Third New International Dictionary, 1986: 411)

Some states are also willing to allow their citizens to become naturalised in another state without giving up allegiance to or rights of protection from the first. In other situations, individuals inherit citizenship of two states from their parents in exogamous marriage. In neither case does citizenship necessarily entail an affective attachment, a cultural loyalty. Being bicultural is different from being bilingual, and both are different again from having dual citizenship.

Culture in Multilingual Classrooms

The question now arises as to what lessons from schooling with explicit concerns for identity and culture, can be learnt for multilingual classrooms where a main concern, as in the SESB schools of Berlin, is with promoting multilingual competence among its students. I have suggested a number of parameters which are important in understanding the former and I now want to consider how they might help us with the latter.

In summary, the 'culture bearing' features of schooling, like that of the Foyer programme, are the following:

- the use of the 'other' language – i.e. other than the official language of the state – as a medium of instruction;
- the presence of native-speaking teachers who embody cultural values, beliefs and practices;
- a curriculum which includes explicit reference to the other culture (see Met, Chapter 3, and Nunan & Lam, Chapter 6 this volume).

The issues raised are:

- the distinction between bicultural competence and bicultural identity;
- the degree to which bicultural identity is experienced positively as a resource or negatively as a source of stress;

- the impact of the social environment on people's sense of belonging to one or more ethnic groups;
- the potential confusion of ethnic identity with national identity, of national identity with citizenship.

Now, if schools which have hitherto focused on developing bi- or multilingual proficiency should wish to give more explicit attention to a cultural dimension, the points just summarised suggest that the presence of native speakers is essential and that this has to be complemented by a syllabus that includes not just the existing state's culture but also the cultures associated with the other languages. In the case of programmes for minority children, the decision is already made as to which of a number of cultures associated with a language should be represented. The culture represented will be that of the parents and of the teachers. In principle, where learners of, say, English have no existing relationship to a particular culture, then the choice is more open. One could decide to link the learning of English with British or American or any English-speaking culture. However, the significance of the native speaker as an embodiment of a culture means that the choice has to be for the culture from which s/he originates. The corollary of this is, furthermore, that to try to expose learners to another culture in such situations will not be successful, or at least far less likely to be successful, if the teachers are not native speakers. For it is in their culture-specific affective relationships with children, particularly at primary school age, that their influence on children's socialisation is strongest.

This approach would transfer some of the methods of schools for minorities, such as those briefly described in the Foyer vignette, to language-oriented schools. At the same time, it implicitly transfers some of the aims: to develop in young people a bicultural relationship with the culture of the home – in this case, the culture of the country itself – and another culture, from a 'foreign' country. There is then the possibility of schools changing the monocultural identity of pupils and their identification with the nation-state. On the one hand, this may not be a real issue, because the influence of a small number of native speakers from another country, even complemented in some situations by native speaker students in the same classroom, is unlikely to be strong enough to counter-balance the influences of the rest of the social environment. On the other hand, schools should have a clear conception of their aims in the cultural dimension and, in particular, whether they wish to encourage a bicultural identity or rather bicultural competence, as described by Paulston.

In introducing the SESB schools, I mentioned that their aims might be described as 'intercultural' in contrast with the bicultural aims of the Foyer programme, and we can now distinguish between Paulston's bicultural competence and intercultural competence. Whereas the former is a means of choosing more or less consciously a combination of cultural values, beliefs and practices in order to adapt to a particular situation or as a basis for a personal philosophy and way of life, the latter involves an even more conscious capacity to 'mediate' between two or more cultures, to see similarities and conflicts, to create a relationship between them for oneself and also for others, to take on the mediator role which Egger describes with respect to young people in Südtirol. Rather than becoming a 'native speaker' of two or more cultures and languages, the mediator is an 'intercultural speaker' (Byram & Zarate, 1994; Kramsch, 1998), someone able to engage with people of different cultures, both for themselves and on behalf of others who do not have that capacity.

Elsewhere we have defined the intercultural speaker as someone who has linguistic competence in two or more languages, and also has four *savoirs*, abilities, skills and dispositions as follows (based on Byram & Zarate, 1997).

Savoir être is the ability to abandon ethnocentric attitudes towards and perceptions of other cultures, and to see and develop an understanding of the differences and relationships between one's own and a foreign culture; this involves affective and cognitive change in learners. It might be evident in such behaviour as:

- attitudes of openness towards and interest in foreign peoples, societies and cultures;
- willingness to relativise and criticise one's own cultural viewpoint and system of values;
- ability to distance oneself from usual points of view with regards to cultural difference, such as that of the tourist;
- ability to take the role of cultural intermediary between one's own culture and the foreign culture, also in situations of conflict.

Savoir apprendre is the ability to observe, collect data and analyse how people of another language-and-culture (Byram, Morgan *et al.*, 1994) perceive and experience their world, what beliefs, values and meanings they share about it. This involves practical skills and a readiness to decentre and take a different perspective. It might be evident in the ability to:

- use the language and concepts of a culture to describe something observed in that culture;
- investigate the perspectives of people in the foreign culture with respect to a particular experience or phenomenon;
- identify the institutions concerned with border crossing and residence in another society when asked to consider mobility from one country to another.

Savoir is the knowledge of different aspects of a culture, i.e. a system of reference points and allusions familiar to natives of the culture, which helps the natives to share beliefs, values and meanings, and to communicate without making explicit those shared assumptions. It might be evident in the knowledge of particular institutions such as schools, or of particular behaviours and customs – and their meaning for those involved – such as first communion or confirmation, but also in values and beliefs which are taken for granted and seldom made explicit in a society.

Savoir faire is the ability to draw upon the other three *savoirs* and integrate them in real time and interaction with people of a specific language-and-culture. It might involve:

- an ability to relate in real time the knowledge, skills and attitudes acquired in the classroom;
- an ability to take into account the specific relationships between the cultural identities of the learner and of people from another country and culture;
- an ability to take account of the perceptions of the learner's own culture and cultural identity which people from another country and culture bring to an interaction.

Implications

If language-orientated schools decide on intercultural competence as their aim, as do the schools in Berlin, the implications include the following:

- The presence of native speaker teachers is crucial if not essential, since intercultural competence involves the ability to relate affectively as well as cognitively to other cultures; non-native speakers do not embody the other culture and do not relate to learners in the same way.
- The curriculum must include explicit reference to the other culture, and this requires a different perspective to that of the

state curriculum with its constant reinforcement of the national culture; indeed, since the methods involved should also include comparison and critique, the national culture will be relativised and criticised, made to appear what it is, i.e. a naturalised but not a natural selection of values, beliefs and practices.

- The use of two or more languages as media of instruction should also include comparative analysis, in pedagogically appropriate methods, of the ways in which different languages express different cultures, so that learners can become aware of differences and relationships which they have to mediate as intercultural speakers (see Met, Chapter 3 this volume).
- The teachers involved must themselves be intercultural speakers, not just native speakers teaching as if their learners were, or were to become, native speakers; although many teachers in multilingual classrooms have developed intercultural speaker intuitions, not all have, and they need training in the applications for the classroom.
- The teachers also need a professional understanding of the cultural values implicit in the curriculum and of the ways in which the explicit introduction of other cultures into the curriculum relativises and challenges the taken-for-granted, natural status of the national or state curriculum.
- Some parts of the curriculum are particularly sensitive to this challenge; the teaching of history, literature and geography in primary school, when students are in the early stages of learning the nation-state's version of the world as seen through these disciplines, needs particular attention. More specifically, it raises a number of important questions. Should there be juxtaposition of conflicting views of historical events or geo-political entities? Should there be complementary stories, poems and folk-tales from different cultures, or only from the national culture? Should the teaching materials be taken from the national production of the other country or specially prepared for intercultural purposes?

The ways in which these various requirements are met and these questions answered will inevitably depend on particular circumstances. It is hard to deny the crucial role of teacher education. Most, if not all, teachers in multilingual classrooms, including those in minority schools, are not trained specifically for the special conditions and educational aims of the school. Whether as teachers of foreign languages or other subjects, or teachers for primary school pedagogy, they adapt their training to the circumstances as best they can. Appropriate training would include acquisition of an understanding of: the particular aims of multilingual classrooms, the distinctions I have pointed out earlier, the implications for the development of instructional materials and methods, the psychological theory which helps them to understand the development of bicultural and intercultural competence, social identities, and the socio-political consequences of curriculum change to meet the cultural learning aims of multilingual classrooms. To emphasise the significance of teacher education and training is not a surprising conclusion, but is no less important for all that. It is an issue that is addressed by others in this volume (see Met, Chapter 3; Lyster, Chapter 4; Nunan & Lam, Chapter 6; Gonzalez, Chapter 9; Hornberger & López, Chapter 10).

Conclusion

In this chapter, I have tried to offer a number of perspectives on different kinds of multilingual classrooms which demonstrate that language teaching is never and can never be only that, whether in traditional foreign language classrooms, in ethnic minority education or in other approaches to developing linguistic competence in two or more languages. Nor is it simply a question of providing information about a country where a language is spoken natively. Exposing children to another language and expecting them to learn it as part of the process of socialisation and acquisition of social identities is not simply a matter of cognitive learning. There are significant affective factors and challenges which include risk and responsibility on the part of teachers and those responsible for education programmes. The more consciously and clearly these challenges are understood, the better the education in multilingual classrooms will be.

Notes

1. The lesson described here was reported at a seminar at the Internationaler Arbeitskreis Sonnenberg in August 1996. I am grateful to Peter Doyé, Catherine Marson and colleagues for their accounts.
2. This description is based on my own observations and reports in Byram and Leman, 1990.
3. Translations of quotations are provided in the Appendix at the end of this chapter.

Appendix: Translations of quotations

One of the fundamental problems for young people from bilingual families seems to arise from the fact that the definition they give of themselves does not coincide with the one members of the language groups give of them. Children from bilingual families would often not wish to declare themselves in favour of one language group or the other. The social environment however seems to be so devoted to the alternative 'German or Italian', that an allocation of the individual to one of the language groups is inevitable. Since the young people themselves do not wish to decide, they are seen by their immediate environment as belonging to the 'other' language group. It is thus the case that the same young people are seen by the German speakers as Italian and by the Italian speakers as German. (Egger, 1985: 175)

- Do you feel Belgian or still Italian?
- Well, it's difficult. We have taken on all the habits here, but it is difficult to say we are Belgian for that reason, just as it's difficult to say that we're not Belgian either. Since the children are here ... so we're neither one nor the other. Here we are foreigners and at home we're foreigners too. Everybody of our age, a whole generation, left Italy, ... so if we return to Italy we're treated like foreigners, since the new generation doesn't know us. (Byram, 1990: 90)

References

Becher, U.A.J. (1996) European citizenship and historical learning. *Evaluation and Research in Education* 10 2&3, 79–87.

Bourdieu, P. (1977) *Outline of a Theory of Practice*. Cambridge: Cambridge University Press.

Bourdieu, P. and Passeron, J.C. (1977) *Reproduction in Education, Society and Culture*. London: Sage.

Byram, M. (1990) Return to the home country: The 'necessary dream' in ethnic identity. In M. Byram and J. Leman (eds) *Bicultural and Trilingual Education* (pp. 77–94). Clevedon: Multilingual Matters.

Byram, M., Morgan, C. *et al.* (1994) *Teaching-and-Learning Language-and-Culture*. Clevedon: Multilingual Matters.

Byram, M. and Zarate, G. (1997) Definitions, objectives and assessment of sociocultural competence. In M. Byram, G. Zarate and G. Neuner *Sociocultural Competence in Language Learning and Teaching*. Strasbourg: Council of Europe.

Churchill, S. (1986) *The Education of Linguistic and Cultural Minorities in OECD Countries*. Clevedon: Multilingual Matters.

Doyé, P. (1996) *Untersuchung des zweisprachigen Unterrichts an der Staatlichen Europaschule Berlin*. Berlin: Berliner Institut für Lehrerfort-und weiterbildung und Schulentwicklung.

Egger, K. (1985) *Zweisprachige Familien in Südtirol: Sprachgebrauch und Spracherziehung.* Innsbruck: AZB Verlag.

Kramsch, C. (1998) The privilege of the intercultural speaker. In M. Byram and M. Fleming (eds) *Language Learning in Intercultural Perspective.* Cambridge: Cambridge University Press.

Leman, J. (1990) Multilingualism as norm, monolingualism as exception: The Foyer model in Brussels. In M. Byram and J. Leman (eds) *Bicultural and Trilingual Education* (pp. 7–29). Clevedon: Multilingual Matters.

Muckle, J. (1988) *A Guide to the Soviet Curriculum.* London: Croom Helm.

Paulston, C.B. (1992) *Sociolinguistic Perspectives on Bilingual Education.* Clevedon: Multilingual Matters.

Smith, A.D. (1991) *National Identity.* Harmondsworth: Penguin.

Chapter 6
Teacher Education for Multilingual Contexts: Models and Issues

DAVID NUNAN and AGNES LAM

Introduction

Multilingualism is a phenomenon in many countries, but multilingual education as a mode of programme delivery is not as widespread as it could be. By multilingual education we mean educational programmes in which more than two languages are taught and academic instruction is presented through more than two languages. For many years, bilingual programmes have been mounted as an attempt to meet some of the educational needs of a multilingual community. In recent years, however, and in various parts of the world, there is a concern that many students really need to acquire proficiency in more than two languages to function effectively in their society (see Hoffmann, Chapter 7; Cenoz, Chapter 8; Genesee, Chapter 11 this volume).

This chapter is an attempt to give an overview of the types of educational models that have been adopted in multilingual communities and to outline the models for multilingual education as defined above. In the discussion of these models, it will be necessary for us to refer to several bilingual education models, not only because they have often been used in multilingual settings but more because they provide useful insights into the sociocultural considerations and the demands on teacher competencies when additional languages are involved in education. In the light of these considerations, an operational framework for teacher preparation is proposed. The framework is not offered as a simplistic solution to the complex problems of teacher education in multilingual settings; it is merely suggested as a set of parameters to be taken into account when planning a teacher development programme. Only local teacher educators are in a position to evaluate what is most appropriate and practicable for the sociolinguistic and educational circumstances in their countries, provinces and institutions.

Language Dominance and Multilingual Societies

With almost 6000 languages in the world but only about 150 countries, it is to be expected that languages should be in competition for social and/or political power (Wardhaugh, 1987). The languages that come to dominate are those used by the political and economic elites within a society. Hence, language dominance is really the dominance of a particular ethnic group over one or more other ethnic groups in a bilingual or multilingual society. Such dominance does not have to be supported by legislation but may be the effect of *de facto* differences in political or economic power. We shall not discuss language dominance or multilingualism any further here. Elsewhere in this book, there are specific examples (see Gonzalez, Chapter 9; Hornberger & López, Chapter 10 this volume). For the purposes of our chapter, a multilingual society is a society in which there are more than two languages or dialects in use and one or more of them may have relatively high social status or more political power (to be referred to as *Dominant Languages* or DLs hereafter) while another or more may have relatively low social status and/or less political power (to be referred to as *Non-dominant Languages* or NDLs hereafter). DLs, so defined, have been termed *majority languages* in the literature; such a definition can sometimes be misleading because a language with social status or political power may not always be the ethnic language of the majority of the population; examples are found in colonial or post-colonial settings. NDLs have been referred to as *minority languages* in the literature and are now redefined here for the same reason. A non-dominant language or dialect (NDL) in a specific multilingual setting can very well be the national language (and hence a DL) in another country. The United States, for example, has, among its population, several immigrant groups speaking languages that have a high status in their countries of origin. (Our distinction between DLs and NDLs bears some similarity to but is not identical with classical diglossia (Ferguson, 1959) because our DLs may be used in all domains by the dominant group.) Speakers of NDLs have traditionally been referred to as *ethnic minorities* but will be referred to as Non-dominant Groups (NDGs) in our discussion, as we wish to emphasise that these groups may sometimes be in the demographic majority or, at least, exist in substantial numbers.

Overt and Covert Policies and the Role of Teacher Educators

Within our broad definition of a multilingual society, it is easy to see why multilingualism or multidialectalism is a phenomenon that has to be reckoned with in education, and hence teacher education, in almost all societies, regardless of whether there is official recognition of the NDLs or an overt policy to meet the language needs of NDGs. It is useful to conceive of multilingualism as a continuum, rather than as an either-or phenomenon. Multilingualism or multidialectalism exists in almost all societies to various degrees. In other words, while some societies have been recognised as multilingual entities and policies supporting some status for NDLs have evolved in these societies, there are many *unofficial multilingual communities* around the world where policy directions are not clear because the multilingual phenomenon is not recognised socially or politically. (As Byram, Chapter 5 this volume, points out, many governments deny that nationality and citizenship can be different.) Teacher educators in these communities, where there is no overt policy to provide for the NDGs, have to contend with everyday multilingual realities when designing teacher preparation programmes. In the absence of an overt policy, they are usually the ones who will have to interpret the covert policy and prepare teachers accordingly, or perhaps in dissonance with the covert policy if they do not agree with it. In countries where multilingualism is not officially recognised as a phenomenon requiring government action, teacher educators of some stature may even be involved in the policy making as well, even as they update their teacher preparation programmes in the light of changing sociolinguistic circumstances. In view of this, it is important that teacher educators should be given every opportunity not only to consider how to implement a teacher education programme based on given policy directions but also to reflect on and make informed choices among the educational models that are available for use in language dominance circumstances.

The Central Issue in Multilingual Education

Whether policies are overtly articulated, covertly implied or invisibly in the making, the central concern in multilingual education appears to be how much status and recognition within the educational system should be given to the languages of minority groups, or, in our definition, NDGs. Cummins (1984: 72), for example, considers this 'the most contentious issue in policy debates in virtually all the western industrialized countries'. The qualification of 'western industrialized countries' is insightful. In non-western industrialised countries, this has not always been the foremost consideration. Language standardisation and codification have sometimes featured more prominently in policy debates than the status and function of NDLs in education. In the People's Republic of China, for example, the most central language issue when the Republic was established in the middle of this century was to establish a standard dialect (Putonghua) for the Han Chinese, the largest ethnic group speaking several dialects, and a simplified script to promote literacy for a vast population. Corollary work on language description for some of the 55 language minorities, a total of 67,230,000 people or 6.7% of the Chinese population (Ma & Su, 1988: 1) was started around the same time as a matter of policy in accordance with the egalitarian ideals in the prevailing political ideology. Where possible, minority languages have been used as media of instruction, apparently with little contention, except during the Cultural Revolution when this was obstructed (Ma *et al.*, 1985: 119). Contentious or not, the role to be played by NDLs is indeed a concern to be reckoned with in the education of multilingual communities.

Educational Models in Language Dominance Contexts

We now examine the programme models that have been adopted for the education of multilingual communities (which, we must emphasise, are more widespread than is generally acknowledged, if we take into account dialectal variation).

These programme models can be classified into one of four types according to two important factors:

- *cultural status*: whether the NDL is valued as a *target language* (a language that one aims to acquire competence in); and
- *function in education*: whether a NDL is used as a medium of instruction.

We have focused on these two factors because often it is the cultural status and educational function of the NDL or a number of NDLs in relation to the role played by the DL or DLs that shape the mode of multilingual education in a particular society.

Of the four types of educational models in Figure 6.1, two will probably encourage *language shift* or the lessening in proficiency, stunted development or eventual disuse of the first language acquired from birth (L1) while an additional or second language (L2) is

NDL is used as a medium of instruction (+)

LANGUAGE SHIFT TYPE B	LANGUAGE MAINTENANCE
TYPE B	TYPE B
Transitional bilingual	Canadian immersion*
programmes	Protected language programmes
Bridging programmes	Language shelter programmes
	Language exposure time
	programmes
LANGUAGE SHIFT	LANGUAGE MAINTENANCE
TYPE A	TYPE A
Cultural sensitivity programmes	Modern language programmes*
DL intensive programmes for	Foreign language programmes*
NDL students	Heritage language programmes
Submersion programmes	

NDL is not valued as a target language (−)

NDL is valued as a target language (+)

NDL is not used a medium of instruction (−)

* Modern or foreign language programmes are not traditionally considered language maintenance programmes as they are open to learners from dominant groups as well, but they can be used by the relevant ethnic groups to affirm their ethnicity. Likewise, if English-speaking children learn French in Toronto through immersion, it is also not a language maintenance programme; the fact that they do, however, enhances the maintenance of French for the French community.

Figure 6.1 Models in language dominance contexts

acquired. The other two types can promote *language maintenance* or retaining competence in and use of the L1 at least in some domains though the L2 may be acquired or needed for communication in other domains in the immediate community. The above definitions of language shift and maintenance only capture the processes from the individual learner's point of view. Most descriptions of language shift and maintenance focus on the collective language use patterns of NDGs (Hamers & Blanc, 1989: 175–79; Paulston, 1985: 7–15).

The four types of models in Figure 6.1 are:

(1) *Language shift Type A*: The NDL is not valued as a target language and is not used as a medium of instruction.
(2) *Language shift Type B*: The NDL is not valued as a target language but is used a medium of instruction.
(3) *Language maintenance Type A*: The NDL is valued as a target language but is not used as a medium of instruction.
(4) *Language maintenance Type B*: The NDL is valued as a target language and is also used as a medium of instruction.

Language shift Type A (–target language, –medium of instruction)
There are several examples of this type:

- *Submersion programmes*: The NDL is ignored completely and NDL speakers are expected to sink or swim in classes for all subjects that use the DL exclusively (Cummins, 1984: 75; Hamers & Blanc, 1989: 189). Since most NDL speakers find it difficult to survive in such classes, they tend to sink, metaphorically speaking.
- *DL intensive programmes*: The situation is a little better than in submersion classes. Although the NDL is not given any status or function in education, it is recognised that NDL speakers have difficulty following classes for academic subjects delivered entirely in the DL. They are given intensive language classes in the DL to improve their DL proficiency so that they can follow DL instruction for other subjects. Such classes may be additional to their regular curriculum.
- *Cultural sensitivity programmes*: This example is slightly problematic in classification. In a cultural sensitivity programme, the NDL is apparently respected but since only the culture associated with the NDL is taught, the language is still not valued as a cultural asset in itself. In actual practice, some learning of NDL may occur in episodic instances, for example, in learning NDL songs as part of a cultural activity, but competence

in the NDL is not a programme objective. (See Cummins, 1984: 75–6, for a range of cultural sensitivity programmes.)

Language shift Type B (–target language, +medium of instruction)
This type has a wide range within the same general mode:

- *Transitional bilingual programmes*: The NDL is used as a medium of instruction for all or some school subjects to help NDL speakers to make the transition to programmes in which the DL is used exclusively for teaching all subjects; the NDL is not valued in itself and is eventually ignored in the educational system. The term *transition* highlights the gap between the NDL used at home and the DL used at school, a gap that needs to be bridged by transitional bilingualism (Cummins, 1984: 75; Hamers & Blanc, 1989: 189).
- *Bridging programmes*: This is arguably a type of transitional bilingual programme in that it tries to bridge the gap usually between one level of education and another. In some countries, the language of instruction between primary and secondary education or between secondary and tertiary is not the same. Hence, there is a need to bridge the gap. In a bridging course, though the teaching materials may be written in the DL (usually the language used in the higher levels of education) and the corollary aim is to create a DL classroom environment as much as possible, most teachers use a mixture of NDL (usually the medium used in the lower levels of education) and DL in actual classroom delivery. They also tend to be very intensive and last from a few weeks to a few months while conventional transitional bilingual programmes tend to be delivered over a few years.

Language maintenance Type A (+target language, –medium of instruction)
Examples of this type are:

- *Heritage language programmes*: The NDL is respected and valued in its own right (Cummins, 1984: 76) but tends to be taught as a special activity outside of regular class time, either as an extra-curricular activity or as part of a community programme (on weekends, for example). It is not used as a medium of instruction. The very name of the programme can be inhibitory, though unintentionally so. Heritage language programmes tend to connote that NDL speakers are learning their ethnic languages only as part of their cultural heritage, not because there is any special use for them in their immediate community. For example, Chinese children enrolled in a Chinese heritage language programme in Toronto learn Chinese as part of their cultural heritage (and possibly to communicate with their grandparents).

- *Foreign or modern language programmes*: A foreign or modern language programme taught as part of a university curriculum has different connotations altogether. It is not impossible for an American-born Chinese to learn Chinese together with other English-speaking Americans in the Asian Languages Department as his or her affirmation of ethnic identity, though these programmes are not planned for heritage purposes. Similar examples are Americans of German descent learning German, or those of Italian descent learning Italian as foreign languages. While heritage language programmes are, by definition, for NDGs, modern language or foreign language programmes are designed for all citizens as a time-honoured educational desideratum to enable them to participate in life in the international community. Though these languages may not have political power locally, some of them are likely to be DLs in the international community.

Language maintenance Type B (+target language, +medium of instruction)

Here are four examples of this type:

- *Language shelter programmes*: A NDL is used as a medium of instruction and the DL is taught only as a subject (Cummins, 1984: 76–7). Superficially, the teaching of the DL in a language shelter programme is not different from other modern language classes, except that the target language is not just any second language but one that has power in the immediate community.
- *Protected language programmes*: In this model, it is possible to go through the whole educational process including university education entirely in the NDL; learning the DL is optional. In China, for example, there has been a policy to encourage minorities to preserve their languages and cultures (Ramsey, 1987: 159). Hence, for some NDLs in China that have had a written form for a long time, such as Mongolian, it is possible to use the NDL even in higher education for some disciplines in a few geographical locations (Ma *et al.*, 1985: 119).
- *Canadian immersion*: This is the classic model of immersion in

which DL speakers are immersed in a NDL environment so that they can learn the NDL. English-speaking children learn French by studying other subjects in French (Cummins, 1984: 77; Genesee, 1987; see also Genesee, Chapter 11; Lyster, Chapter 4 this volume). French is not obviously a NDL since it is one of the two official languages of Canada and has high cultural status, which partly explains why the Canadian immersion programme has been successful (Navarro, 1985: 294). However, it is a NDL because, outside of Quebec, it has little political or economic power. Strictly speaking, the French immersion programme for English-speaking children in Canada is not a language maintenance programme since French is not their ethnic language and they are the dominant group in the country; but the fact that they are learning French helps to promote the status of French and enhance the maintenance of French for the French-speaking community.

- *Language exposure time (LET) programmes*: Both the NDL and the DL are used as media of instruction for different subjects so that students can get simultaneous proportional exposure to both languages (Goh, 1978: 2–2). For example, social studies and other cultural subjects are taught in the NDL while science, maths and other technical subjects are taught in the DL. This is a variant of immersion in terms of the exposure to the DL but is also a type of language shelter programme if one thinks of the exposure to the NDL. Sometimes, it has also been classified as a transitional bilingual programme if the LET of the NDL is slowly decreased to give way to classes taught exclusively in the DL.

Although our typology of programme models as described above bears some similarity to Cummins' (1984: 76) representation of programmes for minority children, it differs from Cummins' in five distinct ways:

(1) While Cummins uses *L1* and *L2* to refer to the languages in the programmes, we include the essential dimension of social status or political power of the languages more explicitly through our terms, *DLs* and *NDLs*.
(2) Our factor of the NDL's function as a medium for acquiring other knowledge is more generally applicable to diverse realities than Cummins' (1984: 75) variable of *transition*, which is apparently restricted to the use of an L1 as an *initial* medium of instruction to bridge the gap between home and school.
(3) Our factors can be conceived of as degrees on continua so that a

NDL can, for example, be _more_ used or _less_ used as a medium of instruction, not just used (+) or not used (−).

(4) We have included other language programmes, like _modern or foreign language programmes_ and _protected language programmes_, in our scheme for direct comparison with other programmes often used to educate ethnic groups with little power (NDGs).

(5) Our categorisation makes apparent which policies are likely to result in _language shift_ and which will promote _language maintenance_.

From Bilingual Education to Multilingual Education

The programme models described above are generally used to cultivate bilingualism but they can also be implemented in various combinations to meet some of the language needs in multilingual settings. Since multilingual education, by definition, demands that more than two languages are used as media of instruction and has language maintenance as one of its central aims, this means that only Language Maintenance Type B programmes can really count. In actual practice, however, some of the other models may also have a role to play at some point in the multilingual programme. What tends to happen in reality is a range of scenarios, especially for multilingual programmes that are just taking off. It can very well be that although more than two languages are used for teaching in a school, in which case it can be called a multilingual school, it may or may not be the case that all learners are expected to become multilingual. Here are four common scenarios for the organisation of a multilingual programme:

- _Scenario 1_: Multilingual programme with the aim of cultivating bilingualism in NDL speakers while DL speakers may remain monolingual. This tends to happen when the dominant group in a multilingual community is extremely large and its language is one used internationally. The school mounting such a programme allows for NDL students, or at least those NDGs with large numbers, to study some subjects in their own language for at least some time. The DL speakers study only in the DL.

- _Scenario 2_: Multilingual programme with the goal of bilingualism for both NDL and DL speakers. This tends to occur in settings in which the DL is not the ethnic language of any NDGs but is a language of power, for example, as in post-colonial settings.

- *Scenario 3*: Multilingual programme with multilingualism as an objective for DL and NDL speakers. Two DLs are used as media of instruction and one or more NDLs is/are taught as a subject to the respective NDL speakers but not used for the instruction of other subjects. This might involve using the Language Exposure Time (LET) model together with a heritage language programme (which has recently been renamed the *international language programme*).
- *Scenario 4*: Multilingualism across the curriculum. More than two languages are used as media of instruction and all students are expected to learn more than two languages and become multilingual, though same levels of achievement for the languages taught may not be expected.

The above list of scenarios is only an attempt towards depicting a cline of realities. To strong proponents of multilingual education, only Scenario 4 is the true form of multilingual education. But in practice, it is entirely possible for a school to target Scenario 4 as an eventual goal while going through one or more of the other scenarios in its early stages. Just as there is a continuum of multilingualism, there is also a continuum of multilingual programmes.

We have attempted to differentiate the types of educational models used in multilingual settings in some detail not because we particularly wish to make some out to be 'better' models than others, but because they have different implications for teacher education. We now wish to make these implications explicit so that teacher educators can make an informed decision for themselves as to what practicable model or combination of models at different levels of education can maximise the resources at their disposal to meet the most urgent educational needs in their local contexts. There are implications at two levels:

(1) Core teacher competencies required for a model.
(2) Operational models to develop these competencies in teachers.

Teacher Competencies for Multilingual Education

Before discussing the special teacher competencies required for multilingual education, we should like to review the position on core competencies for all teachers, regardless of multilingual considerations. What has happened in the last several decades is that teachers have been expected to have more and more competencies, partly because teacher education as an academic discipline has matured and the nature of teaching is better understood, but more because teaching has become more complex as it has been reconceptualised as a profession rather than a trade or craft. Until relatively recently teachers were expected to have two essential qualities: a sound knowledge of what they try to teach, and a good grasp of how to teach it. The 'how' includes anything from syllabus design to the planning of specific lessons and classroom activities. In the last two or three decades, in response to the educational philosophy of *language across the curriculum*, a third component has been added – effective communication skills in the classroom. With the availability of cheaper and faster methods of the production of teaching materials, teachers have also been increasingly encouraged to experiment with writing their own materials. Recent developments in learner assessment and programme evaluation as well as the general movement towards accountability for educational funding have added other requirements: a familiarity with assessment and evaluation instruments and the ability to handle school–community relations. Likewise, advances in technology, especially in information and communication, have made it necessary for teachers to familiarise themselves with various tools in educational technology. Finally, the trend towards school-based teacher preparation and the movement towards lifelong learning have called for motivation for and expertise in continuing professional development.

To summarise, the ideal teacher for the twenty-first century is expected to have:

(1) A knowledge of the discipline.
(2) The capability to employ a variety of pedagogical methods.
(3) Communicative effectiveness in the classroom.
(4) The ability to develop materials.
(5) The ability to design and implement instruments for assessment and evaluation.
(6) The capacity to understand and handle community relations.
(7) Competence in using a range of educational technology.
(8) The motivation and ability towards further professional development.

More elaborate lists may include additional qualities such as: a genuine concern for students, a sound understanding of educational psychology, effective counselling skills, administrative acumen and so forth. Are we fair to the teacher to expect so much? Is it possible for us to expect any less? Similar trends are apparent in other fields that are reconceptualised as professions rather than as crafts or trades. (A relevant example here would be nursing.) To a certain extent, it is the world we live in and the community teachers serve that have become so complex. Complexity in teacher education programmes is a response to the increasing sophistication in the world around us (Lange, 1990; Nunan, 1989: 144). Having said that, we note that the converse is also true. Though in general the world around us has become more complex (especially if we think of urban centres), if the community we serve is still relatively unsophisticated, then the preparation of teachers for that community can be relatively less demanding, but only in certain areas. For example, if most schools in a certain rural community have no educational technology apart from a piece of chalk and a blackboard, then it does not make immediate sense to give teachers in that community a course in computer assisted instruction. It is important, therefore, to take into account local realities and exigencies when drawing up the specific list of desirable teacher competencies for a teacher education programme.

Specific to bilingual teacher preparation, lists of competencies are also available. Often, these are expressed as important elements in a teacher preparation and certification programme. Even two decades ago, the Center for Applied Linguistics (1974) had a comprehensive list, which can be adapted for multilingual teacher preparation. This can be summarised as follows (with possible adaptations for our purposes in italics):

(1) Language proficiency in both the target language (*languages*) as well as the learner's language (*learners' languages*).
(2) A knowledge of linguistics and bilingualism (*multilingualism*).
(3) An appreciation of the learner's culture (*learners' cultures*) and the ability to respond positively to the diversity of behaviour in cross-cultural (*multicultural*) circumstances.
(4) Competence in a range of instructional methods including appropriate collaborative work.
(5) The ability to utilise and adapt curriculum and develop materials.
(6) The ability to design assessment procedures for both self and learners.
(7) Skills in the effective handling of school-community relations.
(8) The demonstration of competencies in supervised classroom experience.

Descriptions of essential components in teacher education programmes available more recently are similar in some ways. An example is Lange's (1990: 248–9) from which the following list is abstracted (italics indicating adaptations for our discussion of multilingual education):

(1) Competence in a second language (*one or more NDL languages*).
(2) Understanding of how the target language is taught (*target languages are taught*).
(3) Practice in the application of knowledge about the subject and teaching in teaching situations.
(4) Opportunities to reach an understanding of both the art and the craft of teaching.
(5) Evaluation of teaching.

Both the CAL list and Lange's have much more detail. We have merely cited the key elements. Comparison of the discussion of each element shows even more similarity though they may be expressed differently. It must be obvious to the reader that both lists have included elements that do not seem to relate specially to multi-lingual education. This is because for many decades, the preparation of teachers for multilingual settings has usually been part of a more general teacher education programme, the competencies for bi-lingual or multilingual teaching having been included only as a subset of skills.

A different type of perspective is Houlton's (1986). His list of desirable competencies is worth noting for two reasons:

(1) It is focused on language-related competencies.
(2) It specifies the competencies according to different teaching phases or situations.

It is possible to recast his list of competencies for multilingual educa-tion. His overview is reproduced below:

(1) *Teachers at nursery/infant level:*
  • Use of mother tongue (home dialect) as an aid to home–school transition, and as a medium of instruction across the curric-ulum.
  • Use of community/standard language for labelling and every-day written communication.
(2) *Teachers at junior level:*
  • Use of mother tongue for classroom communication and instruction.
  • Introduction of literacy skills in community/standard language.
(3) *Teachers at secondary level:*
  • Teaching community/standard language and literature to examination levels.
  • Use of mother tongue for classroom communication.
(4) *All teachers:*

- Awareness of linguistic diversity, and strategies for acknowledging it in the classroom.

(5) *Supplementary school teachers*:
- Use of mother tongue (home dialect) as medium of classroom communication and instruction.
- Introduction of literacy skills in community/standard language.
- Teaching community/standard language and literature to examination levels. (Houlton, 1986: 11–12)

Houlton's terms *mother tongue (home dialect)* and *community/standard language* correspond to our terms NDL and DL in multilingual education. Although Houlton's list is useful in that it differentiates between the relative needs for proficiency in the NDL and the DL according to different levels of education and whether the trainees are language or non-language teachers, it does not differentiate overtly between the needs for different models of multilingual education.

In the light of the lists of competencies reviewed, when designing a teacher education programme for a language dominance setting, we think it would be useful to draw a distinction between teacher competencies relating to the status and role of NDLs in education and other teacher competencies. The teacher competencies relating to the place of NDLs in education are:

(1) Teacher competence in the NDL(s) in relation to whether the NDL(s) is/are taught as (a) target language(s) and/or used as a medium/media of instruction.
(2) Teacher readiness and ability to appreciate the culture(s) of NDL speakers (see also Byram, Chapter 5 this volume).

It is in these two essential aspects that teacher preparation for multilingual education differs from general teacher preparation for non-multilingual education.

Apart from the two key competencies mentioned above, other useful competencies include:

(3) Proficiency in the DL(s), if taught as (a) target language(s).
(4) A knowledge of the theory in language learning and language teaching.
(5) Other competencies as expected of the ideal teacher in the twenty-first century as described earlier.

Let us now focus our discussion on the two key competencies specific to teacher preparation for language dominance settings. How do the types of models (Figure 6.1) differ in terms of requirements for teacher competence in the NDLs and teacher knowledge of NDL cultures? As an initial illustration, let us assume a bilingual education programme with only one DL and one NDL as possible target languages. On the basis of that assumption, from Table 6.1, it is apparent that different language education models make different demands on teachers. If

Table 6.1 Teacher requirements for various language education models

Policy type	Educational model	Competence in NDL	Knowledge of NDL culture
Language shift	Submersion	Not required	Not required
	DL intensive classes	Not required but a little competence desirable	Not required but desirable
	Cultural sensitivity programme	Not required but a little competence desirable	Required
	Bridging course	Not required but some competence desirable	Not required but desirable
	Transitional bilingualism	Required for lower grades	Not required but desirable
Language maintenance	Heritage language programme	Required only for lessons in NDL, not for other subjects	
	Modern/foreign language	Required only for lessons in NDL, not for other subjects	
	Canadian immersion	Required for subjects taught in NDL	
	Language exposure time	Required for subjects taught in NDL	
	Language shelter programme	Required for lessons in all subjects except DL lessons	
	Protected language	Required for lessons in all subjects	

the NDL is not prevalently spoken, as it tends not to be except in colonial or post-colonial settings, then finding or training teachers to become proficient in the NDL is the biggest obstacle to any sort of language maintenance programme. The more a NDL is used across the curriculum for learning other subjects, the greater the problem is. When the target languages include more than one NDL as in multilingual education, the problem assumes geometric proportions. It is therefore not surprising that some multilingual communities have opted for a heritage programme of some sort, rather than a full maintenance programme. Apart from heritage language programmes in the school curriculum or some government funding for similar programmes run by the ethnic communities themselves, there is also the adoption of cultural sensitivity or awareness programmes as partial solutions because they are less demanding on teacher competence. Truly multilingual programmes are very demanding on teacher competence. Multilingualism across the curriculum may be more easily implemented if it is preceded by a certain level of multilingual proficiency and use in the everyday life of the community. If not, for multilingual programmes to work well, then teacher competence in one or more NDLs or at least some domains of the NDL(s) must be a central feature of the teacher preparation programme.

While proficiency in the NDL or knowledge of NDL culture is a major consideration in teacher preparation programmes supporting NDL education, there are other problems relating to teacher proficiency in the DL, if the DL is not the first language of many teachers as in colonial or post-colonial settings. In Hong Kong, for example, the use of English as a medium of instruction has become increasingly difficult because of the inadequacy of teachers proficient in English. Yet, many Chinese parents want their children to study in English because it is the language that promises a better career and international opportunities (Lam, 1994).

From the above discussion, it is evident that teacher competence in the target languages has to be a major consideration in teacher preparation programmes for language dominance contexts. In the absence of an environment where the target languages are widely used, teacher educators may have to consider the options outlined in Figure 6.1 in their attempt to enhance teacher competence in the target languages. They may have to include in their teacher education programme a component of language learning, perhaps an intensive course. The same applies to multicultural awareness training. Teacher trainees not originally from NDG backgrounds may have to participate in multicultural awareness workshops, with input from multicultural or bicultural informants (see also Met, Chapter 3; Byram, Chapter 5 this volume).

Operational Models for Teacher Education

Having identified the two key competencies specific to teacher preparation for language dominance settings, we now consider the operational models that can be used to develop these and other desirable teacher qualities in the prospective teachers. Such qualities have often been included as components in teacher preparation programmes. However, the inclusion of these qualities in a programme does not necessarily guarantee that course participants will graduate from that programme with those qualities. It is useful at this point to review the models of programme delivery that have been in use to consider which of them is more likely to succeed in the task of developing in prospective teachers the required competencies.

For a long time, a popular model has been the *craft model* of teacher education (Wallace, 1991: 6), which conceptualises the teacher as an apprentice learning under a master through supervised teaching and practice. Intending teachers are trained by experts to achieve competence in various areas of their work. Programmes in which they acquire these competencies are referred to as *teacher training* programmes. It is not uncommon for teacher training programmes to be tied to *teacher certification* procedures by a national body. Once trainees complete a teacher training programme successfully, they are considered to have acquired *Qualified Teacher Status* (QTS). In many countries, teachers without QTS are either not allowed to teach at all or, if allowed to do so, teach under less attractive employment terms. Related to but not identical with teacher training models is the *applied science model* (Wallace, 1991: 9) in which teacher training expertise is considered a body of knowledge just like engineering or the hard sciences. Hence, from time to time when new knowledge becomes available, teachers who have already acquired QTS may need to update their knowledge in *in-service* courses (while they keep their jobs as teachers) as distinguished from *pre-service* programmes (before they join the teaching profession).

The craft model or applied science model or the terms *teacher training* (pre-service and in-service) and *teacher certification* (the process of attaining QTS) reflect validation procedures and national standards and requirements external to the individual teacher. A perspective that calls on the internal resources of the teacher (whether novice or veteran) is the *reflective model* (Wallace, 1991: 15). The teacher is expected to synthesise his or her previous experience with any knowledge received, to try it out in practice, to reflect on it periodically and regularly to achieve professional competence. This model is especially useful for, though not exclusive to, in-service *teacher retraining*. The term *teacher education* has also been preferred over teacher training in relation to the development of the reflective model.

The reflective model has also found expression in the genre of *action learning research* (Nunan, 1990), which even veteran teachers may engage in from time to time. A further development from the reflective model is the *professional development model* (Nunan, 1989), which draws on the philosophy of professional and continuing education. A teacher, even if trained and qualified, makes it his or her lifelong goal to develop himself or herself professionally through a variety of activities such as classroom observation, peer review, team teaching, personal reflection, applied or action research and so forth. In other words, while a teacher may already be trained and certified, he or she undertakes to continue to educate himself or herself as a responsible professional. In this individual pursuit, educational institutions may provide a conducive environment in the form of refresher workshops and other avenues for communication. Institutional involvement has to be designed with a certain degree of sensitivity, however; otherwise, professional development procedures may become reporting exercises without the impetus which has to come from within teachers.

To enable teachers to have professional development as a lifelong goal, teacher education programmes have to provide sufficient opportunity for teachers to do individual research towards improving classroom practice. A teacher preparation programme based on the professional development model has the following features (Nunan, 1989: 148–9):

(1) *School based*: Because teachers are educated to serve a certain community, the earlier teachers are put in touch with the community, the better. Hence, teacher education programmes must allow for opportunities to interact with the school community.
(2) *Experiential*: Rather than just take educational theory and practice as given, teachers have to discover insights on their own through actual classroom observation, reflection and practice.
(3) *Problem centred*: The emphasis is on providing the opportunity to tackle real classroom problems, rather than theorising without a specific context in mind.

(4) *Developmental*: Since teaching is a complex undertaking, teachers are not at the same stage of development. Professional development programmes should be able to allow for such differences.

(5) *Open-ended*: Programmes should motivate and enable participants to work towards lifelong development as a teacher.

While the professional development model delineated above is the most talked about model in the current literature on teacher education, all the other earlier models are still in use to some extent in various countries for teacher development at various educational levels. It is not inconceivable for a country to use the craft or applied science model for pre-service training, the reflective model for in-service training and the professional development model for in-service retraining. At the same time, within any one teacher education programme, individual teacher educators may differ in the degree to which they may prefer and adopt one model or another. This is partly because the models are not mutually exclusive, as the later ones are built on the earlier ones according to increasingly sophisticated teacher education philosophies. In view of that, one cannot really say whether one model is better than another, as they tend to meet the needs at different levels of a teacher's development. The craft model may be good for acquiring basic classroom techniques while the reflective model is probably necessary for components such as cultural sensitivity training and the professional model is definitely desirable to motivate the teacher beyond the teacher education programme.

To return to our discussion of language dominance settings, how can we choose among the various models or combination of models for programme delivery? What variables do we have to take cognisance of when considering which model to adopt? Is any one of the programme delivery models more suitable for multilingual education than others? Should we make a distinction between pre-service teacher preparation and in-service teacher development?

We pointed out at the beginning of this chapter that teacher educators in local circumstances have to make their own choices because what is appropriate for one country or one level of education may not be suitable for another. What we can propose are merely some operational guidelines to facilitate the informed choices that teacher educators make for themselves. When planning a teacher education programme, planners may find it useful to consider the following parameters:

(1) *Multilingual policy*: Is there an overt policy of multilingual

education in my country? What is the policy? (Refer to Figure 6.1.) Do I agree with it? Am I in a position to recommend a different one to the government if I do not agree with it? If I do not agree with it and am unable to change it either in policy or in practice, how should I deal with the problem I perceive in the teacher education programme I am planning?

(2) *Language competence*: What degree of NDL or DL competence or cultural knowledge does the multilingual policy require of teachers? Of all teachers teaching in DL(s) or NDL(s)? Of teachers of DL(s)? Of teachers of NDL(s)? (Refer to Table 6.1.) How does that constrain the entry standards I should set in terms of language competence for course participants, assuming that cultural knowledge can be acquired within my programme? On the basis of the entry standards I set, can I attract a big enough pool of suitable applicants for my programme? If not, what about importing teachers from another country and orienting them to local circumstances? In any case, should I do some initial screening on the language competence of applicants? Assuming I have to accept applicants with less than desirable language abilities, how realistic is it for me, within the constraints of the resources at my disposal, to try to improve them to the competence level required for the model adopted? Can I get more resources? If I cannot, what can I build into the programme to surmount this problem? Can I offer an intensive course? Can I transplant the course participants to an environment where the language is widely spoken? Can they afford to do so at their own cost? Should I advise them to focus on some areas of language learning for a start? Can I encourage them to set their own learning goals which may go beyond the programme? Are there self-access packages that I can recommend to help them in this? What strategies can I help to develop in teachers for collaborative work so that teachers of other subjects may be able to reinforce what is done in the language classroom, and vice versa? Are there materials such as bilingual or multilingual subject glossaries that can encourage this?

(3) *Educational level and type of learners*: What educational level am I preparing teachers for? Is this more or less demanding in terms of the language competence of the teachers? Is it a school situation or an adult learning setting? How much learner independence in language learning is it possible to expect? What kinds of relationships are teachers likely to be able to build with their learners? Do the learners come from several different language

backgrounds? Are there cultural behaviours in the classroom that I should alert teachers to observe and consider for themselves? Can I find multicultural or bicultural informants to provide input to some multicultural awareness workshops for them?

(4) *Background of course participants*: What background do these course participants come from? Have they lived or taught in a multilingual environment? Have they ever been in a classroom before? If not, do they need some systematic exposure to and participatory experience in the range of classroom methods and techniques? If they have been, are they novice teachers or veteran teachers? Have they already attained Qualified Teacher Status (QTS)? Have they had enough teaching experience to be able to identify problems in the classroom? What tasks can I design to enhance their ability to do this?

(5) *Qualifications*: Is my programme one that will award a qualification at the end of it? What type of qualification (workshop attendance certificate, certificate or diploma, first degree, postgraduate degree)? How much time and effort are course participants likely to be able to give to the programme? How motivated are they to develop themselves further when they graduate from the programme?

(6) *Community relations*: What does the immediate community the teacher has to face think about multilingualism? What kind of home support for the DL(s) and the NDL(s) is available? What projects can I design in the teacher education programme to encourage teachers to strengthen this support?

Conclusion

The above considerations serve to further illustrate how complex teaching in multilingual schools can be. The best long-term hope is for a teacher education programme to inculcate in teachers the ability to constantly review and reflect upon their teaching and improve on it even beyond the programme. In this sense, the professional development model is ultimately the most appropriate model for multilingual teacher education. Teaching in multilingual contexts calls for great sensitivity to changing circumstances and lifelong perseverance. Unless the teacher is motivated to do so from within, it is hard to maintain effectiveness. Yet, it is not for teacher educators in one setting to tell those in another that the professional development model is the only model that is practicable. It is the ideal model which in reality may be practicable in some teacher education settings and not in others. The interplay of different variables will determine the particular features of teacher education that are likely to be effective in a particular programme. What is useful for one setting may not work for another. Ideal models for teacher education have to be modified and hopefully realised in, more often than not, less than ideal circumstances in the real world of inadequate national resources, cultural and ethnic conflict and changing social and economic structures. But if we have models, at least we know what we can continue to aim for.

Acknowledgements

Both authors wish to thank the University of Hong Kong for various exchange opportunities which have enabled them to appreciate the realities in different countries. Agnes Lam is especially grateful for the time she spent at Lucy Cavendish College, University of Cambridge, which facilitated her contribution to this chapter.

References

Center for Applied Linguistics (1974) *Guidelines for the Preparation and Certification of Teachers of Bilingual/Bicultural Education.* Arlington, VA: Center for Applied Linguistics.

Cummins, J. (1984) The minority language child. In S. Shapson and V. D'Oyley (eds) *Bilingual and Multicultural Education: Canadian Perspectives* (pp. 71–92). Clevedon: Multilingual Matters.

Ferguson, C. (1959) Diglossia. *Word* 15, 325–40.

Genesee, F. (1987) *Learning Through Two Languages: Studies of Immersion and Bilingual Children.* Cambridge, MA: Newbury House.

Goh, K.S. and the Education Study Team (1978) *Report on the Ministry of Education.* Singapore: Singapore Government.

Hamers, J.F. and Blanc, M.H.A. (1989) *Bilinguality and Bilingualism.* Cambridge: Cambridge University Press.

Houlton, D. (1986) *Teacher Education in a Multilingual Context.* Nottingham: University of Nottingham School of Education.

Lam, A. (1994) Language education in Hong Kong and Singapore: A comparative study of the role of English. In T. Kandiah and J. Kwan-Terry (eds) *English and Language Planning: A Southeast Asian Contribution* (pp. 182–96). Singapore: Times Academic Press for the Centre for Advanced Studies, National University of Singapore.

Lange, D.L. (1990) A blueprint for a teacher development program. In J.C. Richards and D. Nunan (eds) *Second Language Teacher Education* (pp. 245–68). Cambridge: Cambridge University Press.

Ma, N. and Su, J. (1988) *China's Minority Nationalities* (R. Ma, S. Zhang, H. Liu and G. Wang, trans). Beijing: China Nationalities Photographic Art Publishing House.

Ma, Y. and editorial panel (1985) *Questions and Answers about China's Minority Nationalities*. Beijing: New World Press.

Navarro, R.A. (1985) The problems of language, education, and society: Who decides. In E.E. Garcia and R.V. Padilla (eds) *Advances in Bilingual Education Research* (pp. 289–313). Tuscon: The University of Arizona Press.

Nunan, D. (1989) Second-language teacher education: Present trends and future prospects. In C.N. Candlin and T.F. McNamara (eds) *Language, Learning and Community* (pp. 143–54). Sydney: NCELTR.

Nunan, D. (1990) Action research in the language classroom. In J.C. Richards and D. Nunan (eds) *Second Language Teacher Education* (pp. 62–81). Cambridge: Cambridge University Press.

Paulston, C.B. (1985, January) Linguistic consequences of ethnicity and nationalism in multilingual settings. Paper presented at the Conference on the Educational Policies and the Minority Social Groups Experts' Meeting organised by CERI/OECD at OECD Headquarters.

Ramsey, S.R. (1987) *The Languages of China*. Princeton, NJ: Princeton University Press.

Wallace, M. (1991) *Training Foreign Language Teachers*. Cambridge: Cambridge University Press.

Wardhaugh, R. (1987) *Languages in Competition: Dominance, Diversity and Decline*. Oxford: Basil Blackwell in association with Deutsch.

Part 3
Case Studies in Multilingual Education

Chapter 7

Luxembourg and the European Schools

CHARLOTTE HOFFMANN

Introduction

This chapter differs from most of the others in this section in that it deals with a continent, or at least part of it, rather than a particular country. Other continents have clearly defined boundaries, but in the case of Europe there is no common agreement as to where her eastern and southeastern frontiers should be drawn as different criteria – cultural, political or geographic – could be used in doing so. For the purpose of the present discussion, the term Europe refers to the geographical and cultural space that makes up the European Union at present.

This chapter deals, in the first place, with the extent to which it is appropriate to talk about multilingualism in Europe, and it points to the different linguistic patterns which have emerged during the twentieth century as a result of migration, Europeanisation and internationalisation. The latter manifests itself primarily in the spread of English as a lingua franca for both international and intra-national communication. This development is speeded along by the advance of new communication technologies and by what has come to be known as the global information society (for the linguistic implications, see Laver & Roukens, 1996).

Following this, two different approaches to multilingual education are presented. The first discusses the education system in Luxembourg where children are taught, at different stages, through the medium of one of the country's three languages. Second, the European Schools are an example of a modern pedagogic model of multilingual education, designed for children from monolingual home backgrounds whose parents have made the conscious choice of having their children educated through the medium of more than one language even though this is not the norm for the country in which they live.

Multilingualism in Europe

Very few countries in Europe could be said to be wholly mono-lingual; most contain linguistic minorities. But Europe does not display the rich linguistic diversity found elsewhere in the world. This is, of course, a very general statement which begs the question of how 'Europe' itself should be defined – whether politically, geographically, culturally or by applying some other criteria. In an article entitled 'How many languages does Europe need?' Lepschy (1994) discusses a list of European languages he prepared based on two sources (Décsy, 1986–88; Grimes, 1988) and arrives at a figure of languages (almost 70), which is roughly double the number of European states (34). An average of two languages per country is not very high.

Lepschy's answer to the question posed in the title of his article seems to combine the views of the linguist who advocates linguistic diversity and those of the pragmatist when he says:

> As many as there are, as spoken languages. People should not be deprived of their speech [i.e. their first language]. But, please, as few as possible, as written standards, languages of culture to be used for scholarly and scientific publication. (1994: 14)

This preference for only a small number of languages seems to be driven by the conviction that too many languages may interfere with cooperation and mutual understanding. This view is reflected in many education systems where pupils, on the whole, receive their education in one language, the national standard variety, and are taught only a limited number of foreign languages as subjects. Whether individuals become bilingual or multilingual often depends, therefore, much more on their personal circumstances than on the education system that they find themselves in.

Many states, particularly in western and northern Europe, look back on a strong tradition of monolingualism. Even those states which constitutionally are multilingual, such as Belgium and Switzerland, base their internal linguistic organisation on the principle of terri-torial monolingualism. In other words, their multilingualism derives from the fact that people with different mother tongues live in the same state, so that there are Flemish-speaking Belgians, French-speaking Belgians and German-speaking Belgians. States where all citizens habitually use more than two languages are rare – only Luxembourg and Malta come to mind (Kramer, 1986). Nevertheless, the phenomenon of multilingualism is present to varying degrees (and always on a modest scale) in different parts of Europe, and different patterns can be identified. Europe's linguistic situation has undergone considerable change in the twentieth century, following different and at times opposing trends. As we move into the next millennium, it is becoming obvious that the forces which most influence change in language behaviour and policy are three:

- a long overdue recognition of indigenous minority languages such as we have seen in the Netherlands, Spain and Britain, among other countries;
- migration, which has affected virtually all states within the European Union; and
- internationalisation, which in effect means the spread of English and its increased use by non-native speakers for a variety of communicative functions.

The introduction and establishment of bilingual and multilingual education programmes has been an arduous process in many European states. Provision for indigenous linguistic minorities has tended to be more successful than for non-indigenous, new minorities, i.e. the foreign immigrants. The formulation and implementation of language policies in the field of education have often been hampered by administrative hurdles, a chronic shortage of funds and resources, and also widespread negative attitudes towards bilingualism. But linguistic realities and people's attitudes are changing. In response to pressures from old and new minorities for wider linguistic rights and provisions, we now find much more bilingualism at official and institutional levels than at any time since the Second World War. In addition, individual bilingualism and multilingualism have been growing rapidly as Europeans become motivated to achieve proficiency in other languages in order to take part in international cooperation, cultural exchanges, and the global information society.

Internationalisation and the spread of English

Within Europe, English has acquired a special position as the language of wider communication, although with important regional variations. In the north, mainly Scandinavia and the Netherlands, it has almost become a lingua franca; in the south, its impact is less strong; and in the German-speaking countries, it occupies a middle position. But everywhere English has been adopted by specialists in all areas for certain functions, such as presentations and publications, and as the language of general communication at international meetings and conferences. Viereck (1996) presents convincing statistical evidence showing how academic publishing in Europe has switched towards English, and he argues that English is also becoming more frequently used for other communicative functions, just as it has also had a profound impact on certain linguistic systems (in particular, German). In fact, he discusses the 'nativisation' of English rather than its spread.

Different styles and registers of English are also making their way into many people's homes and offices in the new formats of electronic communication and information retrieval systems. Communicating via the Internet, electronic mail and bulletin boards requires comprehension and use of informal styles of usage, while making use of information retrieval systems often requires knowledge of formal or highly condensed forms of English. This may present a challenge, but to the non-native user of English there is an advantage: the computer allows the user to dictate his or her own pace so that even a non-fluent user of English may join in the conversation. This form of communication goes even further when it introduces the spoken word – more often than not in English – to those using the new technologies where PC networks are integrated with voice communication.

The prominent status of English is reflected in education as well. Virtually everywhere in Europe, it is now the preferred first foreign language taught in schools, usually introduced at the beginning of secondary education but increasingly at primary level. Even in multilingual states, such as Switzerland or Belgium, there is increasing demand by parents to let pupils study English as the first foreign language rather than one of the country's other national languages. In some countries there is a move towards starting the first foreign language, usually English, early on at primary level, so that children growing up in bilingual areas are introduced to some form of multilingualism soon after starting school; for example, Cenoz and Lindsay (1996), give an account of a project involving the teaching of English to primary pupils in the Basque Country (see also Cenoz, Chapter 8 this volume). English is therefore contributing to multilingualism in Europe.

The growth of multilingualism in Europe is encouraged by a

convergence of 'natural' forces and an important new factor. The natural forces are those of the European linguistic tradition, since some European languages are now developing and spreading thanks to the removal of previous obstacles. The new factor is the need that many people have to use an international language. In fact, multi-lingualism in Europe is now a reality for an increasing number of individuals. But in the European Union there is only one country where it is also a national, institutionalised feature that affects *all* citizens, and that is Luxembourg.

For the individual, multilingual acquisition can usually be attributed to personal motivation and effort, or to external pressure, or to a combination of the two. The route that leads to multilingualism being firmly established in a society is through education. Multi-lingual education can take a number of forms. It can be driven by, and respond to, a variety of factors, such as local needs and the particular linguistic situation of the communities involved. It is also encouraged, in many cases, by the idealism and ambitions of particular language planners and/or parents, as expressed in the linguistic goals that schools may set themselves.

The following case studies outline two distinct models of multi-lingual education. They differ from each other in many aspects, but what they have in common is that they are probably the only examples of genuinely multilingual education to be found in the European Union (I have excluded central and eastern European countries, where the sociolinguistic situation is more complex).

Trilingual Education in Luxembourg

Sociolinguistic background

The Grand Duchy of Luxembourg, situated in the centre of Europe, comprises some 1000 square miles and has approximately 360,000 inhabitants. Since the Second World War, and particularly since the establishment of the European Economic Community (now the European Union), Luxembourg has grown in international importance. Following the decline of its traditional industries – coal, steel and agriculture – it has experienced a major rebuilding programme, including restructuring of its industry and agriculture. It is now among the most prosperous states in Europe (number one in per capita income) and has attracted foreign investment and a considerable number of foreigners, 31% of the population in 1994 (see J-P. Hoffmann, 1996). The capital, Luxembourg City, is the seat of several

European institutions and it is also a major banking and finance centre.

By European standards Luxembourg is a young state. Like Belgium, it was created by the Congress of Vienna (1815) and its present frontiers were settled in 1839 when, under the Treaty of London, the French-speaking part became the Belgian province of Luxembourg. Luxembourg thus became a linguistically homogeneous state where all inhabitants spoke Luxembourgish although French remained the official language.

Luxembourgish, or Lëtzebuergesch, was not always considered a language in its own right given its exclusive use in oral communication with no written tradition and the fact that it had to look to New High German for a written form. The planned development of Luxembourgish as a sort of *Ausbausprache* (i.e. a variety which derives its status as a language not so much from its linguistic but from its social, cultural and political attributes) started in 1839 and was precipitated by the German invasions of the country during each world war and, particularly, in reaction to the enforced Germanisation policies of the Nazis. Luxembourgish became standardised and codified, a process which was completed in the late 1970s with the publication of the Luxembourgish dictionary. From the several regional varieties, a kind of national *koiné* has become recognised. Some authors point to certain linguistic limitations of the language – for instance, in terms of its syntax which shows few subordinate clauses and restricted tense, mood and case variation. This assumes a descriptive framework based on New High German. But there is now widespread agreement that Luxembourgish is to be considered a language in its own right rather than a dialect of German. '... Luxembourgish [...] can be seen linguistically as a Middle German dialect but sociolinguistically has the characteristics of an independent language' (Barbour & Stevenson, 1990: 231). Linguists in Luxembourg, such as R. Bruch and F. Hoffmann, go further than this, demonstrating the independent status for their language on linguistic grounds as well (see Newton, 1987, 1996a, b).

Luxembourg has developed a unique pattern of trilingualism which is supported by the whole population. Jean-Paul Hoffmann refers to it as a linguistic melting pot at the heart of the European Union, and he adds that multilingualism in Luxembourg 'is virtually a matter of inheritance' (1996: 97). It involves the national, unifying language Luxembourgish and, as there are no substantial German or French minorities in the country, the use of the two exoglossic languages (i.e. languages with no native speakers in the population),

French and German. With trilingualism, cultural isolation from its neighbours can be avoided, and close political and economic cooperation is facilitated (Luxembourg has monetary union with Belgium), while at the same time the state can maintain its independence and own identity. No tension exists between the three languages and there is general consensus on the advantages of having three languages. Newton describes the language situation in Luxembourg as being 'characterised by both political and economic exigency, and personal convenience' (1987: 153). Each of the three languages has a particular role to play, not only on a societal level but also on an individual one. Luxembourgish is spoken by all native inhabitants disregarding their social or educational background, and it is looked upon as the language of solidarity; French is the language of power and prestige; and German is seen by many to be the language of convenience. The use of the three languages follows a pattern based on function and tradition. Historically, first French, and then French and German on equal terms, were adopted as official languages. The Constitution, as amended in 1984, does not say anything about the official use of French and German, although it does fix the position of Luxembourgish as the national language – which is to be used 'as far as possible' by government officials in its written as well as its spoken form.

Luxembourg's linguistic situation has come to be described as *triglossia*, where each language has certain functions. Language use has been described in terms of domains and according to whether the written or spoken medium is used (F. Hoffmann, 1996; Newton, 1987). Luxembourgish is used for general conversation in all domains, but its written form is still quite restricted, although its use is expanding. Some use of it is made in schools and the media and, following the 1984 legislation, by government institutions. German is hardly ever spoken, except at school as a medium of instruction, and occasionally in the media or in public lectures. In contrast, written German is used in newspapers and magazines, by the Church and the police, and in schools, particularly in primary education. Spoken French is used in more formal situations by the government, in administration, the courts and a number of domains where Luxembourgish is used in informal situations. As a written medium, French is used in all areas where formal communication is required. 'The uniqueness of the Luxembourg case lies in the discrepancy between oral and written communication', as J-P. Hoffmann (1996) puts it. However, as Newton (1987) points out, the divisions of language use are not as clear-cut as might appear but involve a certain amount of 'shading', i.e. the use of both languages. The degree of such shading depends on the personal motivation and education of the speaker/writer, and on political and social taboos. This is not unusual in diglossic language situations.

Languages in the education system

Most Luxembourgers are monolingual by birth, i.e. they acquire Luxembourgish naturally at home. They become trilingual through education. Because of the intensity with which German and French are taught at school and the important roles these two languages have in the community, they cannot be seen as foreign languages but should be considered as something approximating 'auxiliary mother tongues' (F. Hoffmann 1979: 115).

Within the school system, each of the three languages is assigned a particular role and function. Each is used as a medium of instruction and is also taught as a subject, although Luxembourgish receives little recognition as a subject, while French receives most. With regard to the language of instruction, the pattern over the whole period of primary and secondary education is one of transition from Luxembourgish through German to French. Luxembourgish is often used at all levels of education for communication when speakers have difficulties using the other two languages.

Table 7.1 gives an overview of the Luxembourg education system ranging from pre-school to tertiary education, as outlined.

Pre-school education

Compulsory education starts at four years of age when Luxembourg's children enter nursery school, where they stay for two years. Pre-school education is in Luxembourgish although nursery schools with a substantial number of foreign, non-Luxembourgish-speaking children may use Portuguese or French, as the largest number of foreigners in Luxembourg are Portuguese and French is used by many foreigners as a lingua franca. These schools attempt to teach such children sufficient Luxembourgish to allow transition to primary school.

Primary education

German is introduced as a subject in the first year of primary school, i.e. at age six. Luxembourgish continues to serve as the language of instruction and as a subject; it is taught for just one period per week, out of a total of 30. The teaching of German is intensive, taking between eight and nine periods per week during the first two years and then five periods per week from year three onwards.

Table 7.1 Overview of the Luxembourg education system

Age						Grade
21/20	Institut d'Etudes Educatives et Sociales	Institut Supérieur de Technologie	Institut Supérieur d'Etudes et de Recherches Pédagogiques	'Cycle Court'		
20/21						BTS
19/20				Cours Univer.		
18/19						13
17/18						12
16/17		Vocational secondary education	Secondary education			11
15/16						10
14/15	Complementary education					9
13/14						8
12/13						7
11/12						6
10/11						5
9/10		Primary education				4
8/9						3
7/8						2
6/7						1
5/6		Pre-school education				
4/5						

(Adapted from: Das Schulwesen in Luxembourg, Ministère de l'Education nationale. Unité Nationale d'Eurydice, Louxembourg. Printed in Kraemer 1993: 169)

German is introduced as a medium of instruction progressively throughout the curriculum, a process that varies from school to school and is completed by the sixth grade, when the pupils are 12. French is introduced as a subject in the second half of the second grade (age seven) when it is taught for three hours per week; and this is increased to seven periods per week from year three onwards. The study of French thus takes up more curricular time than that of Luxembourg-ish and German together although the latter, by their use as languages for oral communication within the school, remain prominent in the pupil's daily life.

As can be seen from Table 7.2, primary education is characterised

Table 7.2 Subject distribution by year (adapted from Kraemer 1993: 170)

	I	II 1st sem.	II 2nd sem.	III	IV	V	VI
Religious Education	3	3	3	3	3	3	3
Luxembourgish	1	1	1	1	1	1	1
French	–	–	3	7	7	7	7
German	8	9	8	5	5	5	5
Maths	6	6	6	5	5	5	5
Basic Science	3	4	2	2	2	–	–
History	–	–	–	–	–	1	1
Geography	–	–	–	–	–	1	1
Natural Sciences	–	–	–	–	–	1	1
Art	1	1	1	1	1	1	1
Handicraft	1	1	1	1	1	1	1
Music	1	1	1	1	1	1	1
Physical Education	3	3	3	3	3	3	3
Optional Subjects	1	1	1	1	1	–	–
Supervised Activities	2	–	–	–	–	–	–
	30	30	30	30	30	30	30

by a heavy bias towards language study and the development of linguistic skills, ranging from just under one-third of the curriculum at age six to well over a third (13 out of 30 periods per week) from age eight onwards. Literacy skills are established first in German and then in French. Transfer is assumed to take place in the acquisition of reading and writing skills in Luxembourgish, facilitated by the close genetic relationship between the two Germanic languages.

Secondary education

Transition to secondary education at age 12 is marked by a further language switch as French becomes progressively the language of instruction and all spoken communication in school is supposed to take place in French after the third (secondary) grade, i.e. at age 15, when German is eliminated as a medium of instruction.

Kraemer claims that in comparison to equivalent institutions in other countries Luxembourg schools give pride of place to the teaching of languages: '... le lycée luxembourgois accorde une place exceptionelle à l'enseignement des langues' (1993: 171). One may well believe this if one considers the amount of time spent on languages and the number of languages studied. As regards the former, during the first three years of secondary schooling, the _cycle inférieur_, languages take up between 11 and 16 periods per week out of a total 30 periods (i.e. between 36% and 53% of total teaching time), and in the _cycle supérieur_ approximately half of the school curriculum is given over to the study of languages during the 10th and 11th grade. Time spent on languages during the last two years varies according to the areas of study students choose to concentrate on. Those specialising in sciences spend less time on languages than those following the _classique litteraire_ stream.

In addition to studying their three languages for three periods a week (one period of Luxembourgish, plus one or two of German and French, depending on the stage reached), Luxembourger students learn either one, two or three other languages, starting with English in the second year of secondary school, followed by Latin the year after; those who have opted for the languages and literature stream may also take up Italian or Spanish or Greek. Many students, therefore, study five or six languages in the course of their school career; they all learn at least four. This may sound high to the reader with a monolingual background. But the linguistic reality of trilingual Luxembourg is that everybody will become proficient in the country's three languages and has to learn at least one foreign language at school.

Students who do not attend a _lycée_ but have opted for a more vocationally oriented type of education spend approximately one-third of their timetable on language study, with French and German given roughly equal time. English is taught from the second year (age 13) onwards, and in some schools children may be able to choose another foreign language.

The so-called 'complementary education programmes' are designed for children who leave school at the end of the 9th grade, i.e. when they have reached the end of compulsory education at the age of 15/16. They will have spent only three years at secondary level and they will, therefore, have had no experience of French-medium teaching.

Higher education

There is no university in Luxembourg, but there are some institutions of higher education which provide certain facilities. Most students go to university in France, Belgium or Germany. Their trilingual education in Luxembourg prepares them well for this, and in turn their educational experience will further enhance their positive attitudes to multilingualism.

Teaching content and materials

In both primary and secondary schools, there is considerable emphasis on acquiring and improving grammar, orthography and oral expression. Later on, more time is spent on developing writing and analytical skills, and the study of literature features prominently. In his study on languages in Luxembourg, F. Hoffmann (1979) wrote that the German taught and used in schools is not colloquial modern German 'but the finest literary German, true to the models of the 19th and 20th century' (quoted in Newton 1987: 156). Newton also said that the German used in the Luxembourg press also made very little use of modern German colloquial forms, and he then continued with a comment on the kind of French children were taught: 'very correct French, just as they learn very correct German' (1987: 157). It has not been possible to ascertain what the situation is like today. The 1989 curriculum reform envisaged putting more emphasis on teaching oral and written communication, although this objective was not reached at the expense of grammatical competence, to which a good deal of importance has always been attached.

One might think that a multilingual education system of this kind would be extremely costly in terms of resources, but apparently this is not the case. The textbooks and manuals used at all levels are not specifically designed for trilingual education but tend to be imported from neighbouring countries. The materials are usually in the language of instruction at any given stage so that, for example, in the second year of secondary education a German biology textbook is employed whereas in the last year a French one is used. Some of the teaching materials, for instance for teaching French as a subject, may be produced locally for Luxembourg.

All teachers of languages as a subject must obtain their university qualifications in a country where the language is used; for example in order to teach English one needs to have a British or American qualification. Obviously such a requirement has considerable significance for the quality of a teacher's language competence and therefore the success of language study in general. It also indicates that the only model that the authorities consider appropriate for their students is that of native speakers, i.e. they value authenticity in both linguistic and cultural terms.

Evaluation of the Luxembourg model

Trilingualism in Luxembourg is established by means of a series of language switches that take place at certain stages. These switches are progressive rather than abrupt, and they take place only after the new language has already been introduced as a subject. Schooling is introduced in the pupil's home language, Luxembourgish. Then a related language, German, is introduced as a subject. Progressive use of this second language (L2) as a language of instruction goes hand in hand with the elimination of the use of the first language (L1). French, the third language (L3), is started as a school subject and then at secondary level progressively replaces the L2 as medium of communication while L2 and L3, and a minimum of L1, are kept as formal subjects. As a result of the educational system, a high proportion of the population acquire at least a working knowledge of English. Most educated Luxembourgers are able to speak a second, and often a third, foreign language. Competence in five or even six languages is not uncommon, and a majority of the population is able to use four languages, although of course with different degrees of competence.

The school system, which results in establishing a sound knowledge of the country's three languages, is devised in such a way that, as the students get older, increasing emphasis is placed on French. This reflects a conscious policy decision since it is a trend away from the natural linguistic situation in the country, where there is a greater prevalence of the two related languages Luxembourgish and German. French was chosen for cultural reasons. In Kraemer's own words:

> Comme on le voi, notre apprentisage des langues s'écarte rapidement de notre situation linguistique 'naturelle', vu que l'allemand est beaucoup plus proche du luxembourgois que le français. Cette tendence, qui ne fera s'accentuer dans l'ensegnement secondaire, est la résultante à la fois d'une choix culturel et d'un volunté politique. (1993: 170)

The degree of proficiency in French that is attained depends mainly on the length and type of education the student has received, although other factors may also come into play, such as geographical location and language use of parents. But whatever school type a pupil attends, the school programme develops biliterate trilingualism whereby literacy is initially established in the child's L2 and then in his or her L3. Transfer of literacy skills to Luxembourgish is assumed to take place. Lebrun and Baetens Beardsmore (1993: 106) suggest that the Luxembourg model subsumes Cummins' interdependence hypothesis as well as his common underlying proficiency hypothesis which accounts for successful transfer of literacy skills from one language to another (Cummins, 1984). This widely accepted assumption is common to a number of bilingual education schemes, such as the Canadian or Catalan immersion programmes (Baker, 1993; Cummins & Swain, 1986). The similarity of this model to other programmes ends here, however. The Luxembourg scheme is not like any other bilingual or multilingual education programme aimed at language maintenance or transition, or representing enrichment like the Canadian immersion models. In a way the Luxembourg system contains some element of each, but one should see it primarily as being designed to meet the linguistic and cultural needs of the whole population.

How successful is the programme? Kraemer (1993) seems to be quite optimistic. He points to the admiration it receives from foreigners, and also to its success, which he measures in terms of the proportion of school leavers who progress to higher education in French-speaking countries (60%) and Germany (30%). He considers that this '*mobilité universitaire*' is a source of intellectual and cultural enrichment, an opportunity for young people to develop an *esprit européen*. Luxembourgers often like to see themselves as exemplary Europeans, and they are generally proud of their linguistic attainments. However, Kraemer is conscious of the price Luxembourg's multilingual system entails: a heavy load on pupils at all levels, particularly at primary level, which carries with it the risks that weak or even average pupils may become overburdened. He mentions linguistic shortcomings due to interference, problems of oral expression and 'doubtful accents'.

The point about interference is also taken up by Newton (1987), suggesting that a system which prepares learners to respond in whichever of the three languages they are addressed in will inevitably affect their linguistic performance. 'One can imagine that by the teenage years, interference between these three languages is quite great in the child's mind' (1987: 157). The type and amount of interference, he claims, is shaped by personal motivation, so that more French random vocabulary may appear in some people's Luxembourgish if they have closer ties to the Francophone sphere of interest in terms of cultural or personal ties; and he points to the role of television in particular. Borrowing from German into Luxembourgish is apparently less frequent.

Kraemer and Newton's opinions may also be interpreted in a different way. If monolingual standards of measurement are applied, Luxembourgers' pronunciation of German and French can perhaps be described as 'doubtful'. But in terms of bilingual or multilingual competence, it is to be expected that Luxembourgers should have their distinct phonological features. Similarly, when Newton mentions 'interference', this can probably be taken to refer to code-mixing and code-switching behaviour. I have not been able to ascertain whether any studies on aspects of bilingual speech have been carried out. There are those who have expressed their anxieties about language purity (F. Hoffmann, 1996; J-P. Hoffmann, 1996), but these concerns relate to what is perceived as unwelcome influences (mainly phonological and lexical) from German on Luxembourgish.

It seems that the multilingual education model which provides pupils with equal access to their country's three languages – which represent an essential part of Luxembourg's ethnic identity – cannot be faulted on linguistic grounds. What is educationally more serious, however, is the question of whether *all* children benefit. Whereas Luxembourg's education system itself is quite unique in Europe, it suffers from similar problems as many other countries. As mentioned above, the country has a large proportion of foreign immigrants, a situation which poses particular challenges to the trilingual system, especially as there are large concentrations of speakers of other languages in certain regions. For instance, almost 59% of pupils in nursery schools in the canton of Luxembourg City are children who do not possess Luxembourgish when they enter education. Nursery teachers thus find themselves in a situation where they have to teach these children Luxembourgish in order to help their integration into mainstream schooling, a task they are not trained to carry out. Some children are sent to special reception classes which have been set up for them. There they are taught French or German so that they can use either of these languages as a lingua franca. They are only meant to stay for up to one year in these classes before being integrated into the normal school programme, and for some children their attendance at the preparation classes may not be sufficiently long to equip them well enough linguistically for mainstream school. If so, it is quite likely that they will be affected adversely by this linguistic handicap right through their school days. It is probably no coincidence that in 1985–86 almost 53% of children who left school after completing compulsory education were foreigners (figures taken from Lebrun & Baetens Beardsmore, 1993). This is a much higher proportion than their total numbers as a percentage of the overall population would lead one to expect.

Another area which, according to Kraemer, needs to be addressed concerns pedagogic aspects of language teaching. He makes a plea for a long overdue reassessment of objectives, demanding that communicative competence should be given more prominence than grammatical competence and literature. What is needed in tomorrow's Europe, he argues, is citizens capable of communicating in several languages. A shift in objectives would then also require new teaching methods.

A formal evaluation of the outcomes of Luxembourg's trilingual education system was undertaken by Lebrun and Baetens Beardsmore (1993). The aim of the study was to look at the knowledge of French of 13-year-old students. The test and evaluation procedures used had been adapted from those used in previous research into Canadian immersion and European Schools programmes. Frequent comparisons with these bilingual education programmes are made throughout the evaluation. Thirteen year olds were chosen because the tests had been specifically designed for this age group and because this age represents an important point in the children's education when French begins to take over from German as the main medium of instruction. In intellectual terms it means that French starts to be used for context-reduced, cognitively more demanding tasks. Three tests were carried out, two of them designed to test comprehension and one, a cloze test, aimed at measuring global language knowledge. In addition, a questionnaire was administered aimed at discovering language backgrounds and habits, attitudes and preferences for language instruction and the patterns of use of the three languages inside and outside school.

The authors report that the results were remarkably similar in all three test populations, with higher scores achieved by the Luxembourg and European School students than the Canadian immersion ones. They found that the following factors had contributed significantly to the Luxembourg students' successful acquisition of French: their parents' knowledge of the language acted as an incentive and made the learning of French seem more natural; there was a higher rate of self-initiated use of French both inside and outside school than in Canada (incidentally, both observations were also true in the case of the European Schools); and in Luxembourg the use of French television was higher than any other. Not surprisingly, the questionnaires revealed significant differences reflecting population make-up, setting, attitudes and self-initiated use of French. Among factors favouring good school results in French were: parents' high educational level, self-initiated use of French both inside and outside school, use of French media and positive attitudes – whereas the reverse were seen as negative factors, i.e. low parental educational level, little use of French outside school and slightly negative attitudes towards French. So far, evaluation of the Luxembourg model has not involved an exhaustive assessment, because only French has been evaluated. Studies examining attainment in German and in Luxembourgish have not been published, and there appear to be none that measure general academic achievement. Other areas of evaluation that might contribute towards a full understanding of a multilingual education model would be to look in some detail at the kind of materials and approaches used, and at teacher training.

In conclusion, the Luxembourg model appears to enjoy the support of the country's population. This is not really surprising in view of Luxembourg's unique and stable linguistic situation where, apart from foreign immigrants, there are no linguistic minorities and the education system is aimed at the whole of the school population, not at specific groups as is normally the case where there is bilingual education. The Luxembourg system aims at achieving full bilingualism as far as German and French are concerned, and this becomes achievable because both languages are used in the country's institutions and the media, as well as in formal and informal interactions. On the other hand, Luxembourgish gives expression to the country's nationalist sentiments and thus remains unthreatened by the other two languages. The result is widespread trilingualism.

Many economic, social, cultural and linguistic conditions exist which favour Luxembourg's trilingual education system. Perhaps one can even go so far as to maintain that it is these very conditions which require the country to pursue such a highly complex, and admirable, path towards a truly European education. The question that emerges is whether such highly privileged circumstances are actually needed for trilingualism to be established through the education system. Societal multilingualism elsewhere in the world does not depend upon material wealth, but positive attitudes towards bilingualism and multilingualism may present themselves more easily in regions where different languages are not in competition with each other and where sociolinguistic equilibrium goes hand in hand with the social stability of the country. The underlying principles of linguistic equality and a policy of consensus seem to hold true also in the type of multilingual education to be examined next.

The European Schools

Background

The European Schools represent a good example of schooling designed specifically for establishing and maintaining multiculturalism and multilingualism. They serve a particular type of student in a number of European countries, rather than pupils from a particular national setting. They are international in character and share the same educational philosophy and education programme irrespective of the particular European state in which they are located.

These schools grew out of parental initiative in the early 1950s after the European Coal and Steel Community was founded and employees from different nationalities went to work at its headquarters in Luxembourg. They brought with them their families, including their children, many of them of school age or about to start their school. These children came from varying linguistic backgrounds, and they had different educational requirements. In particular, their parents' employment tended to be of a transitional nature, so that their sons and daughters might, at some stage of their education, have to be moved on to another school in another country or be re-integrated into the educational system of their country of origin. With the establishment of the European Economic Community in 1956, these problems became more pronounced as more civil servants and employees went to work in EEC establishments in different parts of Europe.

What started off as a private kindergarten grew into a primary school and then came to embrace secondary grades as well. The first European School was officially recognised in 1958 after representatives of the original six member states of the EEC had agreed to a common, mutually acceptable programme leading to the European Baccalaureate at the end of secondary education. In the early 1980s, the curriculum and examination for this diploma underwent a reform. Since it was first established, the European Baccalaureate has come to be recognised by all member states, and it allows access to higher education not only within the European Union but in most of the world. At present there is a network of nine European Schools, situated in Belgium (where there are three, two in Brussels and one in Mol), England (Culham), Germany (Karlsruhe and Munich), Italy (Varese), Luxembourg (Luxembourg City) and the Netherlands (Bergen). All schools have the same entry requirements, offer the same curriculum, and prepare their students for the same examinations.

General structure and administration of the European Schools

The schools

The schools rely on public funds from the European Union and on contributions from the host country. Staff salaries are paid by national governments, which are also responsible for the recruitment and secondment of teachers. Each school is run by the Permanent Representative of a Board of Governors made up of delegations from EU member states which include national inspectors for primary and secondary education. This system reinforces the European, international nature of the school while at the same time maintaining close links with the education systems of the individual member states. Each school has a number of linguistic sub-sections representing the linguistic backgrounds of the school population. In the largest school, in Brussels, there are eight different language sections, French and English being the largest. However, since there are more than eight languages spoken within the EU, and since the schools also admit children from non-European personnel, the number of languages spoken by children as home languages is much higher. This means that a child's first school language may not necessarily be his or her native language. It also gives the school an international, not just a European flavour.

The schools provide for pupils from nursery school age up to age 18 and are divided into kindergarten, primary and secondary divisions. Students start school at age six and may leave at different points, for different reasons. The European Schools have been compared to the French Lycée or the German Gymnasium in that instruction is largely taken up with academic subjects (Department of Education and Science, 1985) They award their own diploma, the European Baccalaureate (as distinct from the International Baccalaureate or the baccalaureates of the various European national education systems) which marks the successful completion of the secondary cycle. Students' performance is assessed by a combination of continuous assessment, internal school examinations, and a set of final written and oral examinations. Like many European school-leaving qualifications, the Baccalaureate is a group certificate where the overall mark represents the level attained in all subjects studied in the last year of schooling, including compulsory subjects and electives. The final examination is administered and supervised by an external examination board appointed by the Board of Governors, and it is the same for all schools.

The philosophy of the schools

One of the fundamental principles of the European Schools is that children should be able to receive an education in their native language and culture while being away from their country of origin, thus helping them to develop their own national identity. At the same time, the schools also aim to promote a distinctly European, multi-lingual and multicultural identity capable of overriding national differences. This may seem idealistic given that national differences are quite keenly felt among Europeans. However, as a guiding principle which will enable schools with such a mixed intake to function harmoniously while educating tomorrow's citizens of Europe, it is an important as well as practical proposition. It is the European School's language policy which provides the tool for achieving the two seemingly contradictory goals.

The European School's programme is based on a number of basic tenets which can be summarised in the following way:

(1) The child's distinct national, cultural and linguistic identity must be maintained and therefore most education takes place in the child's dominant language.
(2) Each of the different language sub-sections follows the same time-table and the same curriculum. The notion of linguistic equity is generally accepted and all children, whatever their linguistic backgrounds, are treated equally with regard to language learning requirements.
(3) All children must become proficient in a second and third language through instruction *of* it and *through* it. English, French, German and the language of the host country are the most popular choices as so-called 'vehicular languages'.
(4) The further a student advances in school, the more instruction is presented via the medium of a second and third language. As new languages are introduced, the 'old' ones are also maintained.
(5) From primary school onwards, special curricular arrangements are made to bring students from different linguistic sub-sections together so as to promote the 'European ideal' and to provide opportunities for children to be taught through, and interact in, the medium of multiple languages.

The pupils

The children of parents who work for one of the institutions or organisations of the European Union are given priority of access to the European Schools, but the schools may, and do, admit other pupils if space is available, for instance in order to balance out the numbers in each linguistic sub-section or to allow students from a particular linguistic background to receive an education in their first language. Education is free, but children whose parents are non-civil servants or not employed by a European institution pay a fee which, in hardship cases, may be waived. In 1993 a total of almost 15,000 children were attending European Schools with the proportion of children from European personnel ranging from 11 to 88%. On average, about 60% of places are taken up by children with this sort of background (Bulwer, 1995). But since there are only one or two European Schools per country, it is not particularly useful in terms of average. The social mix of particular schools varies a great deal depending on where it is located. In Britain, for instance, the school is situated near Oxford and attracts children from parents with professional and international backgrounds, often in mixed marriages. It was established to cater for the children of employees of the major European nuclear fission project and, of course, also for the children of the school staff. The fees are much lower than those charged by British private schools, but not insubstantial. The school is always oversubscribed. Within the context of the school system in England with its rather narrow curriculum, it offers an alternative, broader education which many parents with a European outlook find attractive. It is therefore not surprising that the schools have, on occasion, been criticised for their selectivity and social isolation – although others have gone to great lengths to disprove this (Bulwer, 1995).

The teaching staff

As mentioned earlier, teaching staff are seconded from their national education systems for a period of years and, therefore, all teachers are native-speakers of the languages they use. This is particularly important as these teachers serve as linguistic models – often the only authentic one in the student's environment apart from the home. It is, furthermore, a requirement that all teachers be bilingual, as must all support staff. This ensures that all school personnel are aware of the particular linguistic, cultural and psychological problems and demands of bi- and multilingualism faced by the pupils, and it enables students always to find staff who can help them with both linguistic and practical problems. Unfortunately, there are no institutions which prepare teachers for such multilingual education. Some English teachers have a qualification to teach their native language as a foreign language (i.e. EFL), but this may not be true for teachers from other countries. Teachers only receive training while on the job and, in fact, the schools have developed in-service training so that new teaching staff become familiar with the system.

Languages and education in the European Schools

Primary education

Children may enter kindergarten in the language sub-section of their parents' choice at age four. For most children, their first learning experience will be through the language spoken at home, but there are also bilingual speakers, as well as those from different linguistic backgrounds whose languages are not represented by the schools. For these children, kindergarten schooling lays the linguistic foundation for their subsequent learning. Otherwise the first language serves as a medium of instruction for most of primary education and classes are taught by native speakers. In the primary programme, which lasts for five years, a second language is taught to the children as a subject right from the beginning. It is school policy to pay particular attention to the development of the children's L1 as the pupils are not living in the same kind of linguistic environment as their peers in monolingual schools situated in a monolingual region. L1 language classes take a total of 16 periods out of a total of 25 per week in the first two years and nine out of 33 periods per week in Grades 3, 4 and 5. L1 language work is concerned with vocabulary development as well as with acquiring literacy skills, whereas in L2 teaching the main emphasis is on spoken language, basic grammar and lexis.

Promoting multilingual proficiency is pursued in a variety of ways. The method used is not immersion, nor submersion, but rather a highly structured form of slow transition from learning the language as a school subject to learning to use it in cognitively undemanding and highly contextualised situations while at the same time continuing the study of it as a formal subject. First, the L2 is introduced as a subject for two years, always taught by a native speaker. Then, in the last three years of primary school (from Grade 3 onwards) two types of activity involve the L2 as a language of instruction, physical education and the so-called 'European Hours'. Physical education is taught to groups of students with different language backgrounds through the medium of the L2. Although the teacher is supposed to use the L2 only, Baetens Beardsmore (1993) observed that the teachers often provide explanations in other languages in order to proceed more quickly with their class.

The European Hours play an important cultural and ethical role in the philosophy of the European Schools. They are designed to bring students from different L1 groups together for three lessons per week devoted to creative and cooperative tasks (such as cooking, crafts and theme-based project work) and to make them aware of their common

European heritage. Baetens Beardsmore mentions the role they play in social engineering as they aim at breaking down linguistic and cultural barriers created by the existence of language sub-sections (1993: 128). Apart from the social and cultural function of the European Hours, they are also important from a linguistic point of view. The L2 represents the only common language medium among the students and thus gives them the opportunity to use the language that they are learning as a tool for communication. As in the case of physical education classes, the L2 is used in context-dependent circumstances in which the language content is, in cognitive terms, relatively undemanding.

As can be seen from Table 7.3, most of primary education focuses on the children's chosen L1. However, by the end of this stage in their schooling approximately one-quarter of the pupils' timetable is taken up with the L2. This slow progression from L1 to L2 continues, and later intensifies, at the secondary level.

Secondary education

At this level, the 'European ideal' is no longer pursued through European Hours. Instruction during secondary classes takes on a different form which lays more emphasis on illustrating European (rather than national) perspectives. Whereas, for example, history and geography are taught in the L1 in the early years as part of children's acculturation to their national backgrounds, from Grade 8 onwards these two subjects are taught in the L2, and the aim is to make students aware of different interpretations of the same instances of European history or geography. For example, a French pupil with German as the L2 may be taught the history of the French Revolution in German by a German-speaking history teacher.

The secondary school programme lasts for seven years (ages 11/12 to 18/19) and is divided into three phases, the first one lasting for three years, the second and final for two years each. As before, there is a firm commitment to L1 teaching with four periods per week dedicated to its study for the whole of secondary education. Linguistic competence in L2 continues to be promoted through a combination of teaching the second language as a subject, for five or four periods per week in the first phase and three per week in the subsequent two phases, and increasing use of the L2 as a medium of instruction. For three years from Grade 8 onwards, a third foreign language is studied as an obligatory subject for three periods a week; after Grade 10 the L3 may be continued and it may also become the language of instruction of some option courses.

Table 7.3 Primary school curriculum of the European Schools expressed in number of lessons per week and per grade (lessons using the L2 are in *italics*).

Curriculum	*No. of lessons per week*
1st and 2nd Grades	
L1 as a subject	16 × 30 mins
Mathematics	8 × 30 mins
L2 as a subject	*5 × 30 mins*
Music	3 × 30 mins
Art	4 × 30 mins
Physical Education	4 × 30 mins
Environmental Studies	4 × 45 mins
Religion or Ethics	2 × 45 mins
Recreation	7 × 30 mins
Total	25.5 × 30 or 45 mins per week
3rd, 4th and 5th Grades	
L1 as a subject	9 × 45 mins
Mathematics	7 × 45 mins
L2 as a subject	*5 × 45 mins*
Environmental Studies	4 × 45 mins
Art	1 × 45 mins
Music	1 × 45 mins
Physical Education	*1 × 45 mins (mixed languages)*
European Hours	*3 × 45 mins (mixed languages)*
Religion or Ethics	2 × 45 mins
Total	33 × 45 mins per week

Source: Baetens Beardsmore (1993: 131)

During the first three years of secondary school, the amount of work done in a language other than the L1 amounts to up to one-half of the student's timetable. However, the exact proportion of teaching time devoted to language classes depends on the electives chosen – and the possibility of choosing among options increases as the student progresses through the school. Also, some of the options may be taught in a language other than the L1. Total time for languages is never less than one-third or more than two-thirds of a student's programme.

Teaching resources

The most valuable resources in the European Schools are obviously the teaching staff. Because they are native speakers of their respective languages, the teachers serve as linguistic models as well as facilitators of bilingualism and trilingualism. In his study of the European School in Brussels, Baetens Beardsmore (1993) observed that teachers, aware of their students' particular linguistic circumstances within the school, share a number of basic principles and have common attitudes to multilingualism itself. For example, when teachers are involved in L2 classes they try to encourage pupils from different language sub-sections to mix so that using the L2 for classroom interaction occurs naturally. In class, they tend to include linguistic features in their teaching such as explaining special subject-related terminology or providing glossaries, and by spontaneously correcting minor errors in pupils' linguistic production before moving on to the next point. Baetens Beardsmore remarks that these measures do not seem to slow down the natural teaching pace.

Teaching materials produced in the L1 countries for monolingual pupils are used in all classes taught through the L1, so that throughout the school a number of different textbooks are found, depending on the particular language sub-section. In those classes where the L2 or even L3 are spoken, teachers have to rely much more on materials they have produced themselves. So the specific linguistic needs of multilingual students are addressed by the teachers, who are aware of the importance of the way in which the subject under discussion is discussed and the language in which it is being presented.

Evaluation

The European Schools model has a number of distinctive features and, just as in the Luxembourg education system, it does not fit neatly into any of the bilingual education patterns described in the literature. It does not use submersion or immersion methods and it does not aim at achieving transition or maintenance only. The goals of the programme are manifold, involving both maintenance and enrichment, linguistic as well as cultural. The L1 is used throughout schooling and when the L2 is developed this is not done at the cost of the L1. The Luxembourg model is different from the European Schools one in this respect, but then so are the sociolinguistic conditions within which the two schemes function. It is precisely because there is little outside support for the students' L1 that the European Schools are committed to its maintenance, whereas in Luxembourg

Luxembourgish is so omnipresent outside school that the schools do not need to pay so much special attention to it.

The way in which the second and third languages are introduced in the European Schools is similar to the way the Luxembourg model operates. The languages are first introduced as subjects and then, progressively, as media of instruction and inter-class communication while still featuring as a school subject. Again, this tends to be different from immersion programmes where the emphasis is often on using the L2 as a tool for learning and for school communication as quickly as possible (Baker, 1993; Lyster, Chapter 4 this volume).

A further significant characteristic of the European Schools programme lies in the wider cultural aims which it seeks to achieve. In the Luxembourg case, trilingual education is seen as an effective means for enabling young Luxembourgers to acquire the three languages which, together, form an essential part of their national identity. The European Schools cultural mission is more idealistic in that it aims to establish a common supra-national European identity in order to overcome possible prejudice and probable national tensions.

It is difficult to evaluate how successful they are in this aspect of what Baetens Beardsmore calls 'social engineering'. But he mentions one study which is relevant. The study looked at extracurricular aspects of bilingual education (Housen & Baetens Beardsmore, 1987) and found that whereas in primary school most friendships were among children from the same language background, in the higher grades friendship circles moved outside the school's language sub-sections. A sociological investigation into the 'Europeanising' effects of the schools in the long term is called for, to examine for example students' attitudes towards Europe once they have returned to the monolingual and monocultural environment of their country of origin. For instance, in what way (if any) do they develop or change their identities and national loyalties? Of similar interest would be follow-up studies into ex-European Schools students' use of the language acquired through schooling, in order to evaluate the long-term benefit of multilingual education.

The most impressive feature of the European Schools surely lies in its carefully designed academic programme, both with respect to the needs of students and the implementation of its language policy. Although pupils follow the same basic timetable and curriculum, the programmes are set up to fit individual language needs. L2 development is enhanced in a number of ways which are not present in other types of bilingual programmes. It is taught as a subject (i.e. a foreign language) by native speakers, but there are no native speakers of that language among the pupils. When the L2 is used as a tool this is done in carefully controlled contexts. The L2 is used for cognitively demanding tasks only at a later stage. In primary classes, and later on in some classes where the L2 is the classroom language, there may be native speakers among the pupils; this makes using the L2 for communicating more natural. And in the cases where the L2 is also the language of the host country, such as English in the school near Oxford or French in the Brussels school, it provides valuable additional support for L2 learning. Baetens Beardsmore comes to the following verdict: 'Success is determined by the care which has gone into enabling the transition from one language to another to take place, as well as the continuous efforts to integrate the school population in order to achieve the desired linguistic, cultural and inter-ethnic goals' (1993: 153).

In terms of self-evaluation of their achievements, the schools can point to the pass rate of their students in the European Baccalaureate, which is around 90%. This is a high figure, given that admission to the school is not based on any form of selection and that pupils during the first eight years of schooling tend to progress from grade to grade according to age and not test scores. However, after that students may be held back (i.e. repeat a year) if their overall attainment does not meet the educational goals set for the year, and they have to leave the school after having been held back twice. This system, and the fact that those who are less academically inclined tend to leave school after completing compulsory education anyway, ensures a fairly homogeneous population with respect to ability in the upper grades. In these two features (repeating a year of study as a common way of reaching an objective and staying-on power as a factor in achieving homogeneity) the European Schools resemble most European national systems of secondary education – but are different, for example, from the British model.

A number of studies have assessed the linguistic outcomes of the European Schools, comparing the European Schools with other models of bilingual education. (Baetens Beardsmore & Swain, 1985; Baetens Beardsmore & Kohls, 1988; Baetens Beardsmore, 1993). The general assessment of the model has been positive. These studies present the European School programmes not only as different (from the Canadian ones, for instance) but also as providers of an enriching educational experience. Thus, the study by Baetens Beardsmore & Swain (1985) comments on the positive effects of French (the L2 of the school in Brussels which was studied), which was almost used as a lingua franca inside school and further boosted by the fact that it was the predominant language used outside school. In this the European School in Brussels enjoys a considerable advantage over the Canadian immersion programmes: whereas in both models the L2 may serve as the language of wider communication within the school, only the European School has an additional point in its favour, namely that for many children the L2 is also a language spoken outside the school. European School students in Brussels are, furthermore, able to benefit from the fact that the city itself is (officially) bilingual and *de facto* multilingual. In the words of Baetens Beardsmore and Swain: 'Moreover, the multilingual nature of the European School, of the parents' occupational status, and of the wider Brussels context, implies that bi- or multilingual speech habits are a normal part of everyday experience' (1985: 13).

It will be remembered that in their study of Luxembourg's trilingual education system, Beardsmore and Lebrun carried out an investigation of the acquisition of French among 13-year-olds, the results of which they compared to Canadian immersion programmes. There, too, self-initiated use of French by students in and outside school and the presence of the language in the social environment were considered advantageous. Another study posed the question of whether success in L2 acquisition could be related to the fact that the L2 was of immediate communicative usefulness to the students. It came to the conclusion that it could, and it attributed the greater grammatical accuracy attained by European School pupils to the schools' educational model (Baetens & Kohls, 1988). It is worth mentioning that the European School in Brussels has been the target of most studies. A full evaluation of the European School model should include studies of such schools in other linguistic settings and assess attainment in languages other than French. Similarly, a comparison of materials, approaches and human resources across a wider sample of schools should also contribute to a clear picture of the model's success.

The effectiveness of the European Schools can also be judged with respect to their extra-curricular effects. More specifically, students who move from one country to another may find that their school provides the familiarity and security which they do not find in their new environment. The schools offer a large number of extra-curricular and recreational activities which many pupils take advantage of, and which fill their lives and nurture their interests. The enrichment which this provides in cultural, linguistic and human terms when it happens in a supra-national and multilingual context should not be underestimated (see also C. Hoffmann, 1996).

It is noticeable that very little mention is made in the published literature of the L3. Certainly, it features much less prominently in the European Schools programmes as it is a compulsory subject for only three years and its use as a vehicular language is less controlled since it is only used in some of the electives. European Schools students are encouraged to study an L3 as a subject beyond the compulsory stage. However, whatever they choose to do, i.e. whether they continue to study it as a subject in minority time or follow electives where it is the vehicular language, the L3 is likely to remain their weaker language. This, together with the fact that there are no trilingual schemes readily available for a valid comparison within a European context, partly explains the frequent references made to the bilingual immersion model of the Canadian programmes.

The European School model of multilingual education has been thoroughly tried, and deemed to be successful because: (a) it meets the educational needs of the pupils; (b) it contributes to a reasonably effective and continuous response to some of the European problems of the past; and (c) it provides a sound basis for a common European identity at a higher level while at the same time enabling students to develop their own national identities. The European Schools have been the subject of several investigations and evaluations, which together have made a significant contribution to research into multilingual education. Within a Europe that has seen both the enlargement of the European Union in terms of states and resurgent nationalism among its constituent members, the European School remains a model of supra-national Europeanism. As a model of education it is not easily transposable as it is tailor-made for specific pupils with particular requirements living in particular situations – which may partly explain why there are only nine such schools. Also, the European Schools are expensive to operate, both for the EU and the national governments, as they have to be financed separately from the national education systems. But it is not inconceivable that in years to come more of these centres may be created in response to the establishment of new and enlarged European institutions and also in order to meet the demands arising from increased population movements within Europe.

Conclusion

Apart from the two cases discussed above, multilingual education does not feature in European mainstream education. Although for many people who live in European Union countries multilingualism is a *de facto* reality, there is as yet no formal recognition of it at an institutional level. Initiatives regarding publicly supported multilingualism are most likely to involve Europe's prestige languages and a European regional language, rather than a non-indigenous language (see Cenoz, Chapter 8 this volume). A number of European states have already introduced bilingual education policies for their indigenous minorities. Those very same countries also contain large migrant and immigrant communities, such as Turks in Germany, Moroccans in Spain, Algerians in France and Asians in Britain (many of whom are bilingual or trilingual), for whom there is scant provision, if there is any at all, regarding multilingual education.

For historical, geographical and linguistic reasons, some parts of Europe (for instance, Britain) have not experienced the cultural and linguistic repercussions of Europeanisation and internationalisation, trends which have done much to influence language policies in education and people's attitudes towards bi- or multilingualism. English, as one of the working languages of the European Union and as a language of global importance, has found widespread currency in many parts of the European Union. Already one can describe many Europeans as being multilingual with English – although, of course, this does not mean that Europeans are becoming speakers of English with mother tongue or second language competence (Dollerup, 1996; C. Hoffmann, 1991, 1996). This trend looks set to gather momentum, and as it does other languages will come into the reckoning and multilingualism will follow on their heels. It may be a slow process, but language policies are already being discussed at a supra-national level (see, for instance, Coulmas, 1991) and many European Union countries are giving an increasingly high profile to language learning and also to using a foreign language as a medium of instruction.

Despite resurgent nationalism in several member states of the EU and growing reluctance to push European integration further, the consequences of free movement of people, labour and capital will continue to have an impact on European society, and this will necessitate more flexible educational arrangements for parts of the population, both indigenous and migrant/immigrant, in the form of provision for bilingual and multilingual education. Although, as has been shown, the two models of multilingual education discussed here are quite unique, there is much to be learnt from this kind of experience for those planning new programmes elsewhere. Clarity of principles and attention to local conditions are prerequisites.

References

Baetens Beardsmore, H. (ed.) (1993) *European Models of Bilingual Education*. Clevedon: Multilingual Matters.

Baetens Beardsmore, H. and Kohls, J. (1988) Immediate pertinence in the acquisition of multilingual proficiency. *The Canadian Modern Language Review* 44 (2), 240–60.

Baetens Beardsmore, H. and Swain, M. (1985) Designing bilingual education: Aspects of immersion and 'European School' models. *Journal of Multilingual and Multicultural Development* 6 (1), 1–15.

Baker, C. (1993) *Foundations of Bilingual Education and Bilingualism*. Clevedon: Multilingual Matters.

Barbour, S. and Stevenson, P. (1990) *Variation in German*. Cambridge: Cambridge University Press.

Bulwer, J. (1995) European Schools: Languages for all? *Journal of Multilingual and Multicultural Development* 16 (6), 459–75.

Cenoz, J. and Lindsay, D. (1996) English in primary school: Teaching a third language to eight year olds in the Basque Country. *Cuadernos de Filología Inglesa* 5 (1), 81–102.

Coulmas, D. (ed.) (1991) *A Language Policy for the European Community*. New York: Mouton de Gruyter.

Cummins, J. (1984) *Bilingualism and Special Education: Issues in Assessment and Pedagogy*. Clevedon: Multilingual Matters.

Cummins, J. and Swain, M. (1986) *Bilingualism in Education*. New York: Longman.

Décsy, G. (1986–88) *Statistical Report on the Languages of the World as of 1985*, 5 vols. Bloomington: Eurolingua.

Department of Education and Science (1985) *The European Schools and the European Baccalaureate*. DO531SC23A(6).

Dollerup, C. (1996) English in the European Union. In R. Hartmann (ed.) *The English Language in Europe* (pp. 24–36). Oxford: Intellect.

Edwards, J. (1994) *Multilingualism*. London: Routledge.

Grimes, B. (ed.) (1988) *Ethnologue. Languages of the World* (1st edn 1951). Dallas, Texas: Summer Institute of Linguistics.

Hoffmann C. (1991) *An Introduction to Bilingualism*. London: Longman.

Hoffmann, C. (1996) Societal and individual bilingualism with English in Europe. In R. Hartmann (ed.) *The English Language in Europe* (pp. 47–60). Oxford: Intellect.

Hoffmann, F. (1979) *Sprachen in Luxemburg*. Wiesbaden: Steiner.

Hoffmann, F. (1996) The domains of Lëtzebuergesch. In G. Newton (ed.) *Luxembourg and Lëtzebuergesch* (pp. 123–41). Oxford: Clarendon Press.

Hoffmann, J-P. (1996) Lëtzebuergesch and its competitors: Language contact in Luxembourg today. In G. Newton (ed.) *Luxembourg and Lëtzebuergesch* (pp. 97–108). Oxford: Clarendon Press.

Housen, A. and Baetens Beardsmore, H. (1987) Curricular and extra-curricular factors in multilingual education. *Studies in Second Language Acquisition* 9 (1), 83–102.

Kramer, J. (1986) Gewollte Dreisprachigkeit – Französisch, Deutsch und Lëtzebuergesch im Großherzogtum Luxemburg. In R. Hinderling (ed.) *Europäische Sprachminderheiten im Vergleich* (pp. 229–49). Wiesbaden: Steiner.

Kraemer, J-P. (1993) Luxembourg. In U. Ammon, K.L. Mattheier and P.H. Nelde (eds) *Mehrsprachigkeitskonzepte in den Schulen Europas* (pp. 162–73). Tübingen: Niemeyer.

Laver, J. and Roukens, J. (1996) The global information society and Europe's linguistic and cultural heritage. In C. Hoffmann (ed.) *Language, Culture and Communication in Contemporary Europe* (pp. 1–27). Clevedon: Multilingual Matters.

Lebrun, N. and Baetens Beardsmore, H. (1993) Trilingual education in the Grand Duchy of Luxembourg. In H. Baetens Beardsmore (ed.) *European Models of Bilingual Education* (pp. 101–20). Clevedon: Multilingual Matters.

Lepschy, G. (1994) How many languages does Europe need? In M.M. Parry, W.V. Davies and R.A.M. Temple (eds) *The Changing Voices of Europe* (pp. 5–12). Cardiff: University of Wales Press.

Newton, G. (1987) The German language in Luxembourg. In C. Russ and C. Volkmar (eds) *Sprache und Gesellschaft in Deutschsprachigen Ländern* (pp. 153–79). München: Goethe Institut.

Newton, G. (1996a) Luxembourg: The nation. In G. Newton (ed.) *Luxembourg and Lëtzebuergesch* (pp. 5–37). Oxford: Clarendon Press.

Newton, G. (1996b) German, French, Lëtzebuergesch. In G. Newton (ed.) *Luxembourg and Lëtzebuergesch* (pp. 5–37). Oxford: Clarendon Press.

Viereck, W. (1996) English in Europe: Its nativisation and use as a lingua franca, with special reference to German-speaking countries. In R. Hartmann (ed.) *The English Language in Europe* (pp. 16–23). Oxford: Intellect.

Chapter 8
Multilingual Education in the Basque Country

JASONE CENOZ

The Basque Country covers an area of approximately 20,742 square kilometres and comprises seven provinces, three belonging to the French 'Pyrenees Atlantiques' community (Lapurdi, Nafarroa Beherea and Zuberoa), and four to two autonomous regions in Spain (the Basque Autonomous Community, or BAC, and Nafarroa). The total Basque population is approximately three million with 92% being Spanish citizens. The distribution of the Basque-speaking population and the use of Basque in education varies considerably from region to region (Cenoz & Perales, forthcoming). This chapter focuses on bi/multilingual education in the Basque Autonomous Community in Spain.

Although Basque and Spanish are both official languages of the BAC, Basque is really a minority language spoken by approximately only 27% of the population in this territory. There are a number of factors that have resulted in the demographic weakness of Basque. Most importantly, Basque was banned from the public domain for several decades during the Franco regime; it was not until 1979 that the ban was lifted. At that time, Basque was granted official status along with Spanish as an official language in the BAC as a result of the declaration of the Statute of Autonomy. Basque was also weakened as a result of rapid industrial development of the Basque Country in the 1960s and 1970s. This led to extensive in-migration of Spanish-speakers into Basque areas, thereby reducing the percentage of Basque-speakers significantly.

The Basque language is in a process of 'reverse language shift' (Fishman, 1991). Owing largely to the promotion of Basque in schools, there has been an estimated increase of 95,000 Basque speakers from

175

1981 to 1991 (Garmendia, 1994). Since Spanish continues to be the dominant language in most regions of the Basque Country, virtually all Basque-speakers also speak Spanish and, therefore, are bilingual. At present, almost 40% of children between five and 14 years of age living in the BAC are bilingual. Although, taken together, these data represent a relative improvement for the Basque language, it continues to be threatened since Spanish remains the dominant language in most regions of the country while the use of Basque in everyday life is limited to areas of the BAC that are dominated by Basque speakers. Proficiency in Basque is not needed in many regions of the BAC. This makes for a precarious balance of sociolinguistic power.

Apart from Basque and Spanish, English has begun to acquire some importance. Although English is not used in everyday life in the BAC as in other European countries (see Hoffmann, Chapter 7 this volume), English is becoming increasingly important for Basque citizens as a medium of communication for wider scientific, academic, commercial and cultural purposes. Growing interest in learning English has resulted in demands for more English instruction in Basque schools, many of which have a tradition of teaching Basque and Spanish. This emerging form of multilingual education is the focus of this chapter. Before examining this, I will briefly review bilingual education in the BAC since this is the foundation on which multilingual education is being developed.

Bilingual Education in the Basque Country

Bilingual education is not a recent phenomenon in the Basque Country. Some schools were bilingual or even trilingual (in Basque, Spanish, and French) at the end of the nineteenth century. As noted earlier, however, Basque was banned from education during the Franco regime (1939–1975). Despite legal strictures, in the 1960s, groups of enthusiastic parents and teachers in the BAC fought for and succeeded in re-opening a number of private Basque-medium schools (or 'ikastolak'). These schools were not officially recognised in the beginning, but the Franco government was eventually forced to accept them because they had attracted so many students that they could not be ignored.

With the end of the Franco regime, a political climate that was more favourable to Basque and the Basque Country ensued and exists to this day. For example, in 1982, Basque, along with Spanish, was recognised as an official language by the law on the Normalisation of the Basque Language (1982). At that time, approximately only 25% of students attended Basque-medium schools; at present, 73% of elementary school children have Basque as a language of instruction. With the 1982 law, Basque and Spanish became compulsory subjects in all schools in the BAC, and three models of language schooling were established: models A, B and D (there is no letter 'C' in Basque). These models differ with respect to the language or languages of instruction used, their linguistic aims, and their intended student population.

Model A schools are intended for native speakers of Spanish who choose to be instructed in Spanish. Basque is taught as a second language for four to five hours a week. These schools provide minimal instruction and, thus, minimal proficiency in Basque as a second language. In contrast, Model B schools are intended for native speakers of Spanish who want to be bilingual in Basque and Spanish. With this aim in mind, both Basque and Spanish are used as languages of instruction for approximately 50% of school time, although there is considerable variation from school to school (Arzamendi & Genesee, 1997). This model is similar to Canadian models of partial immersion in which French and English are used as languages of instruction for majority group English-speaking students (Genesee, 1987). Finally, in Model D schools, Basque is the language of instruction and Spanish is taught as a subject for four to five hours a week. This model was originally created as a language maintenance programme for native speakers of Basque, but currently also includes a large number of students with Spanish as their first language. Consequently, Model D schools can be regarded as both total immersion programmes for native Spanish-speaking students and first language maintenance programmes for native Basque speakers.

Parents can choose the model they want for their children, and each model is available in the public and private sectors. Access to all three options is limited in some areas of the country, however, where there are not enough students interested in a particular model. The demographic evolution of each model since the Law of Normalization of Basque (1982) is summarised in Figure 8.1.

The data in Figure 8.1 indicate that use of Spanish has undergone a significant decline while the use of Basque as the medium of instruction has attracted an increasing number of students. Model A currently includes less than half as many students as in 1982 (75% v. 34%) while Models B and D which use Basque as the language of instruction have seen a significant increase, from 25% in 1982 to 73% in 1996–97. This trend is the same in all three provinces of the Basque

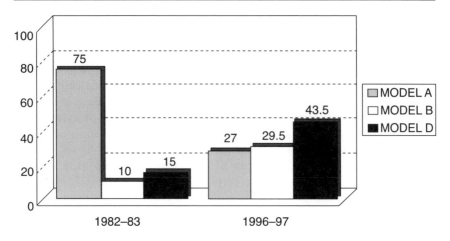

Figure 8.1 Bilingual education models in the Basque Autonomous Community

Autonomous Community (Araba, Bizkaia and Gipuzkoa).

The creation, development and maintenance of bilingual education in the Basque Country has required enormous effort on the part of the Basque Government, individual schools and teachers and has put tremendous pressures on teacher education, materials development and teaching methods. For example, when the Law of Normalization of Basque (1982) was passed, 95% of all public school teachers could not speak Basque at all; the remaining 5% could, but in most cases were not proficient in its use in written form or for academic purposes. The Basque Government now offers extension courses and leaves of absence for teachers who have reached an intermediate level of competence in Basque and want to study Basque full time in order to extend their proficiency. Teachers who complete these courses are required to take examinations to certify that they have attained sufficient proficiency to teach in Basque. At present, over 50% of practising teachers have received this certification (Zalbide, 1994).

Instructional methods in the alternative models vary from school to school depending on whether Basque is used as a medium of instruction or is taught as a school subject. In Models B and D, where Basque is used as the language of instruction, the methodological approach is 'content-based' (see Met, Chapter 3 this volume). Basque is also taught as a subject in Models B and D and, in these classes, instruction focuses on Basque grammar and literature. Basque is a school subject in model A and is taught as a second language. Most teachers in Model A schools adopt traditional second language instructional approaches with relatively structural syllabuses.

Acquisition of Basque is a long, difficult process owing largely to the linguistic distance between Basque and Spanish. Basque, unlike other languages spoken in Spain (Catalan, Galician), is a non-Indoeuropean language. Basque morphology and syntax are complex. It is highly inflected, with 15 different noun inflections, and it includes a complex ergative case system that distinguishes subjects of transitive and non-transitive verbs. Verb morphology is particularly complex; for example, direct and indirect object pronouns are part of the verb forms and different auxiliaries are used with transitive and intransitive verbs. In addition, word order is completely different from Spanish. It is not uncommon for non-native speakers of Basque to have incomplete mastery of the grammar even after many years of study or after having been exposed to Basque as the language of instruction at school (see also Perales & Cenoz, 1996). Another serious challenge facing learners of Basque is that almost all speakers of Basque in the BAC are bilingual and Basque language learners do not need to make the effort to communicate in Basque. Several evaluations of the Basque bilingual programmes have been carried out, with almost 20,000 students having taken part in these evaluations (Gabina *et al.*, 1986; Sierra & Olaziregi, 1989, 1991, Sierra, 1996, etc.). The evaluations have focused on several areas: proficiency in Basque and Spanish, academic development, and foreign language acquisition.

Proficiency in Basque

The results of the Basque evaluations indicate significant differences in Basque proficiency when the three models are compared (Gabina *et al.*, 1986; Sierra & Olaziregi, 1989, 1991; Sierra 1996) – students in Model D are more proficient in Basque than students in Model B who, in turn, are more proficient than students in Model A. Thus, it is apparent that the amount of time devoted to Basque is positively related to level of proficiency in Basque. The lowest levels of proficiency are found among students in Model A schools, where Basque is taught as a subject for only a few hours a week, and the highest levels of proficiency are found among students who are exposed to Basque as a medium of instruction (Gabina *et al.*, 1986; Sierra & Olaziregi, 1989, 1991).

Proficiency in Spanish

Results from evaluations of the students' proficiency in Spanish indicate that there are no significant differences among the models (Gabina *et al.*, 1986; Sierra & Olaziregi, 1989, 1991; Sierra, 1996). Even Model D students, who study Spanish for only four to five hours a week and are in many cases native speakers of Basque, achieve very high levels of proficiency in Spanish. It seems likely that since Spanish is the majority language in the BAC at large, opportunities for extensive exposure to it outside school compensate for reduced exposure to it in school.

Academic development

Evaluations of achievement in mathematics and the natural and social sciences indicate that so far there are no significant differences between students in different models (Aierbe *et al.*, 1974, 1989; Sierra, 1996).

Foreign language

Evaluations of the acquisition of English have found that students who have Basque as the medium of instruction (Model D) attain significantly higher grades than students instructed in Spanish (Model A) (Cenoz & Valencia, 1994; Lasagabaster, 1997; Valencia & Cenoz, 1992).

In general then, results from evaluations of bilingual schools in the BAC corroborate results obtained in Canadian immersion programmes (Genesee, 1987; Swain & Lapkin, 1982) and at the same time extend these results to the case of native speakers of an indigenous minority language.

Multilingual Education: Basque, Spanish and English

Apart from the two official languages, Basque and Spanish, foreign languages have also been a part of education in the BAC. Until the 1980s, the most common foreign language studied at school was French. Recently, however, there has been an important shift in emphasis from French to English and, at present, English is studied as a foreign language by 94% of Basque school children.

Traditionally, students in the BAC have achieved relatively low levels of proficiency in English at school (Cenoz, 1992), so much so that it was popularly believed that English is better learned during visits to English-speaking countries or from private lessons than in school. The poor English language results obtained in school can be attributed to a number of factors, including large class sizes, the use of out-dated or traditional instructional approaches, and the lack of well-trained teachers with adequate proficiency in English. In response to growing parental interest for more and better instruction in English, a great deal of effort has been expended in recent years by the Department of Education of the Basque Government, the Federation of 'ikastolak' (Basque medium schools), and private institutions (Gaztelueta Foundation, Ahizke/Cim) to reinforce and improve the teaching of English within the context of bilingual education, as described earlier. Some of these efforts are described briefly in the following sections.

The Department of Education of the Basque Government, for example, has undertaken to subsidise intensive language learning and instructional methods courses for English teachers both in the Basque Country and in the United Kingdom. The Basque Government has also tried to improve the quality of English teaching by encouraging the adoption of new instructional approaches, especially those that emphasise the acquisition of oral skills, the use of learner-centred syllabuses, and the integration of curricula for the three languages (Cenoz & Lindsay, 1994).

The recent increased interest in English has led to its early introduction in schooling – in kindergarten to 4-year-olds. Traditionally, English was not taught until Grade 6 (11–12 year olds), although the early introduction of English in Grade 3 became compulsory in 1993. The early introduction of English in kindergarten was initiated on an experimental basis in several private Basque schools, or 'ikastolak', in 1991. Enthusiasm for these experimental schools has spawned similar initiatives in a number of public schools. Evaluations of such schools have shown that learning English from such an early age does not adversely affect the students' acquisition of Basque or Spanish or their overall cognitive development (Cenoz *et al.*, 1994). Moreover, questionnaires addressed to parents indicate that they have very positive attitudes toward early instruction in English (Cenoz & Lindsay, 1994; Cenoz, 1996).

Foreign languages (English, French, German) are used as the medium of instruction in some bilingual schools. In these 'foreign language' schools, Spanish and a foreign language are the languages of instruction and Basque is taught as a subject for four or five hours per week. These schools can be considered as examples of bilingual rather than multilingual education because their linguistic objective is that students acquire proficiency in two languages: Spanish and a foreign language.

So far we have referred to bilingual schools in which two languages (Basque and Spanish or, less commonly, Spanish and a foreign language) are used as media of instruction; and we have also referred to experimental projects to improve the quality of third language instruction which treat the third language as a subject. Yet other schools have gone one step further and are using both Basque and English as media of instruction. For example, the A model Gaztelueta School, a private school, has been using English as a medium of instruction for several school subjects (history, science and handicrafts) for a number of years and recently added Basque as a medium for teaching other subjects (history, handicrafts, natural science, computer science). Several public schools have also initiated similar projects, but these projects are still experimental and have a limited scope as compared to multilingual education in Luxembourg or the European schools described by Hoffmann in the previous chapter. In order to better illustrate the main features of such schools, one school that uses Basque, Spanish and English as languages of instruction will be described in some detail now.

Lauro Ikastola

Lauro Ikastola was originally a Basque-medium school. It was founded in 1957 when the use of Basque as a language of instruction was forbidden. It started with 13 students and the enthusiastic support of parents and teachers who wanted to restore Basque as a dominant language of schooling. The school has moved locations several times and is currently located in the village of Loiu, near Bilbao. It is one of the largest schools in the Basque Country. It includes separate buildings for kindergarten, elementary and secondary levels. In 1996–97, over 1800 students were enrolled; 379 in three kindergarten levels (including 3- to 6-year-olds), over 700 in the elementary school (6- to 12-year-olds), and approximately 700 in the secondary school (12- to 18-year-olds). The kindergarten students spend about five hours per day at school, and all other students spend between five-and-a-half to six hours a day at school. There is a maximum of 25 students per class in kindergarten and elementary classes and 30 in secondary classes. Most students live in Bilbao or other small towns near Bilbao and are bussed to school. Lauro is a private 'ikastola' that receives funding from the Basque Government.

The majority of the children come from professional, middle-class families with two incomes. Most students are not native speakers of Basque.

The following are the schools' primary objectives with respect to Basque, Spanish and English:

(1) *Basque*: the students will be fully competent in Basque and will achieve the proficiency of an educated native speaker.
(2) *Spanish*: the students will be fully competent in Spanish and will achieve the same level of proficiency as an educated native speaker from outside the Basque Country.
(3) *English*: the students will be able to communicate in both oral and written English beyond basic survival skills.

Lauro Ikastola devotes different amounts of time to Basque, Spanish and English at each level (see Table 8.1). A brief description of each level of education follows.

Kindergarten

Because Lauro is an 'ikastola', Basque is the only medium of instruction in kindergarten. Approximately 25% of the children attending the school are native speakers of Basque who have had limited contact with Spanish. About 30% have had contact with both Basque and Spanish, although there is considerable variation among the children in their relative levels of proficiency in each language. The remaining students are native Spanish-speakers and are mono-lingual in Spanish upon entry to school. The children are assigned to separate classes according to their proficiency in Basque. There are usually two classes of Basque-speaking children (approximately 50 children in total) and three classes of Spanish-speaking children (approximately 75 children in total) in each of the three kindergarten levels. Children with different first languages tend to remain in

Table 8.1 Time devoted to the different languages

	Kindergarten %	*Elementary* %	*Secondary* %
Basque	100	70–82	55–68
Spanish	0	18–21	13–15
English	0	0–10	16–21
German/French	0	0	0–9

separate classes until the secondary level when they must be aggregated to achieve a minimal class size for optional subjects that normally do not attract enough students with a common first language. The policy of separating native and non-native speakers of Basque is somewhat controversial but has been adopted for the following reasons. Since the school is located in an otherwise Spanish-dominant community, it is hoped that aggregating the native Basque-speakers in the same classes will create a critical mass that can better withstand the assimilating and dominating influences of Spanish. Moreover, housing the native Basque speakers in the same classes is designed to enhance their opportunities to develop strong literacy skills in a context which provides little external support for the development and use of traditional language forms in Basque (oral poetry, story writing, etc.).

All teachers in the school are native speakers of Basque and use Basque with the children. The Spanish-speaking children are generally addressed by the teachers in Basque, but they get some help in Spanish during their first days at school. All children acquire initial literacy skills in Basque and they usually begin to learn to read and write in the third year of kindergarten (when they are five to six years of age).

Elementary education

Throughout the elementary grades, Basque is the medium of instruction for all regular academic subjects, and Spanish and English are taught as separate subjects. The programme of study for the regular school subjects follows the Spanish National Reform curriculum except that the textbooks and other allied instructional materials are in Basque and have been produced and published in the Basque Country. The Basque-medium books used in Lauro Ikastola are the same as those used in most Model D schools.

Basque is taught as a subject for five hours a week. During the first three years of elementary school, students for whom Spanish is the first language are divided into two smaller groups for one of their weekly Basque lessons. During these classes, the regular teacher has the assistance of a Basque-speaking instructional aid who works closely with each small group to develop the students' speaking skills. After the third year, the students have four hours of Basque instruction per week along with a workshop in which they focus on the development of communicative skills. The Basque language teachers are native speakers of Basque with a teaching credential. The instructional aids or assistants are also native speakers of Basque and have a teaching certificate; sometimes, they are teachers-in-training who are about to obtain their teaching credential.

Spanish is introduced as a school subject in the first year of elementary school. In the first and second years, the students receive one hour of Spanish instruction five days a week. In years three to six, they have an additional one-hour workshop devoted to the development of interpersonal communication skills in Spanish. Even children for whom Spanish is not a first language acquire inter-personal communication skills in Spanish easily because of the presence of Spanish in the community at large. Even though Spanish is taught as a school subject, it is not taught as a second language. The Spanish language textbooks are the same as those used with native speakers of Spanish in Spanish-speaking areas outside the Basque Country. Instruction in literacy in Spanish is introduced in the first year of elementary school; Spanish language classes are devoted to grammar, vocabulary and the development of oral and writing skills. The Spanish teachers are native speakers of either Basque or Spanish and are bilingual in Basque and Spanish; they all have specialised training in Spanish language and literature.

English is introduced as a subject in the second year of elementary school and the main objective of English instruction at this time is to prepare students to follow content courses in English in secondary school. They begin with two weekly lessons of 30 minutes each and, from the third to the sixth grades, they have five weekly classes of 30 minutes. English is taught to small groups of students and the English teachers have the help of instructional assistants. All English teachers have a teaching credential in English, and their assistants also have a teaching credential in English or are about to obtain one. As much as possible, Lauro Ikastola tries to employ native speakers of English as assistants, and in these cases English is used as the language of communication among English teachers.

English instruction emphasises the development of interpersonal communication skills. The syllabus is topic-based, including topics such as the city, health, and the human body. Textbooks are not used in elementary school; rather the teachers use materials they have developed with the help of an expert. Written English is not introduced until the last year of elementary school (sixth year), that is three years after the introduction of oral English. Apart from the English classes, the children are encouraged to take home tapes so that they can listen to English songs during their school holidays.

The school also organises summer visits to English-speaking

countries – the United Kingdom, Ireland and the United States. These visits are voluntary and start in the sixth year with summer courses in England. The children live with English families and attend organised classes during the weekdays. Trips to English-speaking countries when the students are in secondary school do not include these organised language classes on the premise that this will force the students to spend less time with one another and more time interacting and practising their language with native-English speakers in the communities and families they are visiting. The students are accompanied by their English language teachers on these trips.

Secondary school

In secondary school, there are four classes with approximately 30 students each. Basque is the main language of instruction at the secondary level and it is also studied as a subject. Spanish is taught for five hours a week. The most important change from elementary school is the use of English as a medium of instruction for two to four hours a week.

English language classes for all four groups at each level of secondary school are scheduled at the same time and the students are grouped according to their level of proficiency in English. The English classes include as much content as possible in areas such as the history of English-speaking countries or geography. The classes are sub-divided into two smaller groups that meet once a week with a native English-speaking instructional assistant. The instructional materials and textbooks emphasise the development of interpersonal communication skills. The English language teachers have specialist credentials in English and have often lived in an English-speaking country for at least one year.

Apart from English language arts classes, three school subjects are taught in English: history of religion, computer science, and science. The first subject they are taught through English is the history of religion. This subject is taught in English in the first and second years of secondary school. It was selected as the introductory class in English for a number of reasons: (1) the students are motivated to know different religions; (2) they already know the concepts and terms in Basque and Spanish; (3) there are appropriate written and video materials available (films, videos, posters); (4) the students are exposed to different religions when they travel abroad and even in the Basque Country; and (5) there are trained teachers to teach this subject in English.

The school is currently experimenting with teaching different subjects in English. For example, as part of a three-year pilot project with the European Institute of Software, computer science is being taught in English in the second year of secondary school. Science was taught in English, on a voluntary basis, for the first time during the 1996–97 academic year; two groups of 20 students participated. This course is recommended only to students who have obtained high grades in English. The rationale for teaching science in English includes the following: (1) the students have already been exposed to much of the vocabulary and content in elementary school; (2) English is an important language of science; (3) it is easy to find a variety of video materials for teaching science in English; and (4) the concepts are not difficult. The science classes are taught by a native speaker of English who has a degree in biology, but no specialised training in second language teaching. She works collaboratively with two Basque-speaking teachers who teach science in Basque to the other students. They prepare their science materials together in order to ensure uniformity of content in the English-taught and Basque-taught science classes. A fourth language is also introduced in secondary school as an optional subject for three hours a week; most students choose to study French or German.

The use of Basque and English is reinforced through other activities, including sports, in the school TV Programme 'Telelauro', and by the school journal *Laurorri*. 'TeleLauro' is a school TV programme produced by Lauro secondary school students. It includes interviews and reports about current world news and news in the community and school. One report is in English and others are in Basque. The school journal *Laurorri* includes news in Basque and Spanish; recently it has incorporated English stories. Laurorri is sent to the students' families and other people involved in the school. Spanish is not reinforced because it is the majority in the community at large.

Evaluation

The progress of the participating students is being assessed by their performance on school-based exams and standardised tests in Basque and Spanish. The standardised Basque test results are being compared to results obtained in large-scale research studies sponsored by the Basque Government (Sierra & Olaziregi, 1989, 1991) and the results obtained by students at Lauro Ikastola in previous years. Results from the latter comparisons indicate that the Lauro students are obtaining good results relative to earlier cohorts of students and large-scale evaluations. Although the students' knowledge of Basque has improved during recent years, there is some concern about the use of Basque throughout the school – all too often they use Spanish to converse with each other. To address this issue, there are efforts to enhance the use of Basque through activities of interest to the students, such as sports, drama, or trips to Basque-speaking farm schools. Unfortunately, these efforts are often frustrated because of the difficulty finding personnel, such as sports directors, who are Basque-speaking.

Lauro students have also been found to obtain very good results in Spanish when compared to Basque students who have had Spanish as the language of instruction and when compared to native Spanish speakers living outside the Basque Country, although their vocabulary results are somewhat lower. Despite such positive results, there is some concern that the students' Spanish skills, and in particular their vocabulary, might deteriorate as a result of decreased exposure to Spanish. Consequently, workshops have been organised to ensure that the students' Spanish language skills are comparable to those of Spanish-speaking students outside the Basque Country. To date, the students' performance in English has not been evaluated, although plans for such an evaluation are underway. The use of English as a language of instruction poses important questions and concerns. On the one hand, while parents at Lauro Ikastola are keenly interested in improving their children's proficiency in English and, thus, heartily support the use of English as a medium of instruction, on the other hand, they also have high expectations concerning their general academic achievement. Thus, a thorough evaluation of the effects of using English as a medium of instruction on both the students' linguistic and academic development is called for, and indeed is planned, to address these concerns. Another challenge of using English as a language of instruction in Lauro Ikastola is the need for teachers who are proficient in English and are qualified to teach academic subjects through English. There are also problems finding materials in English that follow the 'Spanish National Reform' curriculum; when appropriate published materials cannot be found, considerable time and effort are needed to create them locally. Finally, the results of a recent attitude survey among the participating students and their families indicates that, in general, the programme is well regarded.

Ongoing Challenges

The school described in this chapter illustrates the growing importance attached to trilingualism and multilingual education in the Basque Autonomous Community. Basque parents and educators alike believe that knowledge of three languages is important in the day-to-day and future lives of their children. Encouraged by positive results from earlier experiments in Basque–Spanish bilingual education (described earlier), the educational community was aware of the feasibility and effectiveness of using English as third medium of instruction in order to achieve this goal. Promoting multilingualism through the use of English as a third medium of instruction poses serious ongoing challenges to schools in the BAC that seek to implement multilingual education. These challenges have been clearly illustrated at Lauro Ikastola. The greatest challenge by far concerns the availability of teachers with sufficient proficiency in English to use it as a medium of academic instruction. Most Basque teachers, with the exception of English language teachers, have no or very limited knowledge of English and many of them have made a great effort to acquire enough competence in Basque to be able to use it as a language of instruction. At the same time, employing teachers who are native speakers of English is politically unpopular since it poses a real threat to teaching positions in a community with a high rate of unemployment.

An additional challenge posed by multilingual education in the Basque Country is related to the sociolinguistic context of the Basque Autonomous Community. As noted earlier, although Basque and Spanish are both official languages, in fact, Basque has minority status in comparison to Spanish and almost all Basque speakers also know Spanish, thereby undermining the status of Basque further. English is a foreign language needed for broader communication in Europe and worldwide; it is not used in everyday life. There is concern that the gains that Basque has achieved in education after long years of effort and a great deal of human and economic investment will be threatened by the use of English as an additional language of instruction. In contrast, others think that more resources should be spent on English than on Basque because English is an important language of international communication. Schools such as Lauro Ikastola are important test cases for determining whether these challenges can be successfully met and they provide important evaluation information about the likely effectiveness of multilingual approaches to instructional delivery in Basque schools.

References

Aierbe, P., Etxezarreta, J. and Satrustegi, L.M. (1974) Ikastoletako aurren jakite mailaren azterketa konparatiboa. *Zeruko Argia* 603, 1.

Aierbe, P., Arregi, P., Etxeberria Balerdi, F. and Etxeberria Sagastume, F. (1989) Urretxu-Legazpi-Zumarraga Eskoletako Euskararen Egoera. *Kilometroak* 85.

Arzamendi, J. and Genesee, F. (1997) Reflections on immersion education in the Basque Country. In K. Johnson and M. Swain (eds) *Immersion Education: International Perspectives.* (pp. 151–66). Cambridge: Cambridge University Press.

Cenoz, J. (1992) *Enseñanza-aprendizaje del Inglés como L2 o L3.* Leioa: Universidad del País Vasco.

Cenoz, J. (1996) El inglés en preescolar. Evaluación. Unpublished research document. Department of Education. Basque Government.

Cenoz, J. and Lindsay, D. (1994) Teaching English in primary school: A project to introduce a third language to eight year olds in the Basque Country. *Language and Education* 8, 201–10.

Cenoz, J., Lindsay, D. and Espí, M.J. (1994) Plurilingüismo temprano. Evaluación. Unpublished research report. Ikastolen Elkartea.

Cenoz, J. and Valencia, J. (1994) Additive trilingualism: Evidence from the Basque Country. *Applied Psycholinguistics* 15, 157–209.

Cenoz, J. and Perales, J. (forthcoming) The Basque speech community. In M.T. Turell (ed.) *Multilingualism in Spain.* Clevedon: Multilingual Matters.

Fishman, J. (1991) *Reversing Language Shift.* Clevedon: Multilingual Matters.

Gabina, J.J., Gorostidi, R. and Iruretagoiena, E. (1986) *Influence of Factors of the Learning of Basque.* Vitoria-Gasteiz: Central Publications of the Basque Government.

Garmendia, M.K. (1994) *Eusko Jaurlaritzako hizkuntza politikarako idazkari nagusiaren agerraldia, berak eskatuta, Eusko legebiltzarreko iraskunde eta herrizaingo batzordearen aurrean.* Vitoria-Gasteiz: Eusko Jaurlaritza.

Genesee, F. (1987) *Learning Through Two Languages.* Cambridge: Newbury.

Lasagabaster , D. (1997) Creatividad y conciencia metalingüística: incidencia en el aprendizaje del inglés como L3. Leioa: University of the Basque Country.

Perales, J. and Cenoz, J. (1996) Silence, communicative competence and communication strategies in second language acquisition. In G.M. Grabher and U. Jessner (eds.) *Semantics of Silences in Linguistics and Literature* (pp. 67–87). Heidelberg: Universitätsverlag C.Winter.

Sierra, J. (1996) Los modelos de enseñanza bilingüe y el rendimiento escolar en educación primaria. Paper read at the III European Conference on Immersion Programmes. Barcelona : September, 1996.

Sierra, J. and Olaziregi, I. (1989) *E.I.F.E. 2: Influence of Factors on the Learning of Basque.* Vitoria-Gasteiz: Central Publications of the Basque Government.

Sierra, J. and Olaziregi, I. (1991) *E.I.F.E. 3: Influence of Factors on the Learning of Basque.* Vitoria-Gasteiz: Central Publications of the Basque Government.

Swain, M. and Lapkin, S. (1982) *Evaluating Bilingual Education: A Canadian Case Study.* Clevedon: Multilingual Matters.

Valencia, J. and Cenoz, J. (1992) The role of bilingualism in foreign language acquisition: Learning English in the Basque Country. *Journal of Multi-*

lingual and Multicultural Development 13, 433–49.
Zalbide, M. 1994, Bilinguisme scolaire en Pays Basque. *6ᵉ Colloque Flarep* (pp. 41–55). Biarritz: Ikasbi/Flarep.

Chapter 9

Teaching in Two or More Languages in the Philippine Context

ANDREW GONZALEZ, FSC

A Brief History of Education in the Philippines

Public education was established in the Philippines by the Spanish colonial government with the Royal Decree of 20 December, 1863 (Bazaco, 1953). As envisaged in this decree, literacy was to be established in Spanish. For this purpose, two Normal schools, *Escuela Normal de Maestros* and *Escuela Normal de Maestras,* for male teachers and female teachers respectively, were established by the Jesuits in Manila and by the Daughters of Charity in Naga, Camarines Sur. The main goal of these schools was to train Filipino teachers in the Spanish language and other content areas. The curriculum in these schools was composed mostly of catechism and basic reading and writing (and presumably speaking and listening) in Spanish. The Decree of 1863 made use of the infrastructure already established by the Church since 1565 and, in effect, made the parish priest super-intendent of the public schools and placed the public primary schools in the parish complex.

Contrary to the directives of the Crown to teach Spanish to the natives, Spanish missionaries at the time used the local vernaculars to teach religion. Their insistence on using local vernaculars instead of Spanish was not a reactionary move to keep the *Indios* (local Malays) ignorant, but rather arose from practical considerations, specifically the difficulty of teaching a foreign language to non-native speakers in a cultural context where there was no support for the foreign language in the community. The Spanish 'frailes', better educated than the natives, learned the local languages for pragmatic reasons and taught in the local languages rather than trying to teach everyone

Spanish. The move was practical and realistic, but was misinterpreted by many as a move to keep the Indios down. Thus, public education in the Philippines was initially multilingual rather than unilingual, with the colonial language being taught systematically only during the last 30 years of Spanish colonial rule. Bazaco (1953) claimed that by 1898, when the Spaniards ceded the Philippines to the Americans, there were 2000 primary schools as mandated by the Spanish Education Decree of 1863. In the Report of the Commission of Education for the Year 1899–1900 under the new American regime, Lardizabal (1991: 39) reports that there were 2167 primary schools in the country.

The Americans bought the Philippines from the Spanish for 20 million dollars after the Treaty of Paris in 1898. At that time, President William McKinley ordered that initial literacy instruction be presented in the 'dialects' of the Philippines and that English be the language in which content would be taught. Apparently on the Whorfian belief that language determines thought, he believed that by learning English and using it in school, in government bureaucracy and in the courts, Filipinos would internalise the ideals and ethos of democracy.

The instructions drafted by the Minister of War, Elihu Root, to the Second Philippine Commission called for the use of local languages. However, when the American system of public education began in the Philippines – with W.D. McKinnon, chaplain of the First California Volunteers as the first American school superintendent and with American volunteer soldiers teaching under him – education was monolingual rather than multilingual. English was used as the only medium of instruction; none of the 'dialects' were deemed to be adequate media of instruction, even for initial literacy. The Organic Act of 1901 (Act No. 74 of the Second Philippine Commission) made English the sole medium of instruction.

During the first three decades of American colonial administration, Philippine public education was supposed to take place entirely in English, although some Spanish was used since some of the first readers were written in Spanish. However, few of the pupils or teachers spoke English. The private schools administered by Spanish religious orders continued to teach in Spanish, with English being taught as a foreign language. A shift to English as the medium of instruction took place from 1921 onward. Monolingual education in English reigned in the Philippines (along with the teaching of Spanish and other foreign languages) until 1940. Beginning in 1940, the Tagalog-based national language (*Wikang Pambansa* 'National Language' or what is currently referred to as Filipino) was taught for the first time as a subject to teachers in training in the normal schools and as a subject in fourth year high school to Filipino students.

Monolingual education in English, with the Tagalog-based national language being taught as a subject, continued even after independence from the United States in 1946. It was not seriously challenged until 1950 when the importance of education in vernacular languages was popularised by UNESCO (1953). Clifford Prator, a visiting language professor with the Fulbright Programme, investigated the language teaching situation in the Philippines and suggested a total revamping of English language teaching. He suggested that English be taught as a second language and that vernaculars be used for initial schooling as a form of transitional bilingualism (Prator, 1950). Prator's observations were reinforced in part by the success of the recently concluded Iloilo experiment of 1961–1964 in which Hiligaynon was used for initial teaching (instead of English). This approach was found to facilitate the subsequent learning of content in English (Aguilar, 1955; Davis, 1967). Similarly, in the Rizal experiment, students were taught in Tagalog and in their home languages and the use of English as a medium of instruction was delayed for two years, until the pupils were literate in their home language.

The trend towards reforming the language of teaching in the Philippines as a result of the Iloilo and Rizal experiments gave rise to the Vernacular Teaching Programme which prevailed from 1957 to 1974. Under this programme, eight major vernaculars in the Philippines were used as languages of initial education and, in particular, for literacy instruction, with Tagalog and English being taught as subjects. English was used as a medium of instruction beginning in Grade 3.

In the Philippines, Tagalog, Ilokano, and Cebuano are used extensively by speakers who have other vernaculars since these three languages not only have the largest number of native speakers, but they are also used as linguae francae in some regions (Central Luzon, Northern Luzon, the Visayas and Mindanao among the settlers). Other languages used in the schools are: Kapampangan, Bikol, Waray Visayan, Hiligaynon Visayan, and Maranao. These eight languages were selected as languages of instruction because they had at least one million speakers.

The use of the eight major languages as media of initial literacy instruction represented a major policy shift on the part of the Department of Education. However, its implementation was of questionable success, particularly in the private schools of the country. The lack of success was due largely to the lack of adequate materials in the major vernaculars for the two years in which students were expected to achieve functional literacy (see Sibayan, 1967). In the case of the private schools, successful implementation was impeded by the lack of personnel who could carry out the required reforms. Moreover, the few vernacular reading texts that were produced were translations from Tagalog texts and were not particularly appropriate. Despite plausible arguments that the most efficient way of teaching initial literacy and facilitating the transition of students from home to school is to use students' first language (or at least a lingua franca used in the community), there was no clear empirical evidence that demonstrated the superiority of using the vernacular for initial learning or for facilitating the transition from the home to the school. Available evidence was primarily anecdotal and impressionistic and the results from the previous Iloilo and Rizal experiments.

The period from 1957 to 1974 was the only time in this century when a multilingual system of education prevailed in the Philippine education system. The system was changed into a bilingual system in 1974. The only modification to this latter system was made in 1987 when vernaculars were restored as 'auxiliary' teaching languages in the initial months of schooling. A trilingual system (first language, or major vernacular, Tagalog-based Pilipino (renamed Filipino), and English) is now in use, with the main vernaculars being used solely for transitional purposes. Since 1974, the most significant change has been the use of Filipino not only as a transitional language or as a subject of study but as one of two major languages of instruction (the other being English) in a bilingual education scheme. This programme is being implemented from Grade 1 to the fourth year of High School.

The shift towards Filipino as a medium of instruction at all levels of basic education arose as a result of demands from nationalist-oriented students and faculty in the late 1960's and early 1970's to extend the use of the national language across all levels of the school system. As a result, the National Board of Education introduced Department Order No. 25 in 1974. The Order mandated the use of Filipino and English as media of instruction from Grade 1 on. This policy of using English for mathematics and science (and of course for the English language and literature class) and Filipino for all other subjects from Grade 1 to the fourth year of high school and for some subjects at the university level was modified slightly in 1987 – the use of the major vernaculars was restored and the timetable for implementation was made more flexible by taking into account regional needs and conditions (Gonzalez & Sibayan, 1988).

Thus, at present in the Philippines, multilingual education (vernaculars, Filipino and English) is available as a transitional arrangement (up to Grade 3) and, subsequently, bilingual education (Filipino and English) is the norm. The major vernaculars used in schools have increased by one, Maguindanao. The nine major vernaculars are not formally mandated but are used for explanations, especially during the initial months of schooling.

Teaching in Two (or Three) Languages in the Philippines: The Results

The system of language use in the Philippines is currently a bilingual system (Filipino and English) with a third language (one of nine vernaculars, depending on the location of the school) as a transitional 'auxiliary' language. There are at present no public or private multilingual schools where at least three languages are used as media of instruction for teaching content. International schools or embassy schools are monolingual, although foreign languages are taught as subjects. The bilingual scheme for public and private schools in the Philippine education system and the following allocation of subjects to the two main languages of instruction can be seen in Table 9.1. For historical reasons, the base scheme for General Education consists of six years of elementary schooling and four years of high school or secondary schooling. These two levels are mandated by the Constitution to be provided free by the state. Private schools (usually with more affluent students) precede Grade 1 with one or two years of preparatory school (mostly in English except for the use of the vernacular as a transitional language) and an additional year of primary schooling (Grade 7). Thus the number of years of schooling before university may range from 10 to 13, creating a very significant difference in the quality of applicants admitted to post-secondary schooling.

In 1985, after 11 years of the bilingual scheme, a national task force was organised by the Ministry of Education, Culture and Sports, to evaluate the programmes (Gonzalez & Sibayan, 1988). The work of this task force was the most comprehensive empirical study to date of bilingual education in the Philippines. Its findings yielded valuable data for evaluating the impact of bilingual education on a national level after 10 years. Earlier evaluations had been carried out in different parts of the country (Gonzalez, 1984) and uniformly cited problems of implementation. Problems were especially evident for the Filipino component of the programme because of the lack of sufficient materials for teaching social studies at the elementary level

Table 9.1 Media of instruction

Level	Major vernacular (=First language or regional lingua franca)	Filipino	English
Kindergarten	All subjects for first few months		All subjects except Filipino
Preparatory *Elementary* 1 2 3 4 5 6 (7)	Transitional (when needed)	Communication Arts Social Studies (including civics) Physical Education (including Arts & Music) Home Technology	Science Mathematics English Language Arts
Secondary I II III IV	Filipino Communication Arts Home Technology (Work Education) Physical Education Arts and Music	Social Sciences Philippine History and Government Asian History Economics World History	Science General Biology Chemistry Physics Mathematics I, II, III, IV English Communication Arts (including English for Specific Purposes)

and social sciences at the secondary and post-secondary levels. There was also a lack of qualified teachers to handle the transition from English to Filipino in the teaching of social studies and the social sciences.

The 1985 national evaluation sampled 122 schools and 2000 students in Grades 4 and 6, and in the fourth year of high school (Grade 10). Students were tested in English, mathematics, science, Filipino, and social studies/science, and 568 teachers of these students were also tested using proficiency tests in the same subjects to find out the correlation between the student results and those of their teachers. In addition, administrators and teachers were interviewed on the implementation of the programme, the teaching of the instructors, and the support extended by the administrators.

The results indicated poor achievement in English; the impression of many parents, teachers and administrators was that this was attributable to the reduced amount of time allotted to English in the bilingual education scheme. It had been expected that the use of the national language would improve learning of content in the social sciences, but these expectations were not realised. Scores in subjects taught in Filipino were low (hovering around 50%), and there was no correlation between the number of years of implementation of the programme and student test results. Socioeconomic status of the schools (indicated by its private status and its tuition rates), its physical surroundings and location in an urban community (at the cross-roads of a mobile population consisting of many ethnic groups), and the overall quality of the school in terms of library facilities, laboratory equipment, department morale, the qualifications and effectiveness of teachers were all found to be good predictors of high test scores. In quite simplistic terms, quality schools, well run and well managed, where teaching was done by qualified and effective teachers and with good logistic support yielded good results in both English and Filipino as well as in mathematics, science and social studies/science.

Schools were systematically visited and examined by a team of evaluators for the aforementioned institutional indicators. As well, classes were visited by the evaluators to obtain an overall impression of effectiveness. Schools evaluated low on the criteria yielded poor results, and a high positive correlation was found between student achievement and teachers' level of proficiency in subject matter areas. Moreover, when the results of teachers' proficiency were analysed further, it was evident that their overall achievement was low and left much to be desired; the teachers averaged only about 50% in subjects they were supposed to know and teach, except in Filipino (language) where the average was about 65%. The results in physics (taught in the fourth year of high school) were especially poor, averaging only 40%.

The results were not encouraging; by and large, education in more than one language had yielded poor results. However, the evaluation indicated quite clearly that the low test scores were due not to the use of two languages in teaching but to the overall low quality of the teaching conditions in the schools. The results made a case not for discontinuing the use of the bilingual scheme, but for ensuring that the scheme be implemented better by systematic training of teachers, use of suitable teaching materials, and the creation of supportive teaching/learning conditions that motivate both teachers and students. Although there has been little positive evidence of the effectiveness of these programmes with respect to quantitative measures, such as test scores, there have been positive results of a qualitative nature – for example, enhanced esteem for the national language, faith in its eventual capability to facilitate communication and the learning of content, and support for the nationalistic aspirations of Filipinos.

Subsequent testing of student achievement in elementary and secondary schools, including the National College Entrance Examination (from 1973 to 1993), National Elementary Achievement Tests (NEAT), and National Secondary Achievement Tests (NSAT), indicates that the largest problem facing the schools at present is the lack of skills and knowledge among teachers (see Felipe, 1995; Ibe, 1994; Ibe & Coronel, 1995). This situation has arisen as a result of many factors (Gonzalez, 1996a,b). Chief among these is the poor quality of recruits into the system, especially during the period 1975–1985 when it became difficult to attract highly qualified teachers because of poor salaries and working conditions. This led many experienced and qualified teachers to leave the profession to take other jobs.

Thus, the implementation of the programme from 1974 to the present has been affected mainly by the overall decline in the quality of the teaching professionals. The causes of the decline in professional qualifications of the teachers are socioeconomic rather than pedagogical. The perceived decline in English language skills is a product of sociolinguistic conditions more than language education (see Gonzalez, 1993; Sibayan & Gonzalez, 1996). There is now pride in and emphasis on Filipino (the national language). The use of English is now restricted to the domains of international business, tourism, decision-making in local business at the highest levels, and education in mathematics, science, and technology. On the one hand, English is used in a reduced number of domains and has become a language for only some subjects in school and for international trade with foreigners. On the other hand, Filipino has expanded its domains of use to include entertainment, ordinary business transactions, most subjects in school, and all activities outside of the classroom.

Lessons from the Philippine Experience

The Philippine experience with education in more than one language has been both positive and negative. On the positive side, the scheme has resulted in the recognition of the major vernaculars and linguae francae as important media of initial literacy instruction. Moreover, the use of the national language – its legitimisation and the expansion of the domains in which it is used – renders it an expression of nationhood and identity and as a useful medium of communication, especially for the social sciences which contain elements of tradition and Philippine culture which need to be handed down as aspects of the nation's patrimony. On the negative side, contrary to expectations regarding the effectiveness of the national language as a more powerful means of communication in school, the results are less than compelling because of the associated difficulties of finding adequate instructional materials and trained instructors.

The lack of success in the use of the local national language may also have resulted from the fact that it has only recently been used as a medium of academic instruction. The process of adapting a local vernacular for use in formal academic settings is a long and tedious one. Where there is a competing language that is already fully adapted for academic purposes (in this case, English), the local national language (in this case, Filipino) is at a disadvantage. It is not recommended that the local vernacular(s) be abandoned in schooling, but rather that it be given special attention (including the creation of dictionaries, texts, and other instructional materials) to facilitate its use for schooling.

Perhaps the most meaningful insight from the Philippine experience is that while the language or languages used is one factor in the effectiveness of schooling, the relative success of an educational system depends on many factors, some in the classroom (including the very significant factor of the teacher), some in the whole school (library facilities, laboratories, efficient and supportive administration), and others in the community at large (its location in the community, the kind of community it is, and the socioeconomic status of students). Put simply, good schools do a good job of teaching both English and Filipino, and presumably the vernaculars as well, if there is a determined effort to use provide all of the resources that are needed.

Present conditions in the Philippines indicate that no classroom is really monolingual (Santos, 1984; Sibayan, 1982), that it is unrealistic to expect Filipino to be used as a medium of instruction in beginning social studies classes in non-Tagalog speaking areas (since Filipino is Tagalog-based), and even more unrealistic to expect English, a totally new language for non-affluent Filipino children in rural areas, to be used as the medium of instruction for science and mathematics at the beginning levels of formal schooling. Common sense dictates that the teacher ought to use what has been termed a 'bimedial system of instruction', that is, teachers give the gist of the lesson in the language prescribed, Filipino or English, and then explain what is meant in a language the students understand (the local vernacular or Filipino in Tagalog-speaking areas). Bimedial instruction continues with the local language predominant in the beginning whereas English and Filipino are used increasingly as children gain proficiency in them.

Possible modifications to the current model of language use in schools in the Philippines might be either to restore the officially sanctioned use of the vernaculars for the first two years of schooling (or even longer depending on how quickly the students learn Tagalog) or to give official approval to the 'bimedial system of instruction'.

There is evidence (Lingan, 1981) that because of the widespread use of Filipino throughout the islands as a result of migration and the mass media, children are learning basic interpersonal communication skills in Filipino as early as the second year of schooling (Cummins, 1991), although in remote areas, away from main thoroughfares, such skills may not be acquired until the fifth year. Likewise, there is evidence that students from affluent middle-class families in prosperous urban areas learn basic interpersonal communication skills in English as early as the third year of schooling (Uri, 1992). However, among less affluent and less culturally advantaged students, such skills are not attained until the sixth grade and for some, they are never attained. At the secondary school level, there are students who are able to understand basic classroom instructions in English but are unable to use English productively; they answer questions in Filipino even if asked in English. For some who do not use English actively, a form of linguistic simplification or 'infantilism' seems to be common.

Montañano (1993, 1996) has found that most students at the primary level in the Philippines do not attain what Cummins (1979) calls Communicative Academic Language Proficiency (CALP) in Filipino. Only in secondary schools in affluent communities was it found that students were able to answer analytic, synthetic and evaluative questions in Filipino. Thus, although most Filipino students of all socioeconomic classes have attained at least the ablity to answer simple WH- questions and to paraphrase at an elementary level, they cannot engage in higher level cognitive activities (analysis, synthesis and evaluation) in Filipino until secondary school. The ability to engage in higher levels of cognitive activity, as attested by scores on reading tests, seems to be attained much earlier in English in schools that are culturally advantaged, arguably, because of the availability of reading materials in English and the students' familiarity with the language (Ibe, 1994).

Some Final Considerations

In addition to the acquisition of knowledge, the process of education consists of cultivating critical thinking skills and promoting students' ability to think independently. Basic to this task is the competent use of a language for higher order thinking. Based on the Philippine experience, it can be said that whether monolingual, bilingual, or transitionally trilingual schools do an effective job of promoting the acquisition of such skills and knowledge depends on a variety of factors besides language *per se*. These include: the availability of certified teachers who have been trained in quality teacher-training institutions or Normal schools, a supportive school that includes an efficient and fair administration that cultivates morale and provides adequate facilities (e.g. library), an environment conducive to study, institutional order, and discipline. The other ingredients of successful bi- and multilingual education are, of course, highly motivated students and a community supportive of the school and its language-learning goals. Schools located in rural areas often have additional challenges to overcome since these areas may be lacking resources which are readily available in urban areas, for example, easy access to mass media, quality teachers, administrators and teacher-training institutions. The most important insight gleaned from the Philippine experience in bi- and multilingual education is that effective education is dependent on multiple factors. Indeed, effective and efficient multilingual education is being done in Philippine schools under specific and definable conditions. Less effective schools in both rural and urban areas do an inadequate job of teaching content in any language.

The Philippine experience provides additional insights about effective multilingual education. From a sociolinguistic perspective, it is well recognised that all linguistic codes have the potential for a broad range of social and intellectual functions. But, it is also recognised that because certain language varieties have been used for formal educational purposes, they are readily adapted to academic instruction. Other languages or language varieties, in comparison, may not have been used, or may have been used only rarely, in educational domains and thus lend themselves only with some difficulty to the full set of purposes required in school settings. Such language varieties may lack, for example, certain vocabulary that is needed to refer to technical or scientific concepts that are not traditionally referred to in everyday contexts or the language may lack grammatical structures or devices that lend themselves easily to discourse about certain academic topics, for example, of a scientific or mathematical nature, since such discourse is not part of the everyday uses of the language. Moreover, there may be no written texts in the language or no tradition in the language community of producing written texts suitable for academic instruction.

In some bilingual or multilingual communities, the languages are more or less equally functional with respect to academic discourse and usage; that is, both or all languages have traditions of academic discourse. In other communities, this is not the case. In the Philippines, for example, Filipino and English have had very different histories as languages of educational instruction. Filipino is based on Tagalog, a language that was used orally in informal, everyday situations and was only relatively recently adopted as a national language and used as a medium of instruction in schools throughout the country. English, in contrast, has a long history of use in formal education in the Philippines, and elsewhere. The linguistic situation with respect to the use of English and Filipino in the Philippines is very different from the situation in Canada, for example, where French and English both have fully developed academic registers and written corpora of texts for use in education. The Philippines is more typical of the developing world, in which former colonial languages (with histories of academic usage) were often adopted as the languages of schooling in lieu of local national/vernacular languages (with little or no history of academic usage).

In such communities, a great deal of time and effort are needed for corpus planning so that the language which traditionally has not been used for academic purposes can be functionally extended to academic domains. This effort requires not only time and financial resources, but more importantly, human resources. Individuals must be identified who can create textbooks and other curriculum materials in the traditionally less academic language. This must be done for different areas of the curriculum (science and mathematics, for example) to make written sources accessible in both languages at levels appropriate for the target learner groups. When this is done experimentally, on a small scale, there is a good chance of success.

However, when it is attempted on a system- or nation-wide scale, the chances of failure are much greater because of the potential lack of qualified individuals to carry out the task.

A similar challenge arises with respect to training teachers in pre-service and in-service programmes. In the case of the Philippines, where resources are often scarce and unevenly distributed, culturally advantaged schools in multiethnic urban communities do a relatively good job of teaching content in a variety of languages because they have access to the necessary resources. Less advantaged schools and regions of the country do not fare so well.

The future of multilingual education in the Philippines depends on the effective training of a new generation of teachers who can provide instruction in local vernaculars that lack a history of academic usage. The lack of empirically validated, effective techniques and procedures for preparing teachers to teach content in their own indigenous languages has been a major lacuna in the implementation of multi-lingual education in the Philippines. Training future generations of teachers for multilingual education also presupposes that they are knowledgeable in the academic subjects that comprise the school curriculum (see also, Met, Chapter 3; Nunan & Lam, Chapter 6 this volume). Thus, a corollary task is to recruit teachers who are qualified to teach academic material in the local or indigenous languages of their students.

References

Aguilar, J.V. (1955) Vernaculars and English as tools of value structure. *The Philippine Journal of Education* 33, 438–40.

Bazaco, E. (1953) *History of Education in the Philippines*. Manila: University of Santo Tomas.

Cummins, J. (1979) Linguistic interdependence and the educational develop-ment of bilingual children. *Review of Educational Research* 49, 222–51.

Cummins, J. (1991) Conversational and academic language proficiency in bilingual context. In J. Matter and J. Hulstijn (eds) *Readings in Two Languages. AILA Review* (pp. 75–89). Amsterdam: Free University Press.

Davis, F.B. (1967) *Philippine Language Teaching Experiments*. Quezon City: Alemar-Phoenix.

Felipe, A. (1995) If NEAT was neat. Educators speak. *Sunday Bulletin* A11, B8.

Gonzalez, A. (1984) Evaluating the bilingual education policy. In A. Gonzalez (ed.) *Panagani Language Planning, Implementation and Evaluation. Essays in Honor of Bonifacio P. Sibayan on his 67th Birthday* (pp. 46–65). Manila: Linguistic Society of the Philippines.

Gonzalez, A. (1993) The English language in the Philippines after November 24, 1992. Solidarity special issue. Facing the future: A Philippine agenda for Philippine-American relations. *Solidarity* 137–38, 116–21.

Gonzalez, A. (1996a) Language classrooms of tomorrow in the Philippines – Dreams and realities. Paper presented at RELC Seminar, Singapore 22–24 April.

Gonzalez, A. (1996b) Using two/three languages in Philippine classrooms: Implications for policies, strategies and standards. *Journal of Multilingual and Multicultural Development* 17, 210–19.

Gonzalez, A. and Sibayan, B.P. (1988) Policy implications and recommendations. In A. Gonzalez and B.P. Sibayan (eds) *Evaluating Bilingual Education in the Philippines (1974–1985)* (pp. 143–48). Manila: Linguistic Society of the Philippines.

Ibe, M.D. (1994) Student achievement in the New Secondary Education Curriculum (1985–1993). *BSE Research Monograph 2*. Pasig, Metro Manila: Bureau of Secondary Education, Department of Education, Culture and Sports.

Ibe, M.D. and Coronel, I.C. (1995) Determinants of the outcomes of elementary schooling under the program for decentralized educational development. *TANGLAW* 3, 1–22.

Lardizabal, A.S. (1991) *Pioneer American Teachers and Philippine Education*. Quezon City: Phoenix Press.

Lingan, A. (1981) The threshold level in Pilipino as a second language. A Region II sample. Unpublished doctoral dissertation. Philippine Normal College, Manila.

Montañano, R.L. (1993) High order cognitive skills in Filipino. Towards measurable criteria for describing Cummins' CALP. *Philippine Journal of Linguistics* 24, 73–85.

Montañano, R.L. (1996) The cognitive/academic language proficiency in Filipino of honor students at two selected secondary schools. *Philippine Journal of Linguistics* 27, 1&2, 73–81.

Prator, C., Jr (1950) *Language Teaching in the Philippines. A Report*. Manila: United States Educational Foundation in the Philippines.

Santos, T. (1984) Classroom language use in selected public elementary schools in Region III. Unpublished doctoral dissertation, De La Salle University, Manila.

Sibayan, B.P. (1967) The implementation of language policy. In M. Ramos, J.V. Aguilar and B.P. Sibayan (eds) *The Determination and Implementation of Language Policy* (pp. 126–89). Quezon: Alemar-Phoenix.

Sibayan, B.P. (1982) Teaching children in two or three languages. Paper read at the Seminar on Interlanguage Processes in Language Learning and Communication in Multilingual Societies, SEAMEO Regional Language Centre, Singapore.

Sibayan, B.P. and Gonzalez, A. (1996) Post-Imperial English in the Philippines. In J. Fishman (ed.) *Post-Imperial English 1940–1990. Status Change in Former British and American Colonies and Spheres of Influence* (pp. 1–26). Berlin: Walter de Gruyter & Co.

UNESCO (1953) *The Use of the Vernacular Language in Education*. Paris: UNESCO.

Uri, G.V. (1992) Threshold level English and public school pupils: A semi-urban sampling. Unpublished masters thesis, De La Salle University, Manila.

Chapter 10

Policy, Possibility and Paradox: Indigenous Multilingualism and Education in Peru and Bolivia

NANCY H. HORNBERGER and LUIS ENRIQUE LÓPEZ

Introduction

South America, widely known as a 'Spanish-speaking' part of the world, is in fact a region of great linguistic diversity and complexity. Nowhere is this more true than in Bolivia and Peru, with more than 30 and 60 Amerindian linguistic groups, respectively. Compared to the rest of South America, Bolivia has the highest percentage of indigenous language speakers as a proportion of its total population (63%), while Peru has the highest absolute number of indigenous language speakers (6 million) (López, 1995b: 22, 36).[1] In both countries, Quechua and Aymara comprise the largest Amerindian language groups: Quechua speakers number approximately 5.2 million in Peru and 2.5 million in Bolivia and Aymara speakers about 1.6 million in Bolivia and 0.5 million in Peru; there are approximately 60,000 Guarani speakers in Bolivia (Albó, 1995), with an additional 3 million in Paraguay, Argentina, and Brazil (Grimes, 1988: 83, 87, 94, 125). In both Bolivia and Peru, numerous smaller languages, particularly Amazonian languages, make up the remaining indigenous language groups and speakers.

Both Peru and Bolivia have, in the past few decades, undertaken major education reform initiatives that seek, among other objectives, to strengthen and legitimise the indigenous languages and cultures through bilingual education programmes in multiple indigenous languages. While these cases differ somewhat from multilingual education programmes described elsewhere in this volume which explicitly seek to promote proficiency in multiple languages among students, they illustrate a number of pedagogical, sociopolitical, and linguistic issues in common. These issues may be of some importance in similar communities around the world that are contemplating or offering bilingual or multilingual education.

The indigenous languages in Bolivia and Peru have in the last quarter of the twentieth century experienced a reversal of their legal fortunes, after centuries of official prohibition and social denigration dating from the imposition of colonial rule by the Spaniards in the sixteenth century (Albó, 1977; Cerrón-Palomino, 1989; Mannheim, 1984). In 1975, Quechua was declared an official language of Peru, co-equal with Spanish. This policy was later attenuated in the Constitution of 1979, which nevertheless continued to recognise Quechua, and additionally Aymara, as official for specified regions and purposes, as well as according the 'other aboriginal languages' the status of 'cultural patrimony' (see Hornberger, 1988b for more detail). Two decades after the 1975 Quechua Officialisation, the new Peruvian Constitution of 1993 supports the application of bilingual education (Article 17) and accords official status to all Amerindian languages spoken in the country (Article 48), although to date no other specific measures have been taken and it is indeed difficult to foresee how such a co-officialisation could really go beyond a formal declaration of good will.

In Bolivia, similar recognition has been accorded to the indigenous languages, notably a 1984 government decree (*Decreto* # 20227) establishing an official Quechua Alphabet and an official Aymara Alphabet, which in fact opened possibilities for the unification of the alphabets for Quechua between Bolivia, Ecuador and Peru and of the Aymara Alphabet between Bolivia and Peru (Plaza & Albó, 1989: 84; von Gleich, 1992: 55). Additionally, in 1994 an Education Reform Act and Bylaws (*Ley* # 1565 and *Decreto* # 23950) were passed which go beyond the orthography issue, since they declared the obligation of the educational system to offer intercultural bilingual education nationwide, and for a minimum of the eight years that comprise the primary school level. Although in Bolivia there is no official language policy, *de facto* Spanish is the official language and Quechua, Aymara and Guarani are official in certain domains and particularly in education. This situation may soon change, with positive effect for other minority languages, particularly due to the social and political prestige that lowland and rainforest Amerindian language groups (hereafter referred to as East Andean linguistic groups) have gained during the past decade.

As in most of the world, so too in Bolivia and Peru, formal education has been seen as a vehicle for the implementation of language policy; thus the above policies were accompanied by or embodied in language education policies. Indeed, in both cases presented here, initiatives for bilingual education in multiple indigenous languages were embedded in larger and quite ambitious national educational reform efforts. In Peru, the 1975 Officialisation of Quechua was a sequel and complement to the 1972 nationwide Educational Reform. In Bolivia, indigenous organisation leaders, specialists and politicians are considering the need for an official national language policy to complement the principles and bylaws included in the Educational Reform Act of 1994. In both cases, the juncture of language policy and education reform has promised new possibility for the oppressed indigenous languages and their speakers.

In the Andes, in general, the historical relationship of the indigenous languages and their speakers to the schools has by and large been one of oppression and exclusion of the former by the latter (Albó, 1977). Formal education has been directly linked to socio-cultural stratification, with education serving as a source of both 'structural stability and individual change' (van den Berghe, 1978: 293). Although, in fact, only a small percentage of the population attains social advancement through formal education, schooling, and the Spanish language with which it is identified, are nevertheless perceived as the route to social mobility.

In this context, to introduce the use of the indigenous languages into formal education produces paradox, at the very least. Specifically, there are tensions and contradictions inherent in transforming what has been and continues to be a tool for standardisation and national unification into, simultaneously, a vehicle for diversification and emancipation.[2] The challenges of bilingual and multilingual education are often seen as primarily technical – having to do with the development of the languages involved or the availability of materials and teaching personnel; this is particularly so when the languages being introduced into education are indigenous or minority languages, and even more the case in developing countries with limited resources (see also, Cenoz, Chapter 8; Gonzalez, Chapter 9; Dutcher, Chapter 12 this volume). As we will see below, the Bolivian and Peruvian cases are replete with those kinds of challenges, many of which have been met with creativity and success. It is our contention, however, that the essential challenge of multilingual education initiatives is an ideological paradox about roles and possibilities for multiple languages and their speakers. The choices made between conflicting alternatives are ideological rather than technical ones, reflecting the tension between conflicting conceptions of education as a selective and narrowing route to elite power and as a universally available and widening route to a pluralistic society.

As is to be expected and as a result of both internal and external colonialism, the ideological paradox of an inclusive and heterogeneous education versus an exclusive, selective, and standardised one often marks the implementation of cultural and educational policies and projects, once they proceed beyond the level of declarations and legal instruments. This has indeed occurred and could also happen in the future in the two cases chosen for this chapter. In Peru, for example, the 1975 official recognition of the Quechua language constitutes an excellent example of how a law, no matter how well intentioned and technically and politically conceived, represents very little if grass root organisations, the vernacular speakers themselves, and especially those who speak the dominant language do not feel touched by it and are not willing to participate in a change that should ideally involve a multilingual society at large and not only those who speak the languages of lesser prestige. In Bolivia, the inclusion of bilingual education measures in the Educational Reform and of a new school language policy responded to a social demand that had been growing since the country re-adopted a democratic system in the early 1980s (López, 1995c). However, the application of the new linguistic measures constitutes a real challenge for Bolivian society in general, and its social and political organisations in particular, since all Bolivian children, whether vernacular speaking, bilingual or monolingual in Spanish, will be affected by the new school policy. Will the fact that the government has now chosen to go beyond ideology and seeks to change the linguistic structure of society and the exercise of linguistic rights by the minorities enjoy the same social response as when those same rights were only at the level of political arguments and demands one had yet to fight for?

To analyse issues such as these, we describe two major educational initiatives in multilingual settings: the Experimental Bilingual Education Project of Puno, Peru, carried out in the 1980s; and the National Education Reform of Bolivia, in progress in the 1990s. In doing so, we will pay particular attention to their handling of multiple indigenous languages and cultures. In our concluding discussion, we will compare and contrast these two initiatives, in terms of the technical challenges they encounter, the ideological alternatives they represent, and the implications they have for multilingual education initiatives everywhere.

Experimental Bilingual Education Project of Puno, Peru in the 1980s

Peru's 1972 Education Reform had the intention of creating an educational system that would build up the Peruvian nation along humanistic, democratic, and nationalistic lines; and proposed a 'flexible and diversified education that would take into account the social and regional variety of the nation, without giving privilege to any particular member, but with a broad spirit of justice' (Pozzi-Escot, 1981: 113; our translation). The Reform called for profound transformation of pedagogical principles, attitudes, and practices within the school system, a transformation to be implemented by, among others, reorganisation of the educational system into three levels (initial, basic, and higher), decentralisation through the nationwide application of the nuclear school concept, educational extension, and bilingual education.

The 1972 Reform Law provided the rationale for the inclusion of bilingual education: '[There is a] need to overcome the present violent hispanicisation and disparagement of the aboriginal languages by means of the system of bilingual literacy teaching as a preliminary process to easier, surer, and permanent hispanicisation and the understanding and recognition of the cultural patterns of each group' (*Decreto Ley* # 19326). Note that the overriding consideration for including bilingual education was to draw the indigenous groups into the Peruvian mainstream efficiently. It was never clear, however, what this mainstream culture was to be like. Considering the political orientations of the various phases of the Military Revolutionary Government of the time and the nationalistic spirit that ruled the country, surely there was no intention of reproducing the colonial and neocolonial structures that undermined the presence of the poor, the peasant and the indigenous of Peru.

Nonetheless, it would be fair to say that while there was a concern to recognise the rights of the indigenous peoples, the indigenous languages and cultures were not in themselves really seen as true resources – not for their speakers, and much less for the national society as a whole. However, both politicians and intellectuals who supported the new policies hoped that the new legislation would contribute to a drastic change in the highly socially and linguistically stratified Peruvian society so as to foster not only tolerance and respect among language groups but also a new Peruvian culture where Quechua and other indigenous languages and cultures could play an important role in both rural and urban areas of the country (Escobar *et al.*, 1975).

Following the promulgation of the National Bilingual Education Policy (1972), approval of the Bylaws for Bilingual Education (1973), and the creation of the Bilingual Education Unit at the Ministry of Education in Lima (1973), bilingual education units were opened and projects set up in various Quechua-speaking regions of Peru. In the Department of Puno, the Puno Experimental Bilingual Education Project (*Proyecto Experimental de Educación Bilingüe – Puno*, hereafter, PEEB, or the Puno Project) began work in 1977 and operated through the 1980s, with tripartite support from the Peruvian Ministry of Education through its National Institute for Educational Research and Development (*Instituto Nacional de Investigación y Desarrollo de la Educación*, or INIDE), the Departmental Board of Education of Puno, and the (West) German Agency for Technical Cooperation (*Deutsche Gesellschaft für Technische Zusammenarbeit* or GTZ).

From the outset, the Puno Experimental Bilingual Education Project was, in a general sense and despite its name, a multilingual, rather than strictly bilingual, effort. This was so because it sought to implement the use of Aymara and Quechua as well as Spanish as both media and subjects of instruction in the schools of Puno. The area of responsibility of the PEEB was the Department of Puno, one of the most highly indigenous areas of Peru, with large numbers of both Aymara and Quechua speakers. Of a total population (over five years of age) of 750,000 at that time, close to 380,000 (or 50%) had Quechua and 295,000 (or 39%) had Aymara as their indigenous language (1981 Census, as cited by López, 1988: 85). Broadly speaking, the Aymara areas are those both north and south of Lake Titicaca and south of the city of Puno, while the remaining areas are all Quechua. The PEEB set out to provide bilingual primary education to monolingual children in their indigenous first language and Spanish-as-a-second-language, for both the Quechua- and Aymara-speaking areas. However, no efforts were made to accommodate to the various communicative needs of children living in areas where more than one vernacular was spoken, since the implementation of multilingual education at the individual school level was never considered as one of the aims of the Project.

The Quechua and Aymara components of the PEEB operated essentially in parallel. There were separate work teams for each area, as far as native-speaking teachers and local consultants were concerned, but the specialists (both foreign and Peruvian) worked simultaneously with both language areas. Thus, specialists in each curriculum area developed essentially the same curriculum for use with both Quechua and Aymara, and specialists developing indigenous language materials worked in both Aymara and Quechua, always in close collaboration with native Aymara- and Quechua-speaking colleagues.

The PEEB began implementation in 100 schools in 1980. Participating schools were selected by Project personnel according to community-based criteria – such as degree of Quechua/Aymara monolingualism, socioeconomic and educational situation, exposure to and participation in development programmes; and teacher-related criteria – such as level of training, knowledge of Quechua/Aymara, and experience in rural schools. The PEEB was introduced in the first grade during the 1980 school year, and one grade was added each year thereafter, up to and including the sixth and final year of primary school. In the early grades, language arts (reading and writing), mathematics, and the social and natural sciences were all taught in the first language, and students also received instruction in Spanish-as-a-second-language. Reading in Spanish was introduced in the second grade, and the proportion of subject matter taught through the medium of Spanish was gradually increased in the upper primary grades, with instruction through the indigenous first language maintained alongside.

Throughout the 1980s, PEEB coverage reached approximately 4% of the primary school-aged Quechua- or Aymara-speaking population in Puno (López, 1988: 84). A promising initiative of the late 1980s to expand PEEB coverage to hundreds of thousands of children in the Department of Puno and the other southern highland departments of Peru (Apurímac, Arequipa, Ayacucho, Cuzco, and Huancavelica) was aborted when the World Bank stopped loans to Peru in 1989 (cf. López, 1995b: 38).

The work of the PEEB has been described at length elsewhere (Hornberger, 1988a; Jung, 1992; Jung *et al.*, 1989; López, 1988; Milk & López, 1986; Rockwell *et al.*, 1989); it will suffice here to review briefly the five areas of Project activities: research, curriculum, educational materials production, teacher professional development, and community outreach. Our review will pay particular attention to the ways in which the PEEB addressed the two indigenous languages and cultures within their compass, with a view to later highlighting the relevance of this case for multilingual education initiatives elsewhere.

Research

Research included sociolinguistic surveys of the Quechua and Aymara areas, investigations preceding textbook production in each curriculum area, and research on the validity of the bilingual education model itself through observation, survey, and testing in selected PEEB and non-PEEB schools. It is worth noting that earlier experimental bilingual education projects in highland Peru had more often been informed by linguistic, rather than sociolinguistic, research; the PEEB surveys are also noteworthy for the depth and breadth of their coverage (Büttner, 1980; PEEB, 1979).

Similarly, and although more related to curriculum design and educational materials preparation, reference must be made to studies undertaken in the Quechua and Aymara areas to describe the language spoken by five and six year olds before entering the school system. Quechua and Aymara children's speech was recorded in interactions carried out between children and interviewers entirely in the indigenous language; the stories, songs, riddles, and other talk thus recorded were later transcribed and served as a database on the form and content of the children's vocabulary (cf. Châtry-Komarek, 1987: chap. III). Prior to these studies, primers and other textbooks prepared for indigenous bilingual education experiments in Peru had been based on general linguistic descriptions and on the information shared by informants and textbook writers.

Curriculum

Curriculum design involved the incremental development of each area of curriculum (language, mathematics, natural science, social science), one grade at a time, in consonance with both existing curriculum objectives emanating from the Ministry of Education at the national level and the objectives of the PEEB itself. A significant attempt was made to incorporate indigenous knowledge into every area of the curriculum. In practice, this meant that curriculum specialists carried out field research in the communities both before and during development of their curricular approach. As a result, the mathematics curriculum, for example, makes extensive use of a teaching aid especially designed for the PEEB: the *yupana* (Quechua) or *jakhuñataki* (Aymara), an abacus adapted from what is thought to have been an Inca method of calculation (Burns Glynn, 1981: 30; Villavicencio, 1983a,b).

Similarly, the reading materials in the first language present not only the indigenous languages, but also indigenous cultural practices; for example, at the back of the Grade 2 language text *Ayllunchis*, there is a series of readings, one for each month of the year, depicting traditional community practices associated with the agricultural cycle and the celebration of various fiestas throughout the year. As one parent who had stated he was opposed to bilingual education perused this text with one of us, he commented that if young people today would follow some of the traditions described, there would not be so many problems in the communities; he ended by stating, 'If this is bilingual education, I'm in favor of it!'.

Educational materials production

Textbook and educational materials production followed an essentially uniform procedure in each curriculum area, based on cyclical repetition of three essential steps: basic research, drafting (and later revising) the material, and trial use in schools. The work was carried out by teams, each of which aimed to include a spectrum of specialists, including linguists, anthropologists, sociologists, pedagogical, curricular and materials specialists, artists/illustrators, and native Quechua/Aymara-speaking rural teachers (Châtry-Komarek, 1987: 29–30). The Project was prolific and successful in producing texts, particularly those for the natural/social sciences and for first language instruction (Châtry-Komarek, 1987).

Both the initial research and later trialing uses in communities and schools had significant impact on the materials produced; for example the initial reader in Quechua underwent major revision between its first and second versions (Châtry-Komarek, 1987: 19–24). Similarly, as far as the curriculum and textbooks for the natural and social sciences, not only was the content based on themes from indigenous community life, but the eventual combining of the two curricular areas into one (for the first three years of primary school) was largely impelled by the indigenous world view, in which the natural and social orders are seen as integral and inseparable (cf. Dietschy-Scheiterle, 1988; Minssen & Dietschy-Scheiterle, 1987; Valiente, 1988).

It is worth pointing out that the PEEB was the first educational enterprise in Latin America to produce textbooks both in the Amerindian languages involved as well as in Spanish-as-a-second-language for all six years of primary school. Prior experiments had stopped producing materials in the vernacular after the first two years and others had done so after Grade 4. As we will see, the strategy followed by the PEEB in the area of materials preparation was coherent with the view and model of bilingual education adopted by the Project. Furthermore, both the commitment to the use and development of more than one language throughout the years of primary schooling and the strategy of using a corps of curriculum specialists to develop materials in more than one language simultaneously are useful principles applicable to multilingual education initiatives everywhere.

Teacher professional development

Training and supervision of teaching personnel was carried out chiefly through two types of activity: (1) the *seminario* or *cursillo* (short course) for PEEB teaching personnel held in the month before the beginning of the school year; and (2) *seguimiento* (follow-up), consisting of two to three-day visits by PEEB staff teams to each PEEB school once or twice during the year. The PEEB had an uphill battle drawing on teachers' linguistic and cultural knowledge to incorporate and strengthen indigenous language and culture in curriculum and instruction. This was so despite the fact that most Puno teachers were native Quechua or Aymara speakers. In the first place, local practice in assigning teachers to schools took no account of teachers' linguistic knowledge in determining placements. Thus Quechua-speaking teachers were often assigned to Aymara-speaking areas, and vice versa. This, combined with the high turnover rate of teaching personnel in the rural schools (due to teachers' near-universal preference for transfer to more urban areas), meant that the PEEB could not reliably expect continuity of teachers in all the classrooms of all the PEEB schools at all times, even if both predecessor and successor were native Quechua/Aymara speakers. Secondly, although teachers might speak Quechua or Aymara, they had never encountered these languages in written form and in formal settings such as those typical of the learning-teaching process; thus they required training before they could be expected to teach these languages as subject and use them as media of instruction. The need for training was partially addressed through the *cursillos* and *seguimiento* mentioned above; yet this also became a source of frustration, since the PEEB would no sooner train a cohort of teachers than they would be transferred out of the PEEB schools. This latter fact had its positive side too, however, since it contributed to a faster dissemination of certain bilingual education practices among Puno teachers (Rockwell *et al.*, 1989).

The Project also sought other ways to provide teachers with the education necessary to transform their everyday teaching practice. Two successful efforts in this regard were a specialisation in bilingual education at Puno's Normal School, initiated in 1983, and a graduate programme in Andean Linguistics and Education at Puno's National University of the Altiplano, started in 1985. Both of these programmes enrolled significant numbers of students over the next several years, and several of the graduates of the latter programme went on to play important roles in indigenous literature production as well as in the expansion of bilingual education in Bolivia and Peru.

The Normal School programme placed emphasis on the introduction of reading and writing in Quechua/Aymara, the history and culture of the Quechua/Aymara peoples, the Quechua/Aymara language, and exposure to bilingual education theories and practice. Additionally, the University programme introduced students to knowledge of descriptive linguistics, sociolinguistics, applied linguistics relevant to the teaching of and in an indigenous and a dominant language, and to pedagogical and curricular theories and practices necessary for the design, implementation and evaluation of bilingual education programmes. As we shall see later on, through this particular component, the Puno Project largely transcended its initial coverage and undertakings and its influence can still be felt both within Peru and in neighbouring countries.

Community outreach

Community outreach, the fifth and final category of PEEB activities, included a variety of approaches, such as 30-minute serial radio programmes, donations of school furniture, community collaboration in Project investigations, and informative seminars for community leaders. While the original intent here was to 'teach' the communities about the advantages of bilingual education, these efforts to communicate with the communities eventually led to processes of dialogue, which in turn led to increasing collaboration and incorporation of indigenous perspectives in the Project's work. This change was evident in the inclusion of community attitude as one criterion for selection of schools, the extension of Quechua/Aymara materials production to include a series of books on indigenous culture for a post-literate readership, and endorsement of the PEEB by such community-based entities as the Federation of Peasants or Catholic priests and pastoral agents.

Despite the change in orientation towards community participation in the course of the development of the Project, it is important to point out that the approach followed by the Project was a top-to-bottom one and the involvement of parents and community leaders in decision-making was never part of the overall Project strategy. On the one hand, the time was not propitious for innovations of this type, either in Peru or in Puno,[3] and, on the other hand, the mere fact of being an official Ministry of Education Project inhibited Project staff from undertaking more challenging initiatives which no doubt would have contributed to greater community involvement and ultimately the survival of the Project.

Outcomes

Academic, cultural, and political outcomes of the Project have been assessed, by both qualitative and quantitative means. Principal among evaluations of the Project are the PEEB's internal evaluations, summarised by López (1988: 97–99); Hornberger's 1982–83 ethnographic study focusing on the Quechua side of the Project (1988a, 1989a), an evaluation study carried out by a team from the Educational Research Department of the National Polytechnic Institute of Mexico (Rockwell *et al.*; 1989); and a comparative study carried out by post-graduate students in the Andean Linguistics and Education programme in collaboration with GTZ specialists (Jung *et al.*, 1989).

Among the academic outcomes of the Project was a notable improvement in communication of academic content that resulted from increased use of the indigenous languages in the classroom. This was observed by Hornberger in her study of schools in the Quechua-speaking area and was characterised in terms of greater use of Quechua, a more linguistically complete Quechua, more Quechua for primary communication, more Quechua for information content, and far more written Quechua in PEEB classrooms than in non-PEEB classrooms. Improved communication of academic content was evidenced by improved student participation in oral, reading and writing activities and by improved teacher techniques, such as the use of copying assignments for reinforcement rather than as a principal means of instruction, emphasis on logic and reasoning rather than step-following and numeral manipulation in arithmetic, and systematic and separate treatment of Spanish phonology rather than allowing it to interfere with content (Hornberger 1987, 1989b).

In addition to these academic outcomes, the studies point to broader cultural and political outcomes, as well, such as: positive influence on teachers, community members, and the general public in terms of achieving understanding and acceptance of bilingual education; greater awareness among Project personnel of the meaning and role of indigenous cultures; increased use and appreciation of the indigenous languages not only in the schools but in other public domains as a consequence of their presence in the schools; and contributions toward the development of written Quechua/Aymara literatures (Jung, 1992: 131–33; López, 1988: 97–9).

Beyond the outcomes for the students, schools, and communities immediately involved, outcomes of the Project were also felt at national and international levels. We noted earlier that the 1972 Education Reform which served as a backdrop to the PEEB emphasised the role of bilingual education as a means to achieve a less violent hispanicisation of indigenous language speakers; the 1973 National Bilingual Education Policy contained a similar emphasis and posited an essentially transitional model of bilingual education. Early PEEB documents adopted these perspectives on indigenous language as a problem and on bilingual education as transitional, but by the early 1980s a different orientation began to emerge (Hornberger, 1988b; Ruiz, 1984). Distinguishing between transitional and maintenance bilingual education, the PEEB authors of *Modelo de Educación Bilingüe – Puno* (1982), pointed out that the choice to teach only in Spanish implies a policy of hispanicisation; the choice of transitional bilingual education implies a policy of assimilation; and the choice of maintenance bilingual education implies a policy of national integration based on respect for all ethnic groups. They went on to outline a number of long-term effects to which they hoped the maintenance bilingual education model would contribute, including: the development of the indigenous languages, the production of written material in the indigenous languages, cultural integration, the overcoming of social discrimination, reduction of illiteracy, and better use of educational opportunities.

Ironically, as the PEEB moved more firmly toward a language-as-right orientation (Ruiz, 1984) and the concomitant maintenance model of bilingual education (Hornberger, 1991), official language policy in Peru moved in the opposite direction, away from the understanding of language-as-resource that had been evident in the 1975 Officialisation of Quechua, back toward a view of language-as-problem (Hornberger, 1988b; Ruiz, 1984). During the remainder of the 1980s, referred to by social scientists as the 'lost decade' due to the economic failure and social decomposition Peru experienced under the APRA government of Alan García (von Gleich, 1992: 60), the official climate for bilingual education worsened, and when PEEB was eventually dismantled in 1990, official bilingual education in Peru was severely affected since the public sector did not have either the financial resources nor the professional personnel and expertise to go on with bilingual education experiments. In 1992, the Bilingual Education Directorate which in 1988 had succeeded the Bilingual Education Unit created in 1973, was dismantled under the restructuration of the Ministry of Education. This occurred despite the fact that a year earlier a new and thoroughly updated Bilingual Education Policy which to a large extent reflected PEEB's orientation and influence had been approved. A new institutional transformation of the Ministry of Education in 1996 re-established a Bilingual Education Unit as part of the National Directorate of Primary Education, implying that intercultural bilingual education should restrict itself to primary education. Gone are the days when Peruvian academics thought intercultural bilingual education could become an important cross-sectional component of the Peruvian educational system and permeate all levels and modalities of Peruvian education. PEEB's admirable record of success in overcoming numerous technical challenges to present a panorama of new possibilities in indigenous education was not enough to overcome the weight of political failure (Hornberger, 1987).

At the same time, however, more than a dozen bilingual education projects have arisen out of private initiatives and as a result of the involvement of both local and international non-governmental organisations and foundations. The new projects emerged both in Puno and in other vernacular speaking areas, such as Apurímac, Cuzco and Huancavelica. Although of minor scope and coverage, such initiatives generated more local attention and to a certain extent offered better and more realistic possibilities for the development of bilingual education in the Quechua- and Aymara-speaking areas of Peru. The new projects drew on the experience and knowledge accumulated and generated by the PEEB and a few of them began their experiments using the textbooks produced in Puno.

Further, the activities initiated by the PEEB at the Normal School of Puno and at the National University of the Altiplano did not stop when the Project came to an end. Although the Project, as such, stopped its activities in Puno in 1990, the University of Puno continues offering the MA in Andean Linguistics and Education and in September 1996 started the sixth class with 21 professionals – out of 75 applicants – from Arequipa, Cuzco and Puno. As with the primary school activities, the Normal School and University programme initiatives were also replicated, modified, and enriched in other areas of the country. Between 1991 and 1992, the Ministry of Education developed a teacher education curriculum for a specialisation in intercultural bilingual education, to be offered in 10 different normal schools located both west and east of the Andes. The new specialised curriculum relied extensively on the experience gathered in Puno. In three of these Normal Schools, University of

Puno graduates are involved in the implementation of the new curricula. In addition, in 1996, a former director of the Puno graduate programme started a new professional programme, the Andean University College of Cuzco, which offers post-graduate training in Andean Linguistics and Bilingual Education geared to both Peruvian and foreign students.

The fact that some of the PEEB products and the spirit it inspired in Peruvian bilingual education have been recreated by others and that many of the professionals prepared by academic sub-programmes sponsored by the Project are involved in the development of bilingual education in Peru and in neighbouring countries, raises the question whether the Project in fact failed politically or not. The Puno legacy has been a key determinant for the present and future of intercultural bilingual education in Peru, and indeed beyond Peru (Nietta Lindenberg-Montes, personal communication, 1996), even though very little may be happening in any of the schools that the experimental Project served.

The Puno experience offers a number of useful lessons for multilingual education initiatives, particularly those involving indigenous or other minority languages. Among these lessons are the practical responses to technical linguistic and pedagogical challenges, in particular those arising from introducing hitherto largely unwritten languages into the schools. These responses included sociolinguistic surveys and field-based studies of children's speech carried out in order to identify characteristics and patterns of use of the language to inform curriculum development, a cyclical research/draft/trial approach to materials production, and the deployment of a specialist team that worked across more than one language at a time in curriculum and materials development. Other lessons stem from philosophical or ideological stances taken by the Project with respect to the local language being introduced into the school, namely the commitment to use and develop the language throughout all the years of primary school, and the explicit attention to incorporating local linguistic and cultural knowledge into the curriculum. Finally, the case exemplifies the importance of community participation and a favourable political climate for long-term survival of any particular educational programme, while also demonstrating the possibility of spin-off effects (in terms of personnel, materials, and a vision of bi/multilingual education, for example) which can ultimately have a great impact.

National Educational Reform and Popular Participation in Bolivia in the 1990s

We turn now to another case of indigenous education in a multilingual context, the Bolivian National Education Reform of July 1994. The Reform envisions far-reaching institutional and curricular change with the twin goals of making Bolivian education fully intercultural and participatory (López, 1995b: 63). It seeks to make Bolivian education more reflective of Bolivian society in both its long-standing linguistic and cultural diversity and its newly promoted popular participation (see below).

This initiative differs from the Puno case in both scale and complexity. While the Puno initiative was, from the very beginning, regarded as an 'experiment' which encompassed the introduction of two indigenous languages (alongside Spanish) as subjects and media of instruction in a small sample of selected schools of one Peruvian department, the Bolivian initiative consists of a comprehensive transformation of the educational system – including the introduction of *all* of Bolivia's indigenous languages (alongside Spanish) as subjects and media of instruction in *all* Bolivian schools. The PEEB was designed and implemented on a trial basis in search of pedagogical and linguistic answers to improving the educational success of indigenous children. In contrast, the Bolivian Reform, although also a pedagogical and sociolinguistic endeavour, was regarded from the outset as a political measure aiming at radical transformation not only of the educational system, but also of Bolivian society.

Given these differences, the two initiatives also vary in orientation toward the indigenous languages and cultures. Whereas the PEEB Project operated in a vacillating national policy context where indigenous languages and cultures were regarded as, alternately, a problem needing to be surmounted, a right for indigenous peoples, or a resource for the nation as a whole, the 1994 Bolivian Education Reform adopted a clear language-as-resource stance from the outset (see López, 1996a for a summary of the Reform). Such a radical view was possible because the new measures, in fact, responded to an ongoing process of self-discovery and recognition that Bolivian society had been experiencing since 1982, when the country re-adopted a democratic system.

What is interesting to note is that despite such profound differences, the Bolivian process took advantage of the lessons and findings of the Puno experience. Both personnel and material resources were shared across these two initiatives. For example, a small corps of Bolivian indigenous language specialists who had helped their Peruvian and German PEEB colleagues, particularly with teacher training and materials production, now brought their experience and expertise to the Reform. In addition, by the time the Bolivian Reform got under way in the schools in 1995, most of the approximately 70 Bolivian rural teachers who had studied in the Puno graduate applied linguistics programme were incorporated into the Reform at national, regional and local levels. Finally, some of the texts, materials, and methodological guides produced in Puno were included in the classroom and school libraries which are part of the Bolivian Reform.

Bolivia's president and vice-president (the first indigenous vice-president in the Americas) have made the Education Reform, and in particular its intercultural, bilingual and participatory aspects, a top priority of their government. That, combined with unusual support from both vernacular and dominant language speakers, and significant amounts of expertise and funding from international development agencies and banks, bodes well for the successful implementation of the intercultural bilingual education schemes within the Reform.

On the institutional side, the Reform seeks to guarantee transparency, democracy and accountability in the educational system through new mechanisms of decentralisation and community involvement in the everyday running of the school. For the first time, indigenous parents, male and female, will take part in decision-making about the educational system.

In this regard, it is important to realise that the Educational Reform is part of a series of structural changes in Bolivia, among which the Popular Participation Process, launched in 1994, deserves special mention. The Popular Participation Act promotes political decentralisation and the devolution of power; accords official recognition to indigenous traditional authorities; fosters the organisation of indigenous municipalities; and transfers responsibilities and financial resources to local municipalities and grass roots organisations to enable them to make investments in their education and health plans. Such changes in policy are particularly important in a country where 85% of the municipalities are rural and thus in large degree indigenous. Bolivian indigenous, or 'originary' peoples, as they would rather be called, have the possibility for the first time in modern times to take active part in decision-making and in the determination of local policies regarding themselves and also all those who although non-indigenous live or work in an indigenous sphere (López, 1996b: 7

ff.). The changes are taking place so rapidly that in the last municipal elections of 1995, out of approximately 3000 mayors or city councillors elected by popular vote, nearly 500 of them are and recognise themselves as indigenous.

The Popular Participation Act and the Education Reform are an indivisible dyad; together, the two laws constitute the institutional cement for the construction of a new state in which pluralism is seen as a resource and not a problem (López, 1995d: 87). In Bolivia, the form that democracy will take in a predominantly indigenous multiethnic society is at stake. The Popular Participation Process promotes participatory decision-making. Transforming education is crucial to this process because it is both pre-requisite for and integral to that participation; cooperative and participatory pedagogy is in turn seen as a new condition for learning. In the words of former Bolivian Minister of Human Development Enrique Ipiña, 'We have discovered that to survive as a nation and to reach real and just development, we must devolve and redistribute power, knowledge and possibility' (personal communication).

The devolution of power will perhaps allow indigenous and non-indigenous Bolivians to surmount the many problems they will face in constructing a truly bilingual and intercultural education in a multiethnic society. The implementation of the new policies and bylaws in the more linguistically complex and diversified socio-cultural settings, such as those that characterise Amazonian or East Andean Bolivia for example, will certainly require the educational system to go beyond bilingualism to generate various types of multilingual education. Similarly to what happens in other lowland indigenous settings of South America, Bolivian East Andean language minority groups are multilingual and resort to more than two languages to satisfy their basic communicative needs. In such a context and due to the participatory emphasis of the new educational system, one can easily foresee the emergence of pedagogical innovations that include the use of at least two vernaculars – or 'originary' languages as the indigenous peoples prefer to call them – alongside Spanish.

Although the Reform is complex and multi-faceted, we will focus below only on selected aspects of greatest relevance to our topic, indigenous multilingualism and education, using the same five categories of activity we used in reviewing the PEEB.

Research

'Interculturalism for all' is a slogan that clearly characterises the Bolivian Educational Reform. For this to happen in a predominantly indigenous and oral society such as the Bolivian one, popular participation in the educational decision-making process is fundamental. For this reason, the new Bolivian education places emphasis on the identification and ongoing reconsideration of the people's basic learning needs.

Basic learning needs were initially identified and defined in assemblies in which parents (both male and female), local authorities (traditional and political), and local institutions expressed themselves as to the functions and roles the local school should play in the development of the community. In such a context, intercultural bilingual education and even intercultural multilingual education naturally emerged as a demand due to its close relationship, on the one hand, with local needs and ways of being and, on the other, with the need to establish and maintain communicative contact with others beyond the borders of the local community. This process of consultation is scheduled to go on periodically as Reform plans advance, so as to obtain ongoing feedback from the communities themselves. The new curriculum considers the Reform itself as an ongoing communicative process in which communities, parents, teachers and students engage in a continuing re-elaboration of educational content and procedures and, while doing so, are engaged in meaningful interaction in which the vernacular languages assume new roles and functions.

This new orientation is not the result of illuminated professionals but rather of a process of trial-and-error that included the active participation of local communities and grassroots organisations. This has taken place in rural areas of Bolivia for over a decade in conjunction with the implementation of various pedagogical projects and innovations, among which the following deserve special mention: a nationwide literacy campaign in Quechua and Aymara which took place between 1983 and 1988; a multigrade project implemented in almost 4000 rural schools between 1985 and 1995; a successful UNICEF-sponsored intercultural bilingual education programme implemented in 140 Quechua, Aymara and Guarani schools from 1988 to 1995; and the successful Guarani literacy campaign and guaranisation process carried out between 1992 and 1993 by the *Asamblea del Pueblo Guarani* 'Guarani People's Assembly' (López, 1996c).

In addition to the accumulated knowledge from these experiences in Bolivia and the Puno Project, there is also a body of linguistic and sociolinguistic research to draw on. Prime among the research endeavours explicitly commissioned by the Reform is a sociolinguistic mapping of Bolivian society carried out by Xavier Albó in 1993 and 1994 (Albó, 1994).

Curriculum

On the curricular side, the Reform places the learner at the centre of the educational process and emphasises modifications to social relationships in classrooms and schools through changes in pedagogical practice, the reorganisation of classrooms, the reconsideration of learning time and space, and the use of learning modules, learning centres, and cooperative learning strategies. In this regard, the Reform pursues a new educational structure organised in cycles in which learners are grouped according to their personal rhythm and modes of learning. The new Bolivian curriculum promotes the development of an open, active, flexible, cooperative, permanently evaluated and periodically revised educational system. It promotes the implementation of a new pedagogical organisation grounded in flexibility, and an open classroom orientation. It is also based on a concept of the classroom as the principal site of cultural negotiation and meaningful interaction where participatory and cooperative modes of learning contribute to the development of learner autonomy.

The curriculum is designed to incorporate local, indigenous knowledge and to include the indigenous languages as languages of instruction. The dynamically structured curriculum consists of competency standards established at both national and local levels, denominated *tronco común* 'common trunk' and *ramas diversificadas* 'diversified branches' (or *ramas complementarias* 'complementary branches') respectively. The intention behind the two-tiered trunk-and-branch curriculum is that it will allow for the incorporation of local knowledge and ways of knowing, through a feedback process from the branches to the trunk. Thus, the Reform explicitly foresees and invites the inclusion of indigenous knowledge and culture in the national curriculum. Similarly, the inclusion of Quechua, Aymara, Guarani, and other Bolivian indigenous languages as languages of instruction is intended for both indigenous language speakers and Spanish speakers nationwide. For the first time, Bolivians encounter a real possibility for two-way intercultural education.

Generally, it is assumed, and widely accepted in Latin America, that intercultural bilingual education strategies are convenient and necessary to promote educational quality in indigenous areas. Very seldom, however, do educational systems recognise the need for the non-indigenous peoples to learn about indigenous knowledge and cultural and artistic traits. Experience has shown that for bilingual education to prosper it needs at least a sympathetic milieu in which the non-indigenous people learn not only to tolerate but also to respect and understand cultural and linguistic differences. The Bolivian curriculum goes in this latter direction.

Educational materials production

Inclusion of the indigenous languages as subjects and media of instruction is a fundamental aspect of the Reform. To this end, teaching/learning modules are being developed for each of the indigenous languages. The learning modules constitute a new and key unit of learning and teaching for all areas of the curriculum. Modules for the teaching of and in Quechua, Aymara, Guarani, and Spanish-as-a-second-language are currently under development (eight modules for each language for the first cycle – i.e. the first three years of primary education). In these modules, students work with activity-based, integrated materials in mathematics and their first language, in which (alongside content of the specific discipline), topics related to natural and social sciences are integrated. The integration of content and the globalisation of learning are key concepts which materials producers have taken into account in accord with the holistic views of the indigenous cultures and current theories of learning and teaching. The modules promote peer interaction and negotiation about problems to be solved and, hence, promote the development of oral competencies in the students' first language. They also include indigenous knowledge which is presented in Spanish only for monolingual Spanish-speaking children or in any of the indigenous languages. Although based on a common structure, each set of modules is different from its equivalent in a different language. That is, the modules in any of the indigenous languages are not translations of a prior version previously agreed to and written in Spanish, as used to be the case in most bilingual education projects.

The modules for the indigenous languages are being developed by native speakers of the languages who have had extensive classroom experience and a degree of pedagogical and linguistic training. The modules thus have the potential to contribute doubly to the strengthening of indigenous language and culture – by providing a vehicle for native authorship as well as for children's learning. Some have expressed concern that the specialists developing the language modules have limited training in pedagogy or linguistics. Indeed, this reflects the scarcity of specially trained personnel. As a result, the Reform has designed ongoing learning experiences in which young Bolivian professionals learn and specialise in a given field (e.g. linguistics, or mathematics education) while attempting to transform the educational system; this experience takes place under the guidance and advice of foreign professionals who accompany the process from time to time.

In the case of Quechua and Aymara, the materials developers can and do draw on prior linguistic, sociolinguistic and applied linguistic knowledge and experience that has accumulated in the Andes over at least the past three decades, as well as on materials developed, not only by the Puno PEEB, but also in experimental bilingual education projects carried out in Bolivia beginning in the 1970s (Plaza & Albó, 1989). They can also rely on a growing number of publications in indigenous languages and on the Quechua and Aymara children's literature books included in the classroom library programme of the Reform.

In the case of Guarani, modules writers can and do resort to the series of Guarani and Spanish-as-a-second-language textbooks produced in the 1990s under the auspices of the UNICEF project mentioned earlier. They also draw on the experience they gained as teachers in bilingual classrooms and when they were involved in the successful participatory literacy campaign carried out between 1992 and 1993 (López, 1996c). In contrast to their Quechua and Aymara colleagues, the Guarani writers are confronted with more unresolved linguistic questions since the development of Guarani linguistic studies lags behind that of Quechua and Aymara.[4]

Work in the other indigenous languages is comprised at present largely of orthographic and lexical development; this is a step prior to materials production. Although the Reform had planned to include other smaller linguistic groups (about 30) in a second phase to start in the year 2002, social pressure and the political prestige enjoyed by Amazonian and East Andean ethnic organisations moved this work into the first phase. The smaller number of speakers of these 'other' indigenous languages, the insufficient scientific knowledge about the languages (and cultures), and the generalised social and political commitment of these populations and their organisations with regard to their languages and cultures and to the Reform obligated the Reform to put together an emergency plan for them.

The plan comprises, on the strictly linguistic side, the education of young and informed speakers of the languages as field linguists and at the same time an appeal to the academic world to help and study these languages *with* the linguistic communities and the indigenous researchers they have appointed and commissioned to carry out the study of their languages.[5] On the pedagogical side, the plan includes the preparation of indigenous writers of educational materials who will, in interaction and cooperation with Reform specialists who have gained experience with the preparation of modules in any of the four major Bolivian languages and together with other indigenous writers, prepare learning modules for all of the other languages. Finally, on the side of materials production, the plan recurs to the creation of five regional centres, which the Reform will set up and equip for the local production and printing of educational materials. The institutions involved are also including specific courses in educational materials preparation and use for indigenous researchers and writers. These smaller language communities pose a tremendous challenge from a variety of angles. It is possible that once the indigenous communities have produced materials in their own language, they will also see the need for books and materials in other languages with which they are in constant interaction. Hence, the Reform may need to consider multilingual education and a way of institutionalising it.

Teacher professional development

Crucial to the successful implementation of the Education Reform will be the participation of willing and informed teachers. The Reform foresees the importance of teachers in the success of the large-scale curricular change envisioned and proposes an active pedagogical support network to that end. Key players in this support network are the pedagogical advisers. This new corps of educational professionals is made up of 500 experienced teachers drawn from across the nation who are given special training and charged with providing support nationwide to Bolivia's in-service teachers in the implementation of the Reform.

Particularly challenging for teachers and advisers alike is the use of the indigenous languages in the classrooms. Importantly, the first hour of each morning of the pedagogical advisers' seven-month training course was dedicated to classes in the indigenous languages. These classes were geared toward both raising awareness about the languages and providing the necessary technical skills (e.g. grammar, writing) to teach and use them in work with teachers in the schools. Teachers for these classes were drawn from the ranks of the pedagogical advisers themselves, among whom is a growing expertise on indigenous languages. For example, the two teachers of the more advanced Quechua class were graduates of the Puno Andean Linguistics and Education programme. Of particular interest in this class were the teachers' use of Quechua more than Spanish as medium of instruction (as well as subject), including the use of Quechua terms to designate grammatical categories; and the many spontaneous questions and contributions from the students, which revealed a reflective and wide-ranging process of inquiry into their own language.

The indigenous language classes provide grounds for optimism with regard to incorporating and strengthening the indigenous languages and cultures in education. First, the enthusiastic participation of the pedagogical advisers suggests a genuine eagerness to deepen their knowledge of the language and, as a result, increased chances that their use of the language, in both oral and written forms, will expand. Second, the very existence of such classes, and the availability of personnel to teach them, is evidence of the progress already made in the last decade in expanding the knowledge and use of these languages in new, written domains. Yet, there was also evidence of ongoing challenges. In the advanced Quechua class, there were occasional disagreements between teacher and student as to points of grammar or spelling, disagreements reflecting for the most part unresolved aspects in the process of Quechua standardisation. Further, once the pedagogical advisers are versed in these indigenous language skills, there still remains the task of ensuring that classroom teachers are equipped with the necessary knowledge and skills to teach and use indigenous languages.

One of the most important sub-programmes of the Reform is the transformation of Normal Schools into higher level education centres offering training and education comparable to that of university faculties of education. Plans provide for the reorganisation of at least six of the 24 existing Normal Schools to turn them into higher education centres where new cohorts of intercultural bilingual educators could be formed. Two of these institutes would be geared to the preparation of Aymara-speaking teachers, two for Quechua-speaking teachers, one for Guarani-speaking teachers and one would be a multilingual and multiethnic teacher training centre for the East Andean minority linguistic groups. It is possible that in these new bilingual teacher training centres, learning an indigenous language other than that spoken by the student-teachers might generate a certain type of multilingual education; Reform plans also project that student-teachers attending the remaining 18 teacher training institutions will learn the indigenous language of the region they are either studying in or where they expect to work. In both cases, multilingual education will *de facto* emerge, since in higher education Bolivian students are also required to take classes in a foreign language. This means that future teachers will study, alongside Spanish, at least one indigenous language and one foreign language. This opens up unforeseen possibilities to enrich the concept and practice of interculturalism in Bolivia.

It is also worth mentioning that as a result of the emphasis the Reform places on intercultural bilingual education two of the largest and most important universities – San Andrés in (predominantly Aymara-speaking) La Paz, and San Simón, located in a Quechua-speaking region – have recently opened new programmes to train bilingual educators. Both programmes are designed to allow primary school teachers to obtain university first-degrees (*licenciatura*) through a special complementation scheme whereby the years spent at a Normal School – an average of four – and classroom experience count for academic credit. In both programmes, in-service teachers receive, in a two- or three-year period, specialised training in disciplines related to the implementation of intercultural bilingual education. These initiatives have been imitated by other universities, public and private, in various provincial cities, and have resulted in even greater demand for the preparation of teacher trainers.

In spite of all these initiatives and in order for such a complex and long process as the Bolivian Reform to go forward, efforts will have to be made in cooperation with the universities to open specialised professional programmes in a number of academic disciplines. We have seen how in the case of the smaller indigenous languages an emergency plan was put together to partially address the lack of linguistic knowledge. The situation for the three major indigenous languages is also precarious. Strictly speaking, for example, there is no trained Bolivian linguist to attend to the scientific description of the Aymara language, despite the number of foreign researchers who have passed through Aymara communities and worked with Aymara speakers.[6] There is at present only one university in the country, San Andrés, which offers undergraduate training in linguistics and languages, and that with an as yet insufficient and unsatisfactory outcome. Bolivia needs linguists as well as anthropologists and pedagogues to carry out ambitious plans such as the ones the Educational Reform has engaged in (López, 1995a). Thus, serious attention must be paid to human resource development, going beyond activities pertaining to teacher training and the preparation of pedagogical advisers.

Community contexts and participation

Unlike the Puno Project which was intended as an experiment for selected school/communities only, the Bolivian Reform is to be applied nationwide. In keeping with its nationwide coverage and the diverse needs that entails, the Reform foresees the need for at least two modes of bilingual education – the bilingual and monolingual modes (*modalidades*, in Reform terminology).

The monolingual mode is intended primarily for the dominant Spanish-speaking population. In this mode, as its name suggests, children are taught in Spanish and receive instruction in (but not through) an indigenous language as a subject. In light of the history of severe oppression and denigration of the indigenous languages in Bolivia, this monolingual mode of bilingual education, whereby speakers of the dominant language will receive at least some instruction in an indigenous language, represents an initial step toward the possibility of truly two-way bilingual and intercultural education. Nevertheless, it remains to be seen how the specifics will be worked out. One challenge, for example, is lack of experience in teaching indigenous languages as second languages. The Reform language team intends to take advantage of the methodology being designed to teach Spanish-as-a-second-language to promote the oral acquisition of indigenous languages also. Time and effort will have to be invested to make the learning of an indigenous language attractive to children and youngsters who live in urban areas and have been accustomed to disparage indigenous language and culture. Such an effort is essential if the Reform is to embody fully the enrichment bilingual education, language-as-resource stance it espouses.

The bilingual mode of bilingual education in the Reform is directed primarily at indigenous populations. In this mode, children receive instruction through the medium of both their indigenous language and Spanish-as-a-second-language. Underlying this mode is a basic premise of the Reform – the principle that every child should have the opportunity to learn in his or her own language. This is coherent with the child-centred learning conception of the Reform which assumes that new learning should be constructed on the basis of previous knowledge and experiences acquired by the individual.

Consistent with the institutional and popular participation aspects of the Education Reform, decisions as to the mode of bilingual education to be adopted by a particular school will be made locally, at the community or *nucleo* level. Given the diversity of languages and communities involved, however, there are some difficult decisions to be made. For example, in centres of urban migration, such as El Alto, Cochabamba, and Santa Cruz, there are often monolingual Quechua, Aymara, and Spanish-speaking students, as well as various sorts of bilinguals, within a given educational nucleus or even school. In addition to such linguistically mixed communities, there are also communities (e.g. in northern Potosí and La Paz departments) undergoing shift, not just from indigenous languages to Spanish but from one indigenous language to another (Albó, 1995). The question is: in which language(s) should children in these communities be taught? In other words, although it may be clear that the bilingual mode is mandated for such schools, the choice of languages within the mode is far from clear and will necessarily be worked out on a case-by-case basis. Indeed, the situations described above may move the Reform toward inclusion of multilingual, as well as bilingual, programmes at school and community levels.

In fact, to date, little is known about which linguistic and pedagogic strategies are most appropriate and effective with these diverse linguistic combinations. Experiences gained in the Americas in the last four or five decades of indigenous bilingual education have generally been restricted to contexts of indigenous monolingualism or of incipient bilingualism, in line with the tradition of transitional bilingual policies. The real challenge occurs when, as in the Bolivian case, the aim is not to transition students into all Spanish classes, but to maintain and develop their indigenous languages. It is in this context that one becomes acutely aware that there can be no single mode of bilingual education. Reform language specialists are aware of the complexities involved and are in search of the most appropriate strategies to help local decision-makers and teachers find the right linguistic and pedagogical solution. It is also important to point out that the participatory orientation of the Reform movement will help the participants find creative solutions at the local level.

Like the Puno PEEB, the Bolivian Reform offers useful pedagogical, linguistic, and sociopolitical lessons for other multilingual education initiatives elsewhere. The trunk-and-branch feedback design of the curriculum, the collaborative approach to linguistic research and materials development wherein community members share their expertise while acquiring new knowledge from outside experts and vice versa, and the participatory orientation which allows for community-level decision-making as to a monolingual, bilingual (or possibly multilingual) mode of bilingual education, are all model strategies for the incorporation of multiple languages in education.

Paradox and Possibility

In his review of the sociolinguistic foundations of bilingual education, Fishman points out that:

> many problems currently faced in conjunction with bilingual education's socio-educational legitimisation (and operationalisation) of languages/varieties hitherto unrecognised for formal educational purposes ['marked languages'] were previously faced (and overcome) by vernaculars that sought and achieved such recognition in the 17th, 18th, 19th, and early 20th centuries. (1982: 4)

Among these problems, he mentions status disadvantages of the language; corpus disadvantages of the language; unavailability of teachers and lack of texts, educational materials and curricula; and non-local control. Both of the education reform initiatives described above have made significant headway in confronting a number of these linguistic, pedagogical, and sociopolitical issues as they seek to incorporate multiple indigenous languages in education. Below we will review their accomplishments, according to Fishman's four categories, paying special attention to implications for multilingual education initiatives elsewhere.

Status disadvantages of the marked language refers to the fact that it is often viewed as a flawed instrument – inelegant, deformed, and backward. Although the Bolivian and Peruvian indigenous languages and their speakers have traditionally been oppressed and marginalised and have indeed been subject to such attitudes, we have seen that the bilingual education initiatives described here were accompanied by broader language policies and educational reforms aimed at improving the status of the indigenous languages and their speakers. We have also seen that, even within the context of a vacillating language policy at the national level, the Puno Project had favourable impact on the status of Quechua and Aymara in Puno, as evidenced by the greater use of Quechua/Aymara in the schools and other public domains, the development of written literature in Quechua/Aymara, and the greater acceptance of bilingual education among teachers, communities, and the general public. We have also noted the more fully committed Bolivian policy stance, as compared to Peruvian policy, a commitment which, if sustained, can be predicted to have a highly favourable impact on the strengthening of Bolivia's indigenous languages and cultures.

With respect to multilingual education in particular, it should perhaps be mentioned that, in both cases, the differing degrees of recognition bestowed on the larger indigenous languages, Quechua, Aymara and Guaraní, as compared to the many smaller languages, is sure to have an effect on implementation of the languages as subjects and media of instruction. It is possible to foresee conflict and the need for negotiation when a smaller indigenous group meets up against a larger one, as may happen, for example, in the mixed linguistic communities becoming increasingly common due to urban migration patterns in Bolivia.

Corpus disadvantages of the marked languages include, for example, the lack of a standardised orthography or grammar, and/or lexical poverty with respect to matters of science, technology, and higher level abstractions (Fishman, 1982: 4; see also Gonzalez, Chapter 9; Dutcher, Chapter 12 this volume). Here again, significant advances have been made with respect to Quechua, Aymara and Guaraní (see, for example, Godenzzi, 1992; Hornberger, 1995 on Quechua; *Lengua, Nación y Mundo Andino*, 1987, on Quechua and Aymara; López, 1996c, on Guarani); but the smaller languages have farther to go in terms of developing their corpus.

This is not to say that issues of language standardisation are entirely resolved for the larger languages, either. A tension arises here between local authenticity and broader standardisation. In the Peruvian case, the PEEB experienced critical reactions to the Quechua/Aymara texts in some cases where linguistic usage varied from one community to another, even within the Department of Puno; such concerns can be expected (and are likely to be even more exaggerated) in any contemplated dissemination of the PEEB texts to an expanded radius of Quechua communities throughout several southern Peruvian departments. In the Bolivian case, at least one Aymarista voice of concern has already been raised with respect to the dominance of the urban La Paz variety of Aymara (with its tendency to borrow heavily from Spanish) in educational materials and radio programmes (Yapita, 1995).

With respect to multilingual education, a particular concern must be the relative status of the languages introduced as second and third languages, *vis-à-vis* the first. For example, where an indigenous (or ethnic) language is taught alongside a foreign language (as is projected for the case of the Bolivian Normal Schools, above), the status difference between the languages may inhibit motivation for learning the ethnic language, unless specific measures are taken to counterbalance its status and corpus disadvantages.

Fishman goes on to note that the legitimisation of marked languages is further rendered difficult by the unavailability of teachers trained to (or wanting to) function as professionals using these languages and by the lack of suitable texts, educational materials, and curricula (see also Nunan & Lam, Chapter 6; Gonzalez, Chapter 9; Dutcher, Chapter 12 this volume). Relevant here is that the materials be reflective not only of the language but also of local culture. We have seen above that the PEEB explicitly sought not only to contribute to the development of the indigenous languages, but also to be informed by and incorporate local knowledge and ways of knowing, in every one of its activity areas. We have also seen that they succeeded, to a very great degree: one anthropologist's evaluation of the PEEB materials noted that 'essential elements of Andean culture have been presented with respect and understanding, in such a way as to facilitate students' conscious identification of their own world' (Jung, 1992: 121; our translation). Nevertheless, in the final evaluation of the Project, there was also recognition of a need for: (1) greater conceptual clarity in the treatment of culture in Project materials; and (2) more participatory and collaborative relationships with the indigenous communities (Jung, 1992: 132–33).

In this regard, it cannot be emphasised enough that in the Bolivian case, interculturalism constitutes, along with popular participation, the most crucial and fundamental piece of the entire Education Reform. The opening paragraph of Decree #23950 states that the Education Reform conceives of interculturalism as 'a resource and comparative advantage by which to promote a new and harmonious personal and social development for all of the nation's students, as well as to build a national educational system that, at one and the same time, assures unity and respects, recognises, and values diversity' (our translation). We have noted above the intended incorporation not only of the indigenous languages, but also of local, indigenous knowledge. What remains to be seen is how these intentions work out in reality.

With respect to multilingual education, the example of the East Andean communities in Bolivia is instructive. We noted above that these smaller, multilingual communities pose a challenge for the Reform in that they may well need materials development in multiple indigenous languages simultaneously, a need which the Reform will certainly have to address and for which the regional print centres may serve a facilitating purpose.

As for professional development, we have also seen significant accomplishments in both the Peruvian and the Bolivian initiatives, above all in the development of expertise within the indigenous population. Significant here for multilingual education initiatives everywhere is the value of involving local authors in materials development, such that a dual function is served of providing educational materials while also developing local authorship (and ultimately, literature). Furthermore, University, Normal School, and pedagogical adviser programmes such as those described here are all viable models for professional development in multilingual education.

Finally, Fishman mentions that education using ethnically marked languages has tended not to be substantially controlled by the speech communities served. The Peruvian and Bolivian cases above are no exception to this tendency. In both cases, the indigenous educational initiative has emanated from a national policy level, with significant technical advice and financial support from international development agencies. Indeed, in the Peruvian case, we have seen that in the early years, the selection of schools to participate in the Project occurred without regard to community preference; we have also noted, however, that this underwent change over time. Not only did PEEB personnel begin to take community attitude into account, but also communities who had observed the successes of the PEEB in neighbouring schools began to request that it be implemented in their own. While this is still a long way from a self-generated or collaborative effort to incorporate indigenous language and culture in the schools (such as is currently happening in some communities in Ecuador, Hornberger & King, 1996), it nevertheless represents an increasing level of community input to the indigenous multilingual educational programme.

In the Bolivian case, too, the Education Reform emanates from the national level. However, there is a difference here in terms of community participation and control. We have mentioned several times the participatory, or popular participation, aspect of the Education Reform. It is also important to note that, although the Education Reform was formulated at the highest levels of government, it has origins and antecedents in long-standing calls for a linguistically and culturally relevant education from popular organisations and unions (López, 1995b: 22). The tradition of popular activism in Bolivia, the newly instituted mechanisms of popular participation created by the Law of Popular Participation, and the specific provisions for community-level decision-making that are part of the Education Reform, all promise new possibilities for local, indigenous control of educational alternatives. We have already seen that these participatory decision-making processes may well lead to multilingual education initiatives in both the traditionally multilingual lowland East Andean communities and the increasingly mixed linguistic communities in centres of urban migration.

The linguistic, pedagogical, and sociopolitical issues reviewed above comprise a set of technical challenges which are being addressed, and will most likely need to be addressed to one degree or another, in almost any multilingual education initiative. Yet, we maintain that for these initiatives and for multilingual education everywhere, the essential challenge is the ideological paradox with which we opened this paper – the tension between education as a selective and narrowing route to elite power and education as a universally available and widening route to a pluralistic society.

Indigenous communities have long recognised education's role in gaining access to social mobility and power; and have usually 'construed the formal education they have been offered by outside agents as a means of acquiring the language(s) of prestige and power' (Freeland, 1995: 254). Many communities, including the Miskitu of Nicaragua about whom Freeland writes, have, as a consequence, resisted education in the indigenous language 'when offered as part of "outgroup" originated education' (Freeland, 1995: 254). Yet, that is only one option. For those who pursue the alternative, the paradoxical challenge is to incorporate their knowledge and ways of knowing into formal education, without losing them. Fishman puts the paradox this way:

> The school serving minority-group children is in reality a two-edged sword, even when it is minority-community controlled. It leads away, out of, and in a sense, partially undermines the very community it ostensibly serves. (1984: 55)

Throughout the Americas and in other parts of the world, indigenous communities are increasingly taking on the challenge of using formal education as a vehicle, not just for social advancement, but also for their own linguistic and cultural revitalisation (for examples in North, Central, and South America, see Hornberger, 1996; for examples in the Philippines and Eritrea, see Gonzalez, Chapter 9; Dutcher, Chapter 12 this volume). The Peruvian and Bolivian initiatives described here have the potential to do the same.

Yet, we would like to emphasise that the paradoxical challenge is not just for indigenous (or other minority) communities but also for the nation. 'Until this century formal education for indigenous people ... was reserved for the very few,' serving as an 'institutionalised conduit for the channelling into indigenous society, of the language, culture, and values of the nation-state' (Howard-Malverde & Canessa, 1995: 231, 241). Under such conditions, the elite remained firmly in control. In contrast, as can be clearly seen when comparing the Peruvian and Bolivian cases described here, to the degree that a nation seeks to incorporate more and diverse linguistic and cultural traditions within one educational system (and one polity, for that matter), complexity increases in apparently geometric proportions. In a truly egalitarian multilingual education initiative, the voice of the formerly powerful elite can easily be drowned out by the multiple voices of others. Unless that elite is truly committed to pluralism, it is unlikely to long pursue such an endeavour, unless sufficient pressure (whether global, national, or local) is brought to bear to do so.

We have called this an ideological paradox; why ideological? Because it is fundamentally about conceptions of the roles and possibilities for indigenous peoples (and all peoples), their languages and cultures. If to educate is 'to draw out' (from the Latin *educare*), the paradox is that it is so not only in the sense of 'to draw away' – i.e. to lead forth from current experience and understanding to new knowledge and skills, but also in the sense of 'to draw forth' – i.e. to bring out the experience, understanding, knowledge and skills already there. It is this paradoxical challenge which (indigenous) multilingual education must meet if it is to realise the possibilities it promises.

Notes

1. Indigenous languages are defined here as those languages which were already spoken in South America at the time of the sixteenth-century encounter with Europeans and their languages (primarily Spanish and Portuguese).
2. See Freeland and Howard-Malverde (1995) for a discussion of the role of linguistic homogenisation and of education in achieving political unification in Latin America.
3. The implementation of PEEB activities in the 1980s coincided with the growing influence of the Maoist Shining Path movement in the region. This seriously affected Project activities, particularly during the last three years of the Project.
4. The support received by Bartomeu Meliá, a Guarani specialist living in Paraguay, has been particularly important in on-the-job training sessions organised for the teachers working in the Guarani bilingual education project.

5. This work began, in fact, in 1995, when three linguists were invited to work for a semester with informed speakers and leaders of 10 linguistic groups. The linguists were Colette Grinevald (fomerly Craig) of the University of Oregon, and two of her graduate students (Pilar Valenzuela from Peru, and Alejandra Vidal from Argentina), who responded to a request made by Reform authorities via the Harvard Institute for International Development. This work led to the development of nine generally accepted orthographies and 10 teams of indigenous researchers who could start promoting the approved alphabets as well as producing basic reading materials.

An expanded team of linguists (again led by Colette Grinevald, by then at the University of Lyon in France) returned in 1996 and worked with another 10 indigenous teams. Among the tasks realised at this time were: a study of nasalisation in the Guarani languages in order to help improve the Guarani writing system; a course in basic general linguistics and indigenous language writing offered to 35 indigenous researchers from the 20 teams; and additional work with three indigenous teachers (a Besuro speaker and two Moxeño speakers) who had received basic training in linguistics and bilingual education at the University of Puno.

Additional courses will follow in 1998 and it is expected that by the year 2000 Bolivia will be able to count on pedagogical grammars and dictionaries prepared with the direct involvement and participation of the indigenous teams. At the same time, it is anticipated that some or all of the invited linguists will become involved with the Bolivian minority languages and will continue working with them. In the spirit and practice of popular participation, a given linguistic community would give permission to a linguist to study their language only if he/she would commit him/herself to educating and permanently advising that community's language team.

6. The second Bolivian with a PhD in linguistics might come out in 1998 from the University of Liverpool: Pedro Plaza, a Quechua specialist who is now working on a dissertation on language and power in bilingual education. The first, Xavier Albó, a Bolivian sociolinguist originally from Catalunya, has devoted himself to sociolinguistics and anthropology, after obtaining his degree from Cornell University in the early 1970s.

References

Albó, X. (1977) *El Futuro de los Idiomas Oprimidos en los Andes*. Lima, Peru: Centro de Investigación de Lingüística Aplicada, University of San Marcos.

Albó, X. (1994) *Bolivia Plurilingüe: Una Guía para Educadores y Planificadores*. Vols I, II, III. La Paz: CIPCA/UNICEF.

Albó, X. (1995) Educar para una Bolivia plurilingüe. *Cuarto Intermedio* 35, 3–37.

Burns Glynn, W. (1981) La escritura de los Incas: Una introducción a la clave de la escritura secreta de los Incas. *Boletín de Lima*, 12, 13, 14.

Büttner, T. (1980) Diagnóstico Aymara. Unpublished manuscript.

Cerrón-Palomino, R. (1989) Language policy in Peru: A historical overview. *International Journal of the Sociology of Language* 77, 11–33.

Châtry-Komarek, M. (1987) *Libros de Lectura Para Niños de Lengua Vernácula:*

A Partir de una Experiencia Interdisciplinaria en el Altiplano Peruano. Eschborn, Germany: GTZ-Deutsche Gesellschaft Für Technische Zusammenarbeit.

Dietschy-Scheiterle, A. (1988) La enseñanza de las ciencias naturales en el Proyecto Experimental de Educación Bilingüe de Puno/Perú. Unpublished manuscript.

Escobar, A., Matos Mar, J. and Alberti, G. (1975) *Peru, ¿país bilingüe?* Lima, Peru: Instituto de Estudios Peruanos.

Fishman, J. (1982) Sociolinguistic foundations of bilingual education. *Bilingual Review/Revista Bilingüe* 9, 1–35.

Fishman, J. (1984) Minority mother tongues in education. *Prospects* 14, 51–6.

Freeland, J. (1995) 'Why go to school to learn Miskitu?': Changing constructs of bilingualism, education and literacy among the Miskitu of Nicaragua's Atlantic coast. *International Journal of Educational Development* 15, 245–61.

Freeland, J. and Howard-Malverde, R. (1995) Multilingualism, education and politics in Latin America. *International Journal of Educational Development* 15, 205–7.

Godenzzi, J.C. (ed.) (1992) *El Quechua en Debate: Ideología, Normalización, y Enseñanza.* Cusco, Peru: Centro Bartolomé de Las Casas.

Grimes, B.F. (ed.) (1988) *Ethnologue: Languages of the World.* Dallas, Texas: Summer Institute of Linguistics.

Hornberger, N.H. (1987) Bilingual education success, but policy failure. *Language in Society* 16, 205–26.

Hornberger, N.H. (1988a) *Bilingual Education and Language Maintenance: A Southern Peruvian Quechua Case.* Berlin: Mouton.

Hornberger, N.H. (1988b) Language planning orientations and bilingual education in Peru. *Language Problems and Language Planning* 12, 14–29.

Hornberger, N.H. (1989a) *Haku Yachaywasiman: La Educación Bilingüe y el Futuro del Quechua en Puno.* Lima and Puno, Peru: Programa de Educación Bilingüe de Puno.

Hornberger, N.H. (1989b) Pupil participation and teacher techniques: Criteria for success in a Peruvian bilingual education program for Quechua children. *International Journal of the Sociology of Language* 77, 35–53.

Hornberger, N.H. (1991) Extending enrichment bilingual education: Revisiting typologies and redirecting policy. In O. García (ed.) *Bilingual Education: Focusschrift in Honor of Joshua A. Fishman on the Occasion of his 65th Birthday* (pp. 215–34). Amsterdam/Philadelphia: Benjamins.

Hornberger, N.H. (1995) Five vowels or three? Linguistics and politics in Quechua language planning in Peru. In J.W. Tollefson (ed.) *Power and Inequality in Language Education* (pp. 187–205). Cambridge and New York: Cambridge University Press.

Hornberger, N.H. (ed.) (1996) *Indigenous Literacies in the Americas: Language Planning from the Bottom up.* Berlin: Mouton.

Hornberger, N.H. and King, K. (1996) Bringing the language forward: School-based initiatives for Quechua language revitalization in Ecuador and Bolivia. In N.H. Hornberger (ed.) *Indigenous Literacies in the Americas: Language Planning from the Bottom up* (pp. 299–319). Berlin: Mouton.

Howard-Malverde, R. and Canessa, A. (1995) The school in the Quechua and Aymara communities of highland Bolivia. *International Journal of Educational Development* 15, 231–43.

Jung, I., Urban, C. and Serrano, J. (eds) (1989) *Aprendiendo a Mirar: Una Investigación de Lingüística Aplicada y Educación.* Lima and Puno, Peru: Universidad Nacional del Altiplano-Puno and Programa de Educación Bilingüe de Puno.

Jung, I. (1992) *Conflicto Cultural y Educación: El Proyecto de Educación Bilingüe Puno/Perú.* Quito, Ecuador: Proyecto Educación Bilingüe Intercultural and Ediciones Abya-Yala.

Lengua, Nación y Mundo Andino (1987). *Allpanchis* 29/30. Entire issue.

López, L.E. (1988) Balance y perspectivas de la educación bilingüe en Puno. In L.E. López (ed.) *Pesquisas en Lingüística Andina* (pp. 79–106). Lima and Puno, Peru: Consejo Nacional de Ciencia y Tecnología, Universidad Nacional del Altiplano-Puno, and GTZ-Sociedad Alemana de Cooperación Técnica.

López, L.E. (1995a) Intercultural bilingual education and the training of human resources: Lessons for Bolivia from the Latin American experience. In R. Gagliardi (ed.) *Teacher Training and Multiculturalism* (pp. 25–56). Geneva: International Bureau of Education.

López, L.E. (1995b) *La educación en Areas Indígenas de América Latina: Apreciaciones Comparativas desde la Educación Bilingüe Intercultural.* Guatemala: Centro de Estudios de la Cultura Maya.

López, L.E. (1995c) La educación intercultural bilingüe en Bolivia. Ambito para el ejercicio de los derechos lingüísticos y culturales indígenas. *In Cultura de Guatemala* XVI. Special Number: Seminario Internacional sobre Oficialización de los Idiomas de los Pueblos Originarios de América Vols I and II. Vol. 1, 145–200. Guatemala City: Universidad Rafael Landívar.

López, L.E. (1995d) Sigue el debate sobre EIB. *Cuarto Intermedio* 36, 78–100.

López, L.E. (1996a) An ambitious but necessary adventure: The Bolivian Educational Reform. *Education News* [The Newsletter of the UNICEF Education Cluster] Issue No. 15, Vol. 6, No. 1, 30–3.

López, L.E. (1996b) Reformas del estado y política lingüística en Bolivia. *Boletín Internacional de Lenguas y Culturas Amerindias* No. 2, 3–14. Universidad de Valencia, España: Instituto Valenciano de Lengua y Cultura Amerindias.

López, L.E. (1996c) To guaranize: A verb actively conjugated by the Bolivian Guaranis. In N.H. Hornberger (ed.) *Indigenous Literacies in the Americas: Language Planning from the Bottom up* (pp. 321–53). Berlin: Mouton.

Mannheim, B. (1984) Una nación acorralada: Southern Peruvian Quechua language planning and politics in historical perspective. *Language in Society* 13, 291–309.

Milk, R. and López, L.E. (1986) A cross-national comparison of sociolinguistic contexts for bilingual education. *Journal of Multilingual and Multicultural Development* 7, 451–63.

Minssen, M. and Dietschy-Scheiterle (1987) *Ciencias Naturales en la Escuela Primaria Bilingüe en el Altiplano del Perú.* Eschborn: GTZ-Deutsche Gesellschaft Für Technische Zusammenarbeit.

Modelo de educación bilingüe – Puno (1982). Puno, Peru. Working document.

PEEB (1979) *Diagnóstico Sociolingüístico del Area Quechua del Departamento de Puno.* Lima, Peru: Instituto Nacional de Investigación y Desarrollo de la Educación.

Plaza, P. and Albó, X. (1989) Educación bilingüe y planificación lingüística en

Bolivia. *International Journal of the Sociology of Language 77*, 69–91.

Pozzi-Escot, I. (1981) La educación bilingüe en el marco legal de la Reforma Educativa Peruana. In *Acerca de la Historia y el Universo Aymara* (pp. 113–23). Lima, Peru: CIED.

Rockwell, E., Mercado, R., Muñoz, H., Pellicer, D. and Quiroz, R. (1989) *Educación Bilingüe y Realidad Escolar: Un Estudio en Escuelas Primarias Andinas*. Lima and Puno, Peru: Programa de Educación Bilingüe de Puno.

Ruiz, R. (1984) Orientations in language planning. *NABE Journal 8*, 15–34.

Valiente, T. (1988) *La Enseñanza de Ciencias Histórico Sociales*. Proyecto Experimental de Educación Bilingüe – Puno.

van den Berghe, P.L. (1978) Education, class and ethnicity in southern Peru: Revolutionary colonialism. In P.G. Altbach and G. Kelly (eds) *Education and Colonialism* (pp. 270–98). New York: Longmans.

Villavicencio, M. (1983a) Numeración, algoritmos y aplicación de relaciones numéricas y geométricas en las comunidades rurales de Puno. Unpublished manuscript.

Villavicencio, M. (1983b) *Guía Matemática 2 (Quechua-Castellano)*. Lima and Puno, Peru: Proyecto Experimental de Educación Bilingüe (experimental edition).

von Gleich, U. (1992) Changes in the status and function of Quechua. In U. Ammon and M. Hellinger (eds) *Status Change of Languages* (pp. 43–64). Berlin: Walter de Gruyter.

Yapita, J. (1995) Hacia una educación bilingüe en Bolivia. *Revista UNITAS 13/14*, 49–60.

Chapter 11
A Case Study of Multilingual Education in Canada

FRED GENESEE

In this chapter, I describe a number of multilingual schools in Montreal, Canada. These schools are based on the immersion approach to second language teaching. Second language immersion programmes were first instituted in Canadian schools in 1965 to provide English-speaking majority group children better chances of learning Canada's two official languages. As has been described repeatedly and thoroughly in numerous previous reports (Genesee, 1987a; Lambert & Tucker, 1972; Swain & Lapkin, 1982), second language instruction at the time that immersion was introduced was limited to relatively short periods of time each day and focused on teaching basic vocabulary, grammar and communication patterns. The innovation of immersion was the use of the target language to teach regular academic subjects during part of the school day. By integrating second language learning with academic instruction, it was expected that students would learn the target language in much the same way that children learn their first language – to communicate with others about meaningful and important events in their lives. Thus, in contrast to conventional second language methodology, teaching second languages in immersion programmes is incidental to teaching regular academic subject matter, and language learning is incidental to learning the academic material that is necessary to succeed in school. We can now appreciate that the Canadian immersion programmes were among the first content-based forms of second language teaching – an approach that is currently emphasised by many second and foreign language educators (Genesee, 1991; Met, Chapter 3 this volume).

The schools I describe in this chapter extended the immersion approach to promote the acquisition of two second languages: French and Hebrew, along with the students' native language, English (see Genesee & Lambert, 1983, for a complete report). Before describing the schools, I briefly describe the major sociolinguistic features of the national, provincial, and local communities in which these schools are located. I then describe the major features of the schools and the results of a longitudinal study that was undertaken to evaluate them. I go on to discuss some important general educational issues that arise when planning trilingual school programmes of the double immersion type – issues that are related to the status of the native language of the students; the timing of second and third language instruction; commitment to programme development and participation; and teacher qualifications.

The Sociolinguistic Context

The Montreal multilingual schools were private (parochial) schools serving the Jewish community which is one of the oldest in North America. It currently has a population of approximately 100,000; the population of greater Montreal is currently approximately 2,500,000. The Jewish community comprises a broad range of religious orientations and beliefs, including reform to orthodox, and it includes recent as well as early immigrants to the province. Upon immigration, members of the Jewish community have been native speakers of many languages, including French, English, Hungarian, Polish, Russian, and Portuguese. The community has made significant contributions to the cultural, economic, and political life of Montreal and the province at large, and it is a distinctive feature of life in Montreal. Through private philanthropy and public support, the community has developed a full range of services, including a public hospital, libraries, family services, theatres, and schools.

French is the only official language of the province of Quebec itself while English and French are official languages of Canada. There are two public school systems in Quebec: Catholic and Protestant, and each has French-medium and English-medium schools. Distinct Catholic and Protestant school systems were created in Quebec at the inception of Canada in 1867 in recognition of the distinct religious and cultural heritage of the majority francophone community in Quebec. Initially, all non-Catholics, including Jews, were directed toward the Protestant schools which, in effect, became non-denomination. Thus, historically, there has been a tendency for the Jewish community to align itself with the English-speaking population of Quebec.

Approximately 7000 elementary and secondary school students attend private 'parochial' schools which have been a mainstay of the Jewish community from the beginning. These schools emphasise Jewish and Hebrew language studies along with regular academic instruction in mathematics, sciences and language arts. Most parochial schools in Montreal use English predominantly as the day-to-day language of communication. There are currently 22 parochial schools at the elementary and secondary school levels.

Hebrew and French were selected as immersion languages for sociocultural reasons – Hebrew because of its evident religious, cultural, and economic importance for the participating students and their families, and French because of its social, political, and economic relevance in the day-to-day life of Quebec. Thus, the Hebrew portion of the immersion programme could be considered a case of heritage language development while the French portion could be considered immersion for acquisition of an official national and provincial language. In both cases, there are evident and significant material and social benefits for these children becoming trilingual.

The Schools

Two of the three multilingual schools are situated in central Montreal while the third school is situated in suburban Montreal; the latter is relatively young in comparison to the other two. All schools are closely affiliated with a synagogue. The schools serve students in the elementary grades (between five and 12 years of age) and, traditionally, the regular academic curriculum in each school, as prescribed by the Ministry of Education for all public schools in Quebec, was taught in English. When they adopted the immersion model of education, they chose to teach the Hebrew curriculum through Hebrew and the traditional academic curriculum (i.e. mathematics, science, social studies) through French.

Virtually all the students attending these schools are native speakers of English and live in predominantly English-speaking neighbourhoods. They come largely from middle to upper middle class families and would be considered average to above average in academic ability. They are exposed to Hebrew outside school during religious and cultural celebrations and holidays and, in some cases, during visits to Israel. Generally speaking, they do not acquire proficiency in Hebrew for other day-to-day uses. They are exposed to French on the street, in stores, and on radio and television from day-to-day; they may also hear parents, relatives and friends using

French as French is the common language of communication in many, although not all, parts of Montreal. Otherwise, English is the primary medium of communication for the students and their parents outside school. Indeed, despite some sporadic exposure to French and Hebrew, most of these children have relatively little intensive experience in French or Hebrew before coming to school.

The following description focuses on the schools at the time they were evaluated (between 1978 and 1985). The schools continue to provide multilingual instruction but with somewhat different schedules. A schematic summary of the time devoted to each language in the three schools when they were evaluated is presented in Figure 11.1. In two of the schools, all curricular instruction from kindergarten until Grades 3 or 4 was provided in the students' second languages – French and Hebrew; there was no instruction in English during these grades. I will refer to these schools as *early double immersion* schools. The French curriculum consisted of language arts, mathematics, science, and social studies – the traditional subjects of the curriculum. The Hebrew curriculum consisted of language arts, Jewish history, and religious and cultural studies. In the third school, English along with French and Hebrew were used for curriculum instruction from the beginning of schooling. I refer to this school as *delayed double immersion* because the amount of French instruction increased from five hours a week in Grade 1 to 12 hours a week in Grades 5 and 6. As a result, the amount of English and Hebrew instruction in this school decreased somewhat over the same period of time. This is an important distinction among these programmes, one that I return to later when discussing the evaluation results. The instructional personnel in these school are native speakers of English, French, and Hebrew with varying degrees of competence in the other languages.

To summarise, in two of the schools, there was no instruction through English until Grade 3 or 4 (these are called *early* double immersion); in one of the schools, English along with French and Hebrew was used for curriculum instruction from the beginning and in this case the amount of instruction through French increased from kindergarten until Grade 5; this alternative is called *delayed* double immersion.

Programme Evaluation

These schools were the object of a seven-year longitudinal evaluation (see Genesee & Lambert, 1983). Presentation of the evaluation can be summarised according to four major questions.

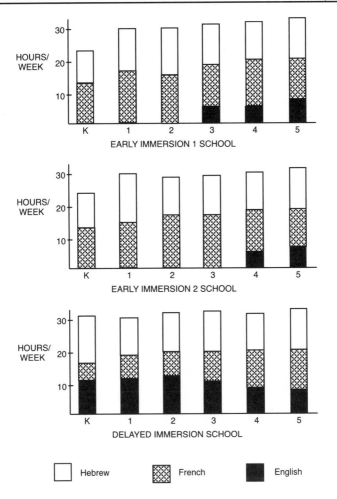

Figure 11.1 Summary of numbers of instructional hours/week in each language in each trilingual school

(1) How effective is double immersion with respect to second language learning?

Research on numerous single language immersion programmes indicates that majority language students in such programmes attain advanced levels of functional proficiency in the target language, although they do not achieve total native-like competence in the language (Genesee, 1987a; Harley, 1992). There is also evidence from evaluations of single language early immersion programmes that second language achievement is less in *partial* immersion where the first and second languages are both used as media of instruction than in *total* immersion where only the second language is used in the beginning. Interlingual interference appears to be more prevalent in immersion programmes that provide simultaneous instruction in both the first and second languages during the primary grades than in programmes that do not. It is not clear whether these results reflect the effects of instruction in two languages at the same time and/or the intrusive effects of a dominant first language on second language learning. Whatever the precise explanation, these results suggest that second language achievement might be less in the trilingual schools, especially if English language instruction is provided at all grade levels, as is the case in the delayed double immersion school.

Also related to second language achievement, researchers have found that, in general, older learners achieve the same or even higher levels of second language achievement than younger learners when learning is school-based (Genesee, 1987a). Other research has shown that this is not the case for language learning outside school settings; when learning occurs outside school, younger is usually better (Genesee, 1981). Comparisons between the early and delayed double immersion schools permitted us to assess the effects of age on the students' acquisition of French and Hebrew in these trilingual schools.

(2) Does simultaneous instruction in two second languages adversely affect first language development?

While there is no evidence that intensive second language learning impedes first language development in single immersion programmes, there is no published evidence to my knowledge concerning the effects of double immersion on first language development.

(3) What is the effect of delaying and reducing first language instruction on first language development?

In many early immersion programmes of the single language variety, instruction in the first language begins in Grade 2 or 3 for some 20% of the school day and often increases to 60% of total instructional time by the end of elementary school (Genesee, 1978). To date, we have found no discernible negative impact on first language development as a result of participation in these programmes. Similarly, Genesee *et al.*, (1985) found that there was no impairment in the English language development of students attending an immersion programme in which English was not introduced until Grade 4 and was taught for only two-and-a-half hours a week in Grades 4, 5 and 6. It is important to point out that these results have been obtained for students who are native speakers of dominant, majority group languages; it cannot be assumed that the same would be true for speakers of non-dominant or minority group languages, such as Basque (see Cenoz, Chapter 8 this volume). In any case, the question arises: would native language development be impaired in trilingual schools that delay instruction in the native language until Grade 4 and provide reduced native language instruction thereafter?

(4) What effect does academic instruction through the medium of two non-native languages have on academic achievement?
The evidence from single immersion programmes has indicated quite consistently that academic achievement does not suffer from instruction via a second language. Can one expect the same for double immersion programmes?

Research design

In order to answer these questions, a battery of tests was administered to students in: (1) all three double immersion programmes; (2) early total immersion schools where French was the only second language; and (3) in English-medium schools. We monitored the progress of the students from kindergarten until the end of Grade 6. Results for the end of Grade 5, the last year when the most complete set of results are available, are reported here. The assessment battery included tests of: (1) English language development; (2) French language proficiency; (3) Hebrew language proficiency; and (4) mathematics achievement. The second language assessment batteries included tests of reading, speaking, and listening. All students in all the schools were native speakers of English. It is important to point out before reviewing the results that the students in all five schools were comparable with respect to general intellectual ability, as determined by standardised tests of intelligence. When the groups were not naturally equivalent, their test results were adjusted using analysis of covariance techniques to statistically account for differences in intellectual ability.

Results

Question 1: How effective is double immersion with respect to second language learning?
This question was addressed by looking at the acquisition of French and Hebrew as second languages; each language was examined separately. With respect to French, the French language

achievement of students in all three double immersion schools was compared to that of comparable groups of students in single immersion programmes. This comparison makes it possible to assess second language learning when there is simultaneous instruction in two second languages, as in the double immersion schools, in comparison with schools where curriculum instruction is conducted in only one second language, as in single immersion schools. We found that, in general, the *early* double immersion students performed as well as the students in the single immersion programme on the French language tests. We also found that there was a tendency for students in the *delayed* double immersion school to score somewhat lower than the others. The rank order of performance for these groups, from highest to lowest, was roughly: **early DI = single immersion > delayed DI**. Thus, early double immersion was as effective as early single immersion, but delayed double immersion was somewhat less effective than early double or early single immersion.

With respect to Hebrew, the Hebrew language achievement of students in the *early* double immersion schools was compared with that of students in the *delayed* double immersion school. The amount of Hebrew language instruction was virtually the same in all three schools. What differed was whether instruction through the native language was present at the beginning or delayed until later. Thus, this comparison allowed us to assess second language achievement in schools that provide equivalent amounts of instruction in a second language but have instruction in the native language from the beginning or delay it to the middle grades. We found that there was a tendency for the *delayed* immersion students to score lower on the Hebrew language tests than the *early* immersion students despite the fact that both groups had had equivalent exposure to Hebrew. These results, along with the French results, suggest that the use of the native language during the early grades of double immersion programmes may interfere with second language learning.

Question 2: Does simultaneous instruction in two second languages adversely affect first language development?

This question was addressed by comparing the English language test results of the double immersion students to those of students in the single immersion programme and to those of students in the all-English programme. There was no evidence that the English language achievement of the double immersion students suffered as a result of participation in the double immersion programme. These findings are consistent with all other evaluations of immersion programmes in

Canada which indicate that English-speaking students do not experience any negative effects to native language development as a result
of immersion (Genesee, 1987a; Lambert & Tucker, 1972; Swain &
Lapkin, 1982).

Question 3: What is the effect of delaying and reducing first language instruction on first language development?

The results pertinent to this question include comparisons between
the two early double immersion programmes – it will be recalled that
in one of these English was not introduced until Grade 4, whereas in
the other school it was introduced in Grade 3. Also relevant to this
question are comparisons between the two early double immersion
schools and the single immersion schools – the early double
immersion schools provided less instruction in English than did the
single immersion schools. Again, there was no evidence that delaying
or reducing instruction in English had any harmful effects on the
double immersion students' native language development. In fact,
these students scored a full grade level above their actual grade level
on most of the tests.

Question 4: What effect does academic instruction through the medium of two non-native languages have on academic achievement?

Here we compared the performance of the early double immersion
students with that of the delayed double immersion students – the
early double immersion students received math instruction in French
while the delayed students received math instruction in English.
There were no significant differences between the groups, indicating
that acquisition of academic skills was not impaired by the double
immersion experience. These results are consistent with evaluations
of academic achievement in single immersion programmes.

Summary

The results of this evaluation indicate that these double immersion
school programmes were effective in promoting proficiency in two
second languages. This was evident in comparisons between the
trilingual school students and students in immersion programmes of
the single language variety and it was especially evident in the case of
the double immersion schools that did not include the use of the
students' native language during the primary grades. That the early
double immersion schools were as effective as the single immersion

schools is particularly striking since the former, in fact, provided less exposure to French than the latter.

There is evidence from evaluations of other immersion programmes that more time in the second language does not always predict more success in second language learning. For example, comparisons of early and late French immersion programmes in Montreal have shown that two-year late immersion programmes can be as effective as early total immersion programmes despite the fact that the late immersion programmes offer considerably less exposure to the second language (Genesee, 1981). Clearly the quality of instruction and the nature of the pedagogy used to teach the language are important factors. Research by Stevens (1983) compared the second language achievement of students in a partial late immersion programme in Montreal with a student-centred, activity-based pedagogical approach to that of students in a conventional total late immersion programme that was teacher-centred and curriculum driven. She found that students in the activity-based programme attained the same levels of second language proficiency as the students in the other programme despite the fact that the student-centred programme provided approximately half as much exposure to the second language.

It is also possible that the French language development of the double immersion students profited from the simultaneous development of skills in French *and* Hebrew. A number of researchers and theoreticians have argued that there are certain cognitive and linguistic advantages associated with bilingualism, particularly if advanced levels of proficiency in the second language are attained (e.g. Ben-Zeev, 1977; Cummins, 1976; Peal & Lambert, 1962; Cenoz & Genesee, Chapter 2 this volume). It might be that the more complex linguistic demands of double immersion in comparison to single immersion promotes general language learning strategies that enhance language acquisition.

Another noteworthy finding from this evaluation was the general tendency for students in the *delayed* double immersion schools to perform less well in both of their second languages than students in the *early* double immersion programme. The advantage of the early immersion students cannot be accounted for entirely in terms of time, because in the case of Hebrew all students had the same amount of exposure to Hebrew. Although we have no definitive explanation of these findings, it is possible that the use of the students' native language, English, impeded or interfered in some way with their second language learning. More specifically, it is possible that when the native language is used there is linguistic interference and/or a type of psycholinguistic dependency on the native language that is not evident when it is absent from the curriculum.

Finally, these results indicate clearly that the native language development and academic achievement of these English-speaking students was not impaired by schooling through two non-native languages. In addition, there was no evidence that the use of English early on, as in the delayed double immersion school, resulted in any significant advantages for the students in those schools. In other words, more English exposure did not result in higher levels of proficiency in English. In addition, as just noted, the use of English early on may even have impeded second language development to some extent. These results are entirely consistent with other research on the impact of immersion on English-speaking children.

General Educational Considerations

I now turn to a number of issues arising from these multilingual schools that deserve consideration by others who may be considering the development of similar trilingual programmes elsewhere. These issues concern: (1) the social status of the languages in question; (2) sequencing and timing of immersion in the second languages; (3) commitment; and (4) teacher qualifications.

(1) Language status

As noted earlier, the students in these multilingual schools were from predominantly middle to upper middle-class homes and would be considered average to above average in academic ability. The question arises: Would these results obtain in schools with students who are less academically and socioeconomically advantaged than the students in these schools? I know of no research at this time that permits an answer to this question. It is also important to point out that the Montreal students were members of a majority cultural group with a socioculturally dominant first language (English). The evaluation results just reported must be interpreted with this feature in mind. More specifically, there was no doubt that these students' first language would survive and continue to be an important medium of social, political and economic communication in their families, communities and the larger world. Such linguistic security is not necessarily the case for students from minority ethnolinguistic groups whose language and culture are not so widely supported and may even be at risk of survival in the community (e.g. Basque, Welsh, or Maori) (see Byram, Chapter 5 this volume).

The status of students' native language can have important implications for the programming of language use in double immersion programmes (Cummins, 1981; Lambert, 1980). To be more specific, while the use of majority group students' native language is not necessary during the primary grades to ensure its normal development, such may not be the case for students who come to school speaking a minority group language that is not widely used or supported outside school (see Cenoz, Chapter 8; Hornberger & López, Chapter 10 this volume). In these cases, the following modifications to the Montreal model may be advisable: (1) incorporate use of the native language into the primary grades of the programme and, in particular, promote literacy in the native language from the outset; (2) provide immersion in only one second language during the primary grades, phasing in literacy development in this language so that it does not coincide with literacy development in the native language; and (3) delay immersion in the other second language until the senior elementary or early secondary grades once full development of the native language has been ensured and advanced levels of proficiency in the initial second language has been achieved.

These recommendations are desirable for a number of reasons. First, they would serve to ensure normal development and use of the students' native language which might otherwise be at risk. This is a matter of both individual and social importance. The recommendation to include the students' native language in the programme from the beginning appears to contradict the results of the present research. However, in my opinion, the risk that use of the native language might interfere with second language learning is off-set by the beneficial effects that would result from the native language development of minority language students. Second, these modifications would reduce the risk of interference in literacy development that can occur if two second languages or three languages are taught simultaneously. The Hebrew–French double immersion schools in Montreal found it necessary to stagger literacy instruction in Hebrew, French and English in order to reduce the possibility of such interference. The risks of interference are potentially higher in the case of languages such as Spanish, Basque, French and/or English because of their orthographic similarities. Third, concentrating immersion in one second language at a time will better ensure that students acquire sufficient proficiency in each language to master complex academic skills and knowledge that are taught through those languages. The double immersion programmes in Montreal had extended their schedule to as much as 32 hours per week in order to accommodate all the demands of trilingual instruction. Phasing in intensive use of each second language in multilingual schools might not require such an extensive school week. However, this is an empirical question that requires investigation. Fourth, the provision of qualified staff and appropriate instructional materials and programme management is streamlined somewhat in multilingual programmes that stagger introduction of the languages.

(2) Timing of immersion in the second languages

Related to the preceding issue is that of timing: what are the consequences of delaying immersion in one second language until the late elementary or early secondary grades? The evaluation of the Hebrew–French immersion schools in Montreal indicated that delayed second language instruction was somewhat less effective than early double immersion Thus, the recommendation to delay immersion in one second language until the secondary grades would appear to run contrary to these results. However, there are reasons to believe that the findings from the Hebrew–French double immersion programmes are specific to these schools. First, numerous other studies of late immersion programmes have indicated that late immersion can be as effective as early immersion (see Genesee, 1987b, for a review). For example, research in Montreal has found that students in two-year late French immersion programmes achieve the same levels of proficiency in French as students in early total immersion programmes despite the fact that the late immersion students had had considerably less exposure to French (Genesee, 1981). Moreover, as Stevens' evaluation of the student-centred late immersion programme demonstrated, less exposure to a second language in school can be compensated for by innovative pedagogy (Day & Shapson, 1991; Lyster, 1994; Swain & Carroll, 1987). Intensive and effective late immersion can be more efficient than early immersion, an important factor to take into account in multilingual education where there is even greater demands made on instructional time. Finally, as noted earlier, delaying immersion in one second language until the early secondary grades would have the added advantages of freeing up time to devote to native language instruction, streamlining programme administration, and facilitating the development of professional staff and instructional materials.

(3) Commitment

The effectiveness of multilingual education is critically dependent on commitment – commitment both from the students and their families and from programme developers and school administrators. Let me explain each of these briefly.

The beneficial effects of bi- and multilingual education are cumulative and are realised only if there is participation for a number of grades, preferably six or seven. Students who do not remain in the programme for its entirety will not acquire the impressive levels of second language proficiency that have been reported in the case of single immersion; they will not acquire sufficient proficiency in the second languages to master advanced academic material; and they will not necessarily show positive transfer to first language development, as has been reported by some researchers (e.g. Cummins, 1978). The success of double immersion, especially a programme that delays intensive use of one of the second languages until later grades, is critically dependent on long-term participation. Parents must be made aware of the importance of such commitment. In a related vein, it is not desirable to admit students to such programmes after the first or second grade since they are likely to lack the accumulated language skills needed to keep up with other students.

Long-term participation by students in multilingual school programmes, in turn, is critically dependent on the provision of a full range of student services, including remedial and enriched forms of special education. In other words, if students are to remain in the programme for its entire duration, they must have available to them all of the support systems that permit them to do this. For some students, this means remedial services; for others, enrichment opportunities. This calls for programme developers and school administrators who believe in and are committed to the programme so that they provide such services. As well, implementation of multilingual education extending over the elementary and secondary grades calls for coordination of secondary and elementary levels of education; this is not always easy in school systems where these two levels of education function autonomously.

(4) Teacher qualifications

Finally, effective multilingual education calls for qualified teachers. Teachers working in multilingual schools where language and content instruction are integrated face the dual challenge of teaching the academic curriculum and a second language at the same time (see also Met, Chapter 3; Nunan & Lam, Chapter 6 this volume). As a result, they require specialised training in language pedagogy, and especially second language pedagogy, along with the pedagogy required of all teachers who teach academic subjects. Moreover, immersion teachers must be qualified to teach the academic curriculum to second language learners in the second language – this means they must have not only native-like proficiency in the target language but also the qualifications to teach in that language. It is not sufficient simply to know a language in order to teach it or to use it effectively to teach academic subjects. This requires specialised training (see Met, Chapter 3; Lyster, Chapter 4; Nunan & Lam, Chapter 6 this volume). This clearly has implications for teacher training institutions and the instructors in those institutions who themselves must know and understand this pedagogy (see also Gonzalez, Chapter 9 this volume). Thus, the decision to embark on the development of double immersion has implications for individual schools but also for teacher training institutions.

Conclusions

The results of our evaluations of a trilingual programme for English-speaking children in Montreal indicate that double immersion programmes can be effective in promoting functional proficiency in two second languages while in no way harming the students' native language development and academic achievement. Double immersion programmes provide a flexible and effective model for promoting multilingualism in communities where there are real advantages to knowing more than two languages. This is becoming increasingly true in the European Union as the countries of Europe build new economic, social and cultural relationships. It is equally true in regions of Asia, Africa and South America where members of bilingual and multilingual communities seek to provide their children with opportunities to acquire proficiency in local, regional and national languages of some importance along with world languages, such as English. Creative use of double immersion offers the possibility of achieving these goals.

References

Ben-Zeev, S. (1977) The influence of bilingualism on cognitive development and cognitive strategy. *Child Development* 48, 1009–18.

Cummins, J. (1976) The influence of bilingualism on cognitive growth: A synthesis of research findings and explanatory hypotheses. *Working Papers on Bilingualism* 9, 1–43.

Cummins, J. (1978) The cognitive development of children in immersion programs. *The Canadian Modern Language Review* 34, 855–83.

Cummins, J. (1981) The role of primary language development in promoting educational success for language minority students. In California State Department of Education (eds) *Schooling and Language Minority Students: A Theoretical Framework* (pp. 1–50). Los Angeles: Evaluation, Dissemination, and Assessment Center.

Day, S. and Shapson, S. (1991) Integrating formal and functional approaches to language teaching in French immersion: An experimental study. *Language Learning* 41, 25–58.

Genesee, F. (1978) A longitudinal evaluation of an early immersion school program. *The Canadian Modern Language Review* 3, 31–50.

Genesee, F. (1981) A comparison of early and late second language learning. *Canadian Journal of Behavioural Sciences* 13, 115–28.

Genesee, F. (1984) Second language learning in school settings: Lessons from immersion. In A.G. Reynolds (ed.) *Bilingualism, Multiculturalism, and Second Language Learning* (pp. 183–202). Hillsdale, NJ: Erlbaum.

Genesee, F. (1987a) *Learning Through Two Languages*. Rowley, MA: Newbury House.

Genesee, F. (1987b) Neuropsychological perspectives. In L. Beebe (ed.) *Issues on Second Language Acquisition* (pp. 81–112). Rowley, MA: Newbury House.

Genesee, F. (1991) Second language learning in school settings: Lessons from immersion. In A.G. Reynolds (ed.) *Bilingualism, Multiculturalism, and Second Language Learning* (pp. 183–203). Hillsdale, NJ: Erlbaum.

Genesee, F., Holobow, N., Lambert, W.E., Cleghorn, A. and Walling, R. (1985) The linguistic and academic development of English-speaking children in French schools: Grade 4 outcomes. *The Canadian Modern Language Review* 41, 669–85.

Genesee, F. and Lambert, W.E. (1983) Trilingual education for majority language children. *Child Development* 54, 105–14.

Harley, B. (1992) Patterns of second language development in French immersion. *French Language Studies* 2, 159–83.

Lambert, W.E. (1980) The social psychology of language: A perspective for the 1980s. In H. Giles, W.P. Robinson and P.M. Smith (eds) *Language: Social Psychological Perspectives* (pp. 415–24). Oxford: Pergamon Press.

Lambert, W.E. and Tucker, G.R. (1972) *The Bilingual Education of Children: The St Lambert Experiment*. Rowley, MA: Newbury House.

Lyster, R. (1994) The effect of functional-analytic teaching on aspects of French immersion students' sociolinguistic competence. *Applied Linguistics* 15, 263–87.

Peal, E. and Lambert, W.E. (1962) The relation of bilingualism to intelligence. *Psychological Monographs*, 76.

Stevens, F. (1983) Activities to promote learning and communication in the second language classroom. *TESOL Quarterly* 17, 259–72.

Swain, M. and Carroll, S. (1987) The immersion observation study. In B. Harley, P. Allen, J. Cummins and M. Swain (eds) *Development of Bilingual Proficiency*. Cambridge: Cambridge University Press.

Swain, M. and Lapkin, S. (1982) *Evaluating Bilingual Education: A Canadian Case Study*. Clevedon: Multilingual Matters.

Chapter 12

Eritrea: Developing a Programme of Multilingual Education

NADINE DUTCHER

Summer Institute of Linguistics

Eritrea, the newest country in Africa, is committed to its development as a multilingual country. In October 1996, at the opening of the first national conference on Eritrean languages, President Isaias Afwerki said, 'Having diverse languages in a country is a blessing.' He urged the people to look at the unifying aspect of linguistic or cultural diversity. (These remarks were reported in an article in *Eritrea Profile* of 24 August 1996.) Officials at the Ministry of Education quote a village elder who said, 'If I speak only one language, I can help my country as only one man. If I can use two languages, I can help as two men. But if I can use all nine languages, then I can work as nine men.'

This chapter will explore the commitment to multilingualism. It will give a brief description of the country, its history, and its language policy. It will discuss how these policies play out in education, and what challenges lie ahead. The chapter is based on information gathered during time spent in Eritrea in the fall of 1996, when the author joined a team from the Summer Institute of Linguistics (SIL) to evaluate the implementation of the mother tongue programmes (or first language programmes) in primary schools. (Ministry of Education, 1996, unpublished report.)

Sociocultural-historical Description

In 1993 after an armed struggle against Ethiopia that lasted about 30 years, Eritrea became an independent country. It has a surface area of about 125,000 square kilometres, roughly the size of England. On the horn of Africa, its neighbours are Sudan at the North and West, and Djibouti and Ethiopia at the South. The Red Sea is on the East, with a coastline of about 1200 kilometres. For centuries its two ports, Massawa and Assab have been important for trade between Africa and the Middle East.

Eritrea has an estimated population of about 3,500,000, including perhaps 500,000 living as refugees in neighbouring Sudan. About 80% of the people are settled agriculturists and nomadic or semi-nomadic herders of livestock (camels, goats and sheep). The remaining 20% live in the urban areas as wage workers, professionals and traders. About half of the population live in the highlands, at elevations of from 1000 to over 2000 metres. Many of them live on the high plateau surrounding Asmara, the capital, at an elevation of 2347 feet. The other half live in the lowlands, in the East, North and West along the Red Sea. About half of the people are Christians, living mainly in the highlands; the other half are Muslims, living mainly in the lowlands, and some animists. (Information from Embassy of Eritrea, 1996; Paice, 1996.)

Eritrea is one of the poorest countries in the world, with a per capita gross domestic product (GDP) of $160–190. The literacy rate is also one of the lowest in the world – estimated at 20% for men and 10% for women. (World Bank News, 1996.)

For thousands of years the area of Eritrea has been home for people of diverse living patterns, religions and traditions. Outsiders have continually tried to extend their influence in the area, the Turks in the sixteenth century and the British, Egyptians, French, and Italians in the nineteenth century. In 1885, the Italians began a successful campaign for control. From 1889–1941 they governed the area as a colony, officially calling it Eritrea for the first time. (According to Paice, 1996, the name may be derived from the Greek word for red. It is mentioned as the Erythrean Sea in the writing of Aeschylus.) By 1910 the country had achieved its present provincial shape. In 1941, the British defeated the Italians and began to govern the country under a military administration. Despite protests from pro-independence groups within the country, in 1950 the United Nations made Eritrea an autonomous unit federated to Ethiopia. In 1955 Ethiopia began steps for annexation, and in 1962 that annexation became official.

From the beginning, there was resistance to control from Ethiopia. In 1961, rebels fought their first battle of the armed struggle, in the western lowlands. Resistance escalated as several groups of rebels rivalled for control of the struggle. In 1977, one group of rebels, the Ethiopia People's Liberation Front (EPLF), held its first congress, and by mid-1981 they were fighting the Ethiopians alone. They gradually liberated all of Eritrea, capturing Asmara in May 1991. Following a referendum in 1993, Eritrea declared itself independent. The EPLF as a fighting force converted itself into a political party, the People's Front for Democracy and Justice (PFDJ). The PFDJ govern the country today, with apparent broad public support, and plan to have multiparty elections soon after ratification of the new constitution. That constitution is now being discussed in its draft form throughout the country.

The long struggle for independence fostered a strong sense of national cohesion. Fighting side by side, the people are now conscious of the importance of unifying the nation with its diversity of cultures and languages. They are fiercely dedicated to strengthening the country so that it does not divide along religious, ethnic or language lines.

Language Policy

Eritrea's language policy reflects the determination to embrace unity within diversity. Eritreans speak nine languages: Afar, Arabic, Bilen, Hedareb, Kunama, Nara, Saho, Tigre and Tigrigna. (See Figure 12.1 for a general idea of the areas of the country where the languages are spoken.)

As a first language, more than half of the Eritreans speak Tigrigna, and about a third Tigre, both Semitic languages. Of the minority languages, estimates are that both Afar and Saho are spoken by about 5% as a first language, and Bilen, Hedareb, Kunama and Nara, about 2%. (Teclemariam Tocrurai, 1995.) (See Table 12.1 for a list of estimates of first language speakers in Eritrea.)

Arabic is estimated to have only one-half of 1% of the population as speakers of Arabic as a first language, but these numbers are controversial. Some experts say that less than 1% speak Arabic as a first language, namely the Rashaida in the north; others claim that with the return of Eritreans from the Sudan after the war, the children born in that Arabic-speaking country speak Arabic as a first language. Still others argue that in the areas of the country where there is much contact with Arabic-speaking neighbours, some children speak Arabic almost as if it were a first language.

The government's language policy is to develop all languages – to forge a national unity within linguistic diversity. The policy is based on the sense of cohesion that was developed during the armed struggle and the belief that the diversity of languages is a national

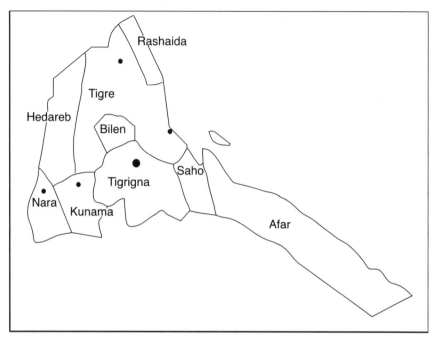

Figure 12.1 Sketch map: Languages of Eritrea
(*Source*: Teclemariam Tocrurai, 1995)

Table 12.1 First language speakers in Eritrea

Language	*Percent of first language speakers*
Afar	5.0
Arabic	0.5
Bilen	2.0
Hedareb	2.5
Kunama	2.0
Nara	1.5
Saho	5.0
Tigre	31.0
Tigrigna	50.0
(The percentage total is not 100 because of rounding.)	

(*Source*: Teclemariam Tocrurai, 1995)

wealth. Interviewed before the first National Conference of Eritrean languages, Abella Jaber, head of Organisational Affairs at the PFDJ said, 'The abundance or fewness of languages spoken within a country has nothing to do with the degree of its unity, identity and development. All these depend on efficient administration and management. In fact, diversity of languages is by itself a national wealth.' (Mr Jaber's remarks were quoted in the English-language newspaper, *Eritrea Profile*, 27 July 1996.)

Therefore, the government has not established an official language. All languages are equal, although Arabic and Tigrigna function as widely used languages, with English as the language for wider communication. The three – Arabic, Tigrigna, and English – are used in many public communications. For instance, many signs in Asmara are in three languages with their three separate scripts – Tigrigna at the top, Arabic in the middle, and English below. However, not all of the Eritrean languages are equally developed in terms of writing. (See Table 12.2 for a summary of the writing status of these languages.)

Education Language Policy

Educational coverage in Eritrea is one of the lowest in the world for all levels:

Table 12.2 Status of writing of languages of Eritrea

Language	Script	First written
Afar	Latin now	1840 Latin
		1981 Fidel
Arabic	Arabic	1000 years ago
Bilen	Fidel	Early 19th century
Hedareb	No	No
Kunama	Latin	100 years ago
Nara	Latin	1988
Saho	Latin	100 years ago
Tigre	Fidel	1889 Bible
Tigrigna	Fidel	13th or 14th century

Note: Fidel is a syllabic writing system, used also by Amharic, the official language of Ethiopia. Tigrigna contains over 200 such syllable forms, which students in Grade 1 are expected to memorise before they can be promoted to Grade 2.
(*Source*: Interviews with Language Panel heads, Ministry of Education)

- Primary (Grades 1–5; students seven to 11 years old): 27%.
- Junior secondary (Grades 6 and 7; students 12 to 13 years old): 9%.
- Senior secondary (Grades 8–11; students 14 to 17 years old): 6%.

These numbers indicate that of the young people eligible by age to attend school only a few do attend. At the primary level (ages seven to 11 years) only about three out of every 10 are in school. At the higher levels, far fewer of the appropriate age groups are in school. However, the numbers are higher if one considers over-age students. In that case the enrolment ratios for primary are closer to 50%. (Ministry of Education, 1995, statistics.)

The low net coverage is the result of many causes, especially the neglect of public education during the colonial administrations. For instance, according to Paice (1996), during the Italian period only 24 public primary schools existed, and there were no secondary schools. During the Ethiopian period, the authorities barred Tigrigna and Arabic as official teaching languages, and replaced them with Amharic, the official language of Ethiopia, but not a language commonly spoken in Eritrea.

During the struggle for independence, the EPLF began the establishment of what would become a national education system. As they gradually gained control of areas of the country, they set up primary schools, first to teach the young fighters how to read and write, then to teach the civilians. By 1977 there were 200 such schools in operation.

The use of the students' first language (or language of the community's choice) was a cornerstone of the EPLF educational philosophy. The fighters wrote textbooks in Tigrigna and Tigre and gradually translated them into five of the other languages – Afar, Arabic, Kunama, Nara and Saho.

The present education policy continues the emphasis on the students' first language in primary school, with English as the medium of instruction beginning in junior secondary, or Grade 6. For primary school, the policy states that, 'Every nationality has the right to its own language or any other language of its choice as the medium of instruction in primary school'. Like the EPLF fighters, Ministry officials are convinced of the importance of the use of the first language. During the SIL evaluation of the first language programmes, staff of the Ministry of Education cited the following reasons for the use of the first language: (1) The students can understand; (2) the students can learn the culture; and (3) the students can get confidence.

For secondary school, the country has chosen English as the medium of instruction. In the words of Zemhret Yohannes, Secretary of the Constitutional Commission:

> Our national policies have been formulated to speed up development. To this end, we have opted to use English as a medium of instruction in all secondary schools. In addition, since Arabic is spoken by a large number of Eritreans as well as by peoples of several neighbouring countries, and since Tigrigna is widely spoken in Eritrea, it has been decided that both languages be taught in all Eritrean schools. (Quoted in *Eritrea Profile*, 26 October 1996)

Thus there are three aspects to the language policy:

(1) Primary language: students' first language as medium of instruction for Grades 1 to 5.
(2) Secondary language: English, the medium of instruction from Grade 6 on, through secondary school and the university.
(3) Other national language: provision for teaching either Arabic or Tigrigna at all levels.

In primary school, the schools may teach Arabic as a subject when the medium of instruction is not Arabic; they may teach Tigrigna as a subject when the medium of instruction is not Tigrigna.

Implementation of the Education Language Policy

The Ministry of Education has implemented the language policy in a careful manner, first by ensuring that communities are able to choose the languages used in their schools, and then by carefully documenting the progress of implementation. The Department of National Pedagogy is engaged in a bilingual/multilingual education project of four phases: first, evaluation of the first language programmes (in which the author participated); second, survey of dialect problems; third, survey of script problems; and fourth, plans for a campaign at the community level to mobilise support for the language policy.

In primary schools in the Tigrigna-speaking areas of the highlands, the communities have chosen Tigrigna as the media of instruction. Surveys indicate that they are happy with that choice. However, in the lowlands, where Tigre and the other languages are spoken, most have opted for either Arabic or Tigrigna, not the students' first language. Arabic has been especially popular because it is useful for trade with neighbouring countries and because it is associated with

Islam, the religion of many of the people in the lowlands.

Thus, not all the communities have opted for the first language as the medium of instruction. In fact, the SIL team estimated that to date only about 60% of the schools are teaching in the student's first language. This choice appears to be related to the parents' desire that their children learn languages with perceived economic and social value higher than their own. (See Table 12.3 for a summary of primary schools by medium of instruction.)

In secondary schools, the language of instruction is English. The author was told that in junior secondary school (Grades 6 and 7), there is little direct use of English as the medium of instruction, but that by senior secondary school (Grades 8 to 11), English was indeed used directly as the medium of instruction. Because the author's work dealt only with the primary level, she was not able to verify this evaluation with her own observations.

At all levels, the schools attempt to teach the two widely used national languages, Arabic and Tigrigna. In the case of Arabic, this is constrained by the lack of teachers proficient in Arabic, or, as with the other languages, by the lack of financial resources to produce educational materials in Arabic. The Ministry has recruited Eritreans

Table 12.3 Primary schools by medium of instruction, 1995–96

| Language | Government and Non-government Schools | |
	Number	Percentage
Afar	0	0
Amharic	2	–
Arabic	117	22
Bilen	0	0
Hedareb	0	0
Italian	1	–
Kunama	13	2
Nara	0	0
Saho	17	3
Tigre	28	5
Tigrigna	364	67
Total	542	100
(The percentage total is not 100 because of rounding.)		

(*Source*: Planning Office, Ministry of Education, Eritrea, 1996)

educated in Arab-speaking countries to fill some of the demand for Arab-speaking teachers.

Within the Ministry of Education, the Division of Curriculum Research and Development has been responsible for promoting acceptance of the first language in primary schools, and for writing and translating textbooks. There has been discussion of establishing a centre for national languages but no definitive steps have been taken as of this writing.

The textbooks in use are mainly those written in the field during the armed struggle. Based on a study which began in 1996, the Ministry is now revising the curriculum for all levels. They plan to write new textbooks based on the new curriculum, adapting them for all the languages currently in use as either medium of instruction or subject. There are widespread shortages of textbooks for all grades and for all languages. (Few of the students in the classes the author observed used textbooks in their classroom work.) English language textbooks are the exception because British overseas assistance is producing textbooks and training teachers at all levels.

The primary school year consists of 180 school days, each day four hours long. Much of the class time is dedicated to language instruction. Grade 1 covers four subjects: the first language, mathematics, science, and games. Grade 5 covers eight subjects: the first language, English, Arabic, Tigrigna, geography, history, mathematics, and science. As an example of the weekly schedule, in one school in the Saho area the teachers said that during one week the Grade 5 teachers would use Saho as the medium of instruction, but teach the other languages as a subject, with English for seven periods, Arabic for three periods, and Tigrigna for two periods.

Primary school teachers receive their training at the country's one teacher training college (Teacher Training Institute or TTI). There has been an overall shortage of trained teachers because before independence over 50% of the nation's teachers were from Ethiopia, and after independence they left and had to be replaced. TTI short-term and summer courses have made up some of the deficit. Although the TTI programme includes provision for training in teaching the mother tongue, most of the TTI students are native speakers of Tigrigna because there has been a shortage of candidates from the other language groups.

Both the curriculum survey and the SIL first language evaluation noted that teaching methods consist mainly of teacher talk and student copying from the board. Teachers rely on repetition and learning by rote.

Critical Issues

In implementing its multilingual education, Eritrea faces at least three daunting challenges: low levels of education, low level of educational inputs, and a heavy cognitive load for the students.

Eritrea begins with a low starting point for education. The estimated 80% of adults who cannot read and write mean that many parents will not be able to help their children achieve success in school, except by offering their considerable moral support to the endeavour. Enrolments at all levels will increase as the government is able to build schools and train teachers. At issue is whether that increase can be fast enough and deep enough to accommodate the government's hopes for multilingual education.

Educational inputs in terms of teachers and materials are at low levels. Teachers, even those who are qualified by their training at TTI, lack skills to work with students in a way which optimises the learning capacity of their students – which takes advantage of the fact that the students can understand and communicate with the teacher in a common language. Furthermore, except for the teachers trained through efforts of the British overseas assistance, few teachers possess the skills necessary for teaching a second or third language. In addition, there is a shortage of teachers, especially for Arabic and for the minority language groups, such as Nara, Saho, and Tigre. There is a widespread shortage of textbooks for all languages, somewhat less acutely for English.

Students face a demanding cognitive load. In Grade 2 some students have to manage four languages. For instance, if the first language is not the language of instruction, they may be receiving instruction in Arabic as the medium of instruction, and studying Tigrigna and English as subjects. This would seem to be a difficult load for students in any part of the world, but especially burdensome for students coming from families where the older family members have received little or no education and the teachers are not trained in methods of language teaching. In addition, the three school languages require three different scripts: the syllable-based Fidel for Tigrigna, Arabic for Arabic, and Latin for English. This author, educated through only the Latin script, wonders how Eritreans will achieve the mass education of their ideals with such cognitive demands on the students. There are educated Eritreans who can use Tigrigna, Arabic and English, both orally and in writing, but it is difficult to believe that they represent more than a tiny fraction of the society.

Hopes for the Future

The issues cited above are mitigated by several factors: governmental will, evidence that many Eritreans do manage three or more languages on a daily basis, and availability of financial and technical help from abroad.

The government is determined to maintain the country's unity by embracing ethnic and linguistic diversity, and to afford all people the opportunity for a meaningful education in their first language as well as the opportunity to learn the two major national languages, and English, the language of higher education.

There is much anecdotal evidence that Eritreans can and do speak three or four languages. For them, learning the other languages of people with whom they must speak is a necessary aspect of living in a multilingual society. Learning those languages is not the miracle that it appears for individuals living in countries like the United States, where one language is sufficient for daily and professional life.

Many outside organisations are prepared to give their financial and technical support. To name just a few: the Danish aid agency is helping with curriculum development, teacher education, textbook production, as well as the implementation of the mother tongue policy. The German aid agency is building schools. UNICEF has a project for girls' education, and a project for improving life skills. The World Bank has plans to help with the construction of schools and the printing of textbooks in Arabic, Kunama, Saho and Tigre. The Summer Institute of Linguistics has evaluated the first language education programmes, and is now working on dialect and orthography issues for the expansion of the language programmes.

References

Embassy of Eritrea (1996) *ERITREA, Africa's Newest State.* Washington, DC: Information Section, Embassy of Eritrea.

Eritrea Profile (27 July, 24 August and 26 October, 1996). English-language newspaper published in Asmara, Eritrea.

Ministry of Education, Eritrea (1996) Assessment of mother tongue education in Eritrea. Unpublished report of Klaus Wedekind and Nadine Dutcher, Summer Institute of Linguistics, in collaboration with the Language Panels of the Curriculum Research and Development Division of the Ministry of Education.

Paice, E. (1996) *Guide to Eritrea.* Bucks, England: Bradt Publications.

Teclemariam Tocrurai, D. (1995) The use of mother tongue education in Eritrea. Unpublished manuscript submitted to the International Linguistics Consultants Seminar, Kenya.

World Bank News (7 March 1996) *World Bank Contributes to Post-Conflict Recovery in Eritrea.* Washington, DC: The World Bank.